*The Immigrant Heritage of America Series*

Cecyle S. Neidle, *Editor*

# The DANISH AMERICANS

by

GEORGE R. NIELSEN

Concordia College
River Forest, Illinois

TWAYNE PUBLISHERS
A DIVISION OF G. K. HALL & CO., BOSTON

Published in 1981 by Twayne Publishers,
A Division of G. K. Hall & Co.


Printed on permanent/durable acid-free paper and bound
in the United States of America

*First Printing*

**Library of Congress Cataloging in Publication Data**

Nielsen, George R.
The Danish Americans.

(The Immigrant heritage of America series)
Bibliography: pp. 230–32
Includes index.
1. Danish Americans. I. Title.
E184.S19N53 973'.043981 81-63
ISBN 0-8057-8419-5

To Lois

and our children,

Laura, Erik, and Christina

# *Contents*

# *About the Author*

A native of Texas, George R. Nielsen received the B.A. degree from Concordia College, Seward, Nebraska, and the Ph.D. from the University of Iowa. Since 1959 he has taught American history at Concordia College, River Forest, Illinois, where he has specialized in ethnic and immigration history and in the history of the American West. His articles have appeared in the *Southwestern Historical Quarterly*, *Business History Review*, *Capitol Studies*, and the *Encyclopedia of American Ethnic Groups*. Two earlier books by the author are *In Search of a Home: The Sorbs (Wends) on the Australian and Texas Frontiers* (1977) and *The Kickapoo People* (1975). Professor Nielsen has been the recipient of a Fulbright grant and awards from the National Endowment for the Humanities.

# *Introduction*

Even though the Danish Americans have not received extensive examination from historians, there is a consensus in all the existing studies that the Danes were among the most rapid assimilators of the American ethnic groups. It is only fitting that the Danish Americans, by focusing their attention on the new home, failed to concern themselves with their heritage or its preservation, thereby compounding the problem of writing their history. There is no central depository of Danish American sources in the United States, no ethnic museum, no single-volume study of these people in English, and there was no permanent Danish American historical society until 1977.[1]

By all standards of assimilation the Danes have been incorporated into American life and not simply acculturated.[2] Although the Danes generally avoided the South in the earlier years, they quickly dispersed throughout the remainder of the United States. In contrast to the Norwegians who were so concentrated that in 1890 50 percent of the migrants were located in two states, the Danes scattered, and it is necessary to collect the Danish-born Americans from five states to arrive at one-half of the Danish population in America. This scattering aspect of the Danish settlers can be illustrated another way by showing the states with the greatest Danish and Norwegian population and the percentage of the total in the United States.

| *Danes* | *Norwegians* |
|---|---|
| Iowa 11.7% | Minnesota 31.4% |
| Nebraska 10.8% | Wisconsin 20.4% |
| Wisconsin 10.4% | Illinois 9.4% |

The Danes also readily accepted the English language, and in 1911 97 percent spoke English, an impressive statistic when compared to 53 percent for the other ethnic groups. By 1930 99 percent of the Danish-born could speak English.[3] This same loyalty to their new homeland is reflected in the naturalization statistics. In 1930, 75 percent of the 179,474 Danes in America had been naturalized, and that amount, once again, was the highest for any national group in the United States.[4]

A further indication of the Dane's assimilation is his selection of a church and a spouse. Only about 9 percent of the Danish Americans and Americans with at least one Danish parent were members of the Danish Lutheran churches in 1920.[5] Some Danes joined other Lutheran synods, but many became members of "American" churches including the Mormon, Baptist, Methodist, and Adventist bodies. When choosing a spouse the Danish man may have preferred a Danish woman, but disproportionately few females migrated. The marriage to non-Danish spouses reflected the Danes' ability to assimilate and at the same time helps explain why they assimilated so rapidly. A study of Chicago Danes shows that 27 percent married spouses outside their ethnic group as compared with 19 percent of the Swedes and 8 percent of the Norwegians.[6]

There is no consensus on any single factor causing this propensity for assimilation, although several causes have been suggested and supported with convincing arguments. Yet not one is ironclad. One view holds that the migrants left Denmark when that nation was declining as a world power and that those people who left could not justify pride in their heritage. Why should the Danish immigrant trouble himself to preserve a memory that was one of defeat and weakness? A Danish American historian identified this feeling among his people in 1896 when he wrote, "The sentiment of patriotism and national pride too is waning . . . and a feeling of national helplessness is becoming dominant."[7] While this theory appears reasonable it nevertheless falls short when it is applied to other ethnic groups. There were too many ethnic groups, such as those from eastern Europe, that originated from nations less significant than Denmark who struggled to preserve their heritage and resisted assimilation.

Another alternative explanation is the timing of the Danish migration. The Norwegians and Swedes, for example, came earlier than the Danes when the hazards of travel encouraged people to organize groups of families and follow a leader to America, where they formed a settlement. By the time the Danish migration had built momentum, transportation had become more reliable and the Danes generally migrated as individuals and not as families or in groups. This meant that there would be few centralized settlements to begin with and that there were not many magnet communities to attract the migrants who followed. Because the Danish migration was predominantly male, the husband-to-be was less likely to marry an eligible girl in the Danish American community, but settled instead for a non-Danish woman if he was not willing to return to Denmark for a bride.[8] At the same time, however, there were other ethnic groups, including the Finns, who like the Danes arrived late, but did not scatter or readily assimilate.[9]

The third reason is based on the motivation for Danish migration. The majority migrated because of economic reasons, and to that goal all subsequent actions would be subordinated. Assimilation produced a bigger financial pay-off than maintaining the Danish culture. Learning the English language and taking land and jobs where the best opportunities presented themselves were logical responses. The Danes had received excellent training in the construction trades and were in demand as workers; by following the building booms, they left the Danish communities and became Americanized more readily.[10] Again, this explanation, though logical, is not completely satisfactory. Danes who migrated for noneconomic reasons also assimilated rapidly, and there were individuals of other ethnic groups, such as the Italians, who came for economic reasons, and then returned to Italy without absorbing much of America at all.

The receptive nature of American society toward ethnic groups whose values and physical characteristics coincided with their own has also been cited as a factor encouraging Danish assimilation. The Danes were traditionally Protestant, so they experienced less hostility than did the Irish Catholics. They were also Caucasians so they avoided the racial abuse endured by the Chinese. In nearly every way, including their values and the desire for economic success, the Danes fit the American system. Danes understood the democratic system, at least in principle, which included a written constitution, political parties, social reform, and toleration. Although Danes experienced the individual abuse that all "greenhorns" suffered, and endured the hostility of the foreign-language foes of World War I, they found a receptive society that did not force them into ghettos but permitted them to find homes anywhere. Like other Americans, Chicago Danes moved out of neighborhoods that were becoming Polish, Jewish, or black. Morris Salmonsen, a Danish Jew and head of the marriage-license bureau in Chicago, reflected the attitudes of the time when he objected to the marriage of a Swedish girl to a Chinese man.[11] Doors to American institutions, churches, lodges, political parties, and neighborhoods were open to the Danes. The receptive aspect of the host community does show how little change was necessary and how limited was the extent of the response, but it does not explain the Danish acceptance of the invitation.[12]

Without detracting from any of these explanations, but with the purpose of rounding out the picture to show the interaction of all these aspects, I would like to identify strife and divisiveness within the Danish American community as still another reason for assimilation. Strife and divisiveness are standard features of the human condition and existed in the experiences of other ethnic groups. Theodore C. Blegen has even used it as a possible explanation for the Norwegian-American's high level of loyalty to the Lutheran tradition. In contrast to the Norwegians, the Swedes aligned themselves into one Lutheran synod in America, while the Norwegians formed fourteen separate synods in competition with each other. The options made available by the variety of synods gave the discontented Norwegian an alternative Norwegian Lutheran synod in the event of theological alienation, while the Swede, if he became dissatisfied, would have no choice but to leave the Lutheran church.[13]

Conflict within institutions can lead to the strengthening or weakening of that agency. Conflict can build loyalty and clarify goals and objectives, but it can lead to schisms, ill-will, and a weakening of the institution's vitality. The problem is to maintain a healthy balance between conflict and consensus. When does the discord and conflict become excessive so that the institution can no longer utilize it or absorb it? The stronger the institution the more readily it can tolerate conflict, but the life of Danish American institutions was tenuous. The Danish Church was weak from the very beginning, Danish families never had the size or the cohesiveness of the traditional Italian family, and Danish societies were loosely organized and small. Had there been more Danes in more concentrated communities perhaps the conflict would have been less debilitating, but the institutions that could have provided stability for Danish Americans and retarded assimilation were wracked with discord that discouraged loyalty and participation. A solution was dispersal, separation from the Danish community, and a more rewarding fellowship within American institutions. This view does not argue that Danes were any more irascible and independent than persons of other nationalities or that they became that way because of the new American environment, but that the Danes did not have the luxury to indulge in disagreements in the new setting if they hoped to maintain their Danish heritage.

The reason for this type of Danish response is much harder to explain than it is to identify it and show its impact. The existence of the conflict was noticed by Danes of that time and became part of their humor. One Dane, for example, observed that when two Greeks get together they start a restaurant, but when two Danes meet they start a fight.[14] Another Danish American commented that a Dane could not bear to see one of his countrymen getting ahead of another. Any Dane would help another Dane down on his luck, but the Dane would more readily support an Irish politician than a fellow Dane who was seeking the same office.[15]

A problem that arises from highlighting controversy is that it detracts from the positive and cheerful aspects of the Danish American people, and that quality must not be forgotten. We also remember the Danish Americans for their good humor, hospitality, humanitarianism, and the development of cooperative societies. Both conflict and goodwill existed, but the conflict was extensive and pervasive and it weakened the cohesion of Danish society and institutions and thereby encouraged more rapid assimilation.

# *Acknowledgments*

In the preparation of this book I have received valuable assistance that must be recognized. Financial support for the project was provided by the National Endowment for the Humanities through a Summer Seminar at the University of California, Davis, and by the Aid Association for Lutherans, Appleton, Wisconsin.

Libraries, archives, and historical societies that made available their holdings include the University of Chicago, Newberry Library, the University of Wisconsin, Northwestern University, the State Historical Society of Wisconsin, the Chicago Historical Society, Bancroft Library of the University of California, Berkeley, the University of California, Davis, Lutheran School of Theology at Chicago, Grand View College, Dana College, Nebraska State Historical Society, the State Historical Society of Iowa, New-York Historical Society, Wartburg Theological Seminary, Minnesota Historical Society, South Dakota State Historical Society, Københavns Universitet, and Det Kongelige Bibliotek. I am particularly grateful for the assistance of Gladys Guebert of Concordia, River Forest, and Inger Bladt of the Udvandrerarkivet at Aalborg.

I have also benefited from the counsel of the following persons who have read all or sections of the manuscript: Pastor Enok Mortensen, Arnold N. Bodtker, editor of the *Bridge*, Erik Helmer Pedersen of the University of Copenhagen, and Henry L. Letterman of Concordia. Finally I wish to acknowledge the advice and direction of the late Cecyle Neidle, who not only painstakingly examined and corrected this manuscript, but brought to bear the years of experience gained from her work in immigration history.

GEORGE R. NIELSEN

*Concordia College*
*River Forest, Illinois*

# Part I: *The Danish Heritage*

CHAPTER 1

# The European Setting

THE title of this book, *The Danish Americans*, presents an image of opposites. Danish history, for example, goes back before the Vikings, who lived a millennium ago, while the United States only recently celebrated its bicentennial. Considering geographical area, the present country of Denmark is one-half the size of the state of Maine. Topographically Denmark's terrain is flat or rolling while the United States has an infinite variety, including ranges of mountains. The temperature of maritime Denmark has moderate fluctuations, quite unlike the extremes in the continental climate of the United States. The contrasts are endless.

Even though the geography of Denmark and its history have little in common with that of the United States, a comparison of the citizens of the two countries shows many similarities. Denmark's race is Caucasian, the religion Protestant, the language Germanic, the citizens literate. The Danish people have had experience with democracy both in the days when the Viking chiefs were selected by common consent and in our contemporary century when Denmark concerned itself with economic equality. The similarities are numerous.

Because the Danish immigrant is the product of history and brings part of that experience along with him, a brief examination of Denmark's history is necessary. A reasonable point of departure would be the rule of Christian IV, the king who assumed the throne in 1588 when he was eleven years old. At that time the kingdom of Denmark and Norway was the strongest power in the Baltic sphere and Denmark enjoyed the wealth resulting from the dues collected from ships that sailed through the Sound connecting the North and Baltic seas. In keeping with the financial policy of other European nations, Denmark followed the policy of mercantilism as a way of making itself strong economically. The crown encouraged the creation of industries, textile factories, and mines in order to provide goods for the Danish market, and the formation of trading companies for foreign exploration and trade. The East Indies Company, for example, started a small colony in Tranquebar during this time. The mercantilist policy also provided the motivation for Christian IV (1588–1648) when he commissioned Jens Munk to search for the Northwest Passage to the Orient. This leader and his crew were the first Danes on the North American continent since the days of the Vikings.[1]

But in the 1620s, while the Pilgrims were beginning to build homes in Plymouth, the power of the king and that of Denmark declined. It began when Christian IV, attempting to secure the north German coast, became involved in the Thirty Years' War. Instead of victory for Denmark, the enemy forces under Wallenstein defeated the Danish army and invaded Jutland.[2] The war further drained the economic resources of Denmark and led to suffering and distress among the lower classes. The king, still aggressive, then turned his attention to restricting Sweden's growing power in the Baltic and another war resulted in 1643. Sweden's army had also fought in Germany, but instead of losing, it had become battle-hardened, and together with its growing navy turned the two years of fighting against Denmark into victory. Denmark was forced to yield some provinces in the southern part of what is now Sweden and to reduce the dues collected on the Sound.[3]

Even though Sweden had become powerful in the North, Sweden realized that it could gain no more power in the Baltic until it captured the remaining Danish provinces in the southern part of its peninsula and gained control of the northeastern shores of the Sound. The occasion came in 1657 when Frederik III was king. During that year the Swedish army became so deeply involved in a war on the Polish coast that Frederik believed he could regain some of the lost provinces in southern Sweden. Charles Gustavus X, however, brought his army from Poland up to Jutland and, taking advantage of frozen seas, crossed the Little Belt and the Great Belt on foot and invaded Zealand. The Danes were defeated and yielded the remaining provinces in southern Sweden.[4] The inhabitants of these Scanian provinces had been Danish and spoke the Danish language, but they became Swedes and Denmark lost one-third of its land and population. The country of Denmark itself was terribly ravaged by the invading troops.

In an attempt to consider ways of reviving Denmark, the Estates of the Realm, the deliberative body of that time, met in Copenhagen in 1660. The king, aware of his limited power in comparison to that of the nobility and realizing the desire of the townspeople of Copenhagen for a strong leader, formed an alliance with the burghers against the nobility. The office of the king was made hereditary, thereby depriving the nobles of their control over that position and establishing an institution that lasted for 175 years. The burghers enjoyed some relief from the tax burden because the nobility was required to share the payment of taxes.[5] The only other significant concession the burghers gained was the appointment of some members of their group to administrative positions in the government. This dramatic growth in power by the king, however, must be seen in the context of Europe, because the leading nations had already adopted the concept of the hereditary monarchy. Only Poland continued the election of the king, and that government was disintegrating.[6]

It was during the administration of Frederik III that the Danish West Indies Company acquired the island of St. Thomas. The company occupied the island in 1672 but the enterprise was not successful even though the company imported slaves from Guinea. In 1754 the crown assumed control of the island and opened it to all Danish citizens. That action immediately stimulated the development of tobacco plantations and later contributed to the cultivation of sugar and cotton.[7]

When the productivity of St. Thomas declined, the settlers, instead of resorting to fertilizers, migrated to St. John, which had been occupied in 1717. Finally in 1733 Denmark purchased St. Croix from France and the governor moved his residence to that island and the town of Frederiksted became the seat of government.[8]

While the early treatment of the slaves was harsh and a slave uprising in 1733 reflected the oppressive conditions, the attitude of the Danish government was more enlightened than that of the resident planters. Denmark was the first country to abolish the slave trade by law in 1792. More legislation followed and in 1803 the slaves were given the right to receive instruction in Christianity and were encouraged to enter into legal marriage. The Moravian Brethren had sent missionaries to St. Thomas as early as 1732, having planted colonies on the American mainland during that same period. Although the Moravians were the first to take an interest in the welfare of the slaves, the Lutheran church soon dominated the religious life of the Danish West Indies, including that of the slave population. The Danish government also introduced educational programs among the slaves to prepare them for a projected freedom in 1860, but a rebellion on St. Croix in 1848 led to the abandonment of a gradual timetable and the slaves were granted freedom immediately.[9]

Even though there were times when the islands were an asset to Denmark, the twentieth century and the long-range steamships passed the islands by. Denmark in 1917 negotiated the sale of the islands to the United States for the price of $25,000.[10] The number of Danes brought into the United States was not particularly significant, but throughout the 250 years of Denmark's control of the islands, Danish citizens found their way to the United States for education, business, or to establish new homes.

In spite of the passage of some positive domestic legislation for Denmark and the improvement of administration under the absolute monarchy, much remained undone. Aristocratic landowners continued to dominate the countryside, collecting taxes and administering justice. In about 1700 the peasants constituted approximately 80 percent of the Danish population but owned about 2 percent of the land. The nobles and the crown controlled the fields, and the peasants, who lived in villages, cultivated the land as tenants. The nobles often did not live on the estates at all, but tried to extract as much wealth as possible from their holdings.[11]

One of the worst aspects of the feudal system was the obligation of villeinage service. This clause in the peasant's contract required him to serve at the manor house without compensation. While the peasant suffered, the landowner profited not only from the free labor but also from the higher prices for the grain carted long distances by peasant labor to more favorable markets. The landowner could improve his flocks and fields while the peasant was reduced to marginal life. The peasant also suffered from the general difficulties experienced by the nation. The peace of 1720 ended the Great Scandinavian War, but also brought a depression in the prices of grain and cattle. Then in 1733 the *Stavnsbaand* was introduced, prohibiting peasants between the ages of fourteen and thirty-six from leaving the district of their birth. It was virtual serfdom and limited the opportunities of advancement.[12]

About the middle of the eighteenth century, rulers in Europe, as well as A. P. Bernstorff and Christian Ditlev Reventlow, advisors of Christian VII, turned to the problem of the peasantry. Reports prepared on peasant life drew attention to the bad conditions, old-fashioned farming methods, communal farming, and villeinage. It was the beginning of agricultural reforms that included the repeal of the *Stavnsbaand* in 1788 and once again permitted the peasant to leave the estate of his birth. The old strip farming was abolished so that the peasant could collect his land into a contiguous area and then transfer his residence to his property. The ambitious farmer, therefore, could buy land and then farm it progressively without being held back by neighbors. The School Law of 1814 also was important because it provided free schooling for rural people. Although the facilities and teachers were initially inadequate, literacy became the rule.

Even though reform legislation was passed, the countryside did not experience immediate improvement. The manor estates could not do without workers so the owners laid out little plots for cottagers (*husmaend*) who were employed as day laborers. They formed a large class, but received little benefit from the new laws. Legislation permitting the farmer to purchase land contained no provisions to assist the farmer in financing the endeavor. Neither was the mentality and outlook of the farmer modernized by legislation, so change was implemented slowly. Economic recession also discouraged additional reforms simply because of uncertainty, and landowners became more cautious of further change. Finally, in 1845, when the farmers had become more enlightened and willing to press for reform, the king forbade political meetings of farmers unless they had received previous police permission.[13]

The economic condition of the farmer and the agricultural environment were extremely important in explaining the background for the migration to America. Agricultural conditions were improving, but life was difficult and the prospects for attaining prosperity were not bright. The agricultural reforms had an impact on the religious life and attitudes of the Danish immigrant. When the farmer moved his residence from the village to the land he worked, he was deprived of membership not only in the social community but in the religious one as well. Church attendance dropped and extra effort was necessary to attend worship services. The church became less and less a part of the peasant's daily life, and the isolated residence in the country, either as cottager or farmer, made him more independent both socially and religiously.[14]

From the perspective of power politics, the nineteenth century was not one of Denmark's most successful eras. During this time Denmark experienced military defeat, lost 40 percent of its territory, suffered a financial depression, and witnessed the departure of over 300,000 of its citizens.

The problems began with the turn of the century when Denmark, like the United States, found it impossible to remain at peace while the major countries of Europe, especially England and France, were at war. Denmark had joined a league of Baltic powers organized to protect neutral shipping, but England objected and in 1801 sent a fleet to Copenhagen, where it destroyed much of the Danish navy. Six years later, in 1807, England demanded the remainder of the Danish navy so that Napoleon could not take it, and destroyed much of Copenhagen to underscore its demands. King Frederik VI yielded, but from then on supported Napoleon. More misfortune followed, because when Napoleon was in turn defeated, Norway was taken from Denmark and given to Sweden. Financially the times were also harsh because trade was disrupted by the war and in 1813 the national bank (*Kurantbank*) of Denmark declared itself bankrupt. The government created a new currency, the *rigsdaler,* based on confiscated land, but the winning of confidence in the new currency took twenty years. The conclusion of the war did not bring prosperity either, because the prices for Denmark's grain dropped during the period from 1818 to 1824.[15]

The Danish economy and its trade slowly revived in the second quarter of the century, and Denmark continued to control Greenland, Iceland, the Faroe Islands, the Virgin Islands, and some trading stations on the coasts of Guinea and India. In addition Denmark took a step toward democracy when in 1848 Frederik VII granted the demands of liberals and gave his approval for drafting a constitution.[16]

But the same movement that provided the basis for Danish democracy also revived a latent problem over the control of Slesvig in southern Jutland. Because Slesvig occupied the southern frontier, the duchy in past years had been granted special advantages, both politically and culturally. Over time, moreover, the successive dukes zealously guarded their rights and yet were drawn more closely to Holstein than to Denmark. German knights from Holstein obtained holdings in southern Slesvig and the German language and culture spread northward, especially to the market towns. The local noblemen wished for the unification of the two duchies, and Christian I of Denmark, who had become the royal duke of both Slesvig and Holstein, had signed a document in 1481 that proclaimed the permanent unity of the two duchies. Even though Christian I was ruler of Denmark, the duchies were under German jurisdiction. German was spoken in courts and government offices and in most churches and schools. Only in North Slesvig was Danish the predominant language. Danish continued to be the language of the home and the Danish-speaking population resented both the emphasis on German and the developing German nationalism. Finally, in the 1830s, the Danes demanded that Danish be made the language of law in their part of Slesvig. The general assembly in Slesvig acceded to the demand, but the nationalistic revival could not reverse the inroads German had made in South Slesvig. At least the Danes would try to keep what they had, and in 1833 a Danish newspaper was founded in Haderslev, and in 1844 a Danish folk school opened at Rødding.[17] (The folk school is more fully treated in Chapter 10.) Even though Slesvig and Holstein were independent states under the duke, who also happened to be the Danish king, some nationalists began supporting the incorporation of Slesvig into Denmark.

When, on January 20, 1848, Frederik VII granted permission to draft a constitution, the nationalistic ministry envisioned the constitution for all of Denmark including Slesvig. The Germans in Slesvig objected and instead applied for Slesvig's admission to the Germanic Confederation, a group to which Holstein belonged. At the same time, they realized Denmark would not consent, and hence they proclaimed a provisional government which rose in revolt against Denmark.[18] Denmark mobilized to hold Slesvig, while German volunteers crossed into South Slesvig to assist the rebels. Although the fighting went on intermittently for three years, the Danish forces won a significant battle against the ducal forces on July 25, 1850, at Isted Heath.[19] Probably more important was the help from other European powers such as England and Russia, who helped restrain Prussian intervention. Eventually in 1850 the Treaty of London was signed that stipulated the return to the status quo of the region, with clear limits on the extent of Danish control of the provinces. Some diplomats had suggested a division of Slesvig according to language, but Frederik VII had opposed it.[20]

In 1863, when most observers realized that the nonpartition policy was unrealistic, the National Liberals broke the treaty and wrote a constitution that extended Danish sovereignty over Slesvig. Bismarck, recognizing the possibility of exploiting the act to further his program of German unification, sent troops across the Ejder on February 1, 1864. Another conference was called for London, and again the partition of Slesvig was proposed, but A. F. Krieger of the National Liberal party objected.[21]

Without a reasonable alternative and without foreign pressure against Bismarck, Prussia won a quick victory. First the Danes took the position along Dannevirke, an ancient defensive wall, but, realizing the vulnerability of their position, retreated to the fortification at Dybbøl. Following an eight-week siege, the Germans launched an attack and captured the fortification. One thousand seven hundred Danes and 1,200 Germans lost their lives. Denmark was forced to yield Slesvig, Holstein, and Launenburg to Austria and Prussia.[22]

With the defeat, 150,000 Danish-minded people were placed

under German rule. German became their official language and young Danes were required to serve in the German army. The unwillingness to undergo Germanization combined with the disillusionment with Denmark and a loss of faith in the future caused many Danes to think of migration. The Slesvigers fleeing German rule along with the Mormons seeking the new Zion supplied the majority of Danish migrants during the decades in the middle of the nineteenth century. Many migrated directly to America through Hamburg and were identified as German subjects, while others crossed the boundary into Denmark where they lived for varying periods of time before they also migrated. Some scholars estimated the number of Danes leaving Slesvig to be as high as 50,000, and the majority went to America.[23]

The Germans were not unhappy with the departure of the Danes, because Germans bought the farms and filled the vacancies. In 1884, however, Germany prohibited Danish agents from recruiting emigrants in Slesvig and that helped retard the migratory trend.[24] By 1900 the feeling of futility changed among the Danes and their young men were encouraged to stay in Slesvig and complete their military obligation. Because Danish was excluded from schools, a language society was organized that provided books for home study. Danes also were elected to the German parliament.[25]

The final episode over Slesvig took place after World War I, when new countries in Europe were created and boundaries drawn to coincide more closely with the ethnic composition of regions. Because Danes were living under German rule, a vote was taken in Slesvig as to the preference between the rule of Germany and Denmark. Seventy-five percent of North Slesvig voted to become part of Denmark, but in South Slesvig, south of the Tønder-Flensborg line, every parish voted to remain with Germany.[26]

During the last part of the nineteenth century Denmark avoided military involvement and instead turned toward internal reconstruction. Most phenomenal was the transformation of the nonproductive heath land into farms and forests. The Danish Heath Society was formed in 1866 to promote this endeavor. Through the adding of lime and careful husbandry, the soil was made to produce crops. Another revolutionary change in Danish agriculture was made in the period from 1875 to 1895. Denmark had been a grain-exporting nation and as the population in Europe increased and became industrialized the profits on Danish grain increased. But then railroads tapped the plains in the United States and inexpensive wheat flowed into Europe at lower prices than Danish wheat. With the destruction of their grain market, the Danish farmers changed to the production of dairy products, eggs, and bacon, and became themselves purchasers of American grain.[27]

To help in the venture of making agriculture more profitable the Danes utilized the cooperative concept. The idea of a cooperative had its origins in England in 1844 with the Rochdale Equitable Pioneers. A group of weavers established a store that would offer goods at lower prices. The Danes took this idea developed in an urban, working-class setting, and adapted it to fit the agricultural conditions.

The person who carried the idea from England to Denmark was Dr. F. F. Ulrich of Thisted. He described the venture in England to Pastor Hans Christian Sonne, who was called the provisions pastor. Sonne had displayed a great concern for all his parishioners, including the poor, and held meetings in a warehouse for workers who stayed away from church because they believed their clothes to be too shabby. The cooperative idea appealed to Pastor Sonne because it suggested another way for meeting some of the temporal needs of the people. Sonne studied the matter further in British journals and in 1867 wrote a pamphlet on cooperatives.[28]

Ulrich and Sonne helped organize the Thisted Society, the cooperative agency that opened a store in 1866. Bread was one of the chief items sold, but soon the cooperative opened a library and established allotment gardens. The next year a society was founded at Randers, and by 1874 there were 92 societies in Denmark.[29]

The first cooperative creamery was founded in 1882 at Hjedding. A traveling dairyman had suggested that the farmers mix cream from various farms before they churn if they wished to improve the quality of their butter. The farmers considered the advice and agreed to form a cooperative. Three of them sat up most of a night and drafted some rules for their organization.

So practical was this document that it became the pattern for many other dairies. Under this system each farmer had one vote without considering the size of his herd, but the profits would be distributed in proportion to the utilization of the dairy. The butter, made from the cream, was sold and the separated milk returned to the farmer for feeding his pigs. The development of creameries was practically impossible until the construction of the first centrifuge (separator) by L. C. Nielsen in 1879. From then on milk could be handled in large quantities and by 1886 there were 176 cooperative creameries in Denmark. Many of the Danes familiar with the procedure and trained in butter-making migrated to America, where they provided the direction for the development of the dairy industry.[30]

Another dimension of the change in Denmark in the last part of the nineteenth century is tied to the activity of political parties. The defeat by Prussia in 1864 influenced Denmark in ways other than through the loss of land and population. The defeat brought about a change in the constitution. The National Liberals, primarily urbanites, academics, and intellectuals, were blamed for the defeat and the king turned to the great landowners for leadership. The elections of 1866 gave a majority to the conservative element and the constitution was revised in such a way as to consolidate conservative power. While not much was changed in the Constitution relating to the *Folketing* (Lower House), the method of selecting members of the *Landsting* (Upper House) was made more restrictive, thereby insuring conservative control. Even more significant was the provision allowing the king to select his ministers from either house.[31] Opposition to the change came primarily from the common people, who insisted that the ministry come only from the lower house selected by the people. Even the religious figure N. F. S. Grundtvig appealed to the king to retain the feature of the old constitution, but he was not granted an audience.[32]

The politicians on the conservative side composed of landowners and intellectuals formed the right-wing party *Højre* and eventually called themselves the United Right. The king supported this group, much to the disapproval of many Danish Americans, and on numerous occasions Danish Americans expressed their affection for Denmark but not for the king. The

Right held power until 1901 and in an attempt to protect their government and interests, restricted freedom of the press, jailed leaders of the opposition, and used excessive police powers.[33]

The various groups of small and large farmers belonged to the party further left called the *Venstre*, or, eventually, the United Left. This liberal party demanded a more equitable tax policy, agricultural reforms, and a return to the 1849 constitution. While in many countries the farmers are apt to be conservative, the Danish farmers associated with the liberal views. In addition, because the Danish farmers depended on foreign trade they benefited from free trade and open competition instead of from a high tariff policy. Many of the farmers who migrated to the United States brought their political views with them and were sympathetic to the programs of reform candidates and parties.[34] In 1889 the Left advanced a platform calling for such programs as assistance to the aged, limits on the number of hours of work, state aid to smallholders for the purchase of land, and a reduction of military expenditures.[35] The Left gained control of the *Folketing* by 1872, but not until 1901 did the king go to the lower house to choose his ministry. Nevertheless some of the programs of the Left, such as the aid to smallholders and procedures for collective bargaining, were passed prior to 1901.[36]

In the meantime, in 1871, a third party, the Social Democrats, was formed to the left of the *Venstre*. This party, composed of industrial workers, civil servants, some owners of small farms, and shopowners, hoped to gain power and establish a government on Socialist principles. The leader of the socialists, Louis Pio, organized a Danish International and gained 700 members in Copenhagen by 1872. In April of that year he led the bricklayers out on strike and called for a mass meeting of all unions. The government banned the meeting and when Pio would not change his course of action, he was arrested. The police dispersed the workers and Pio served a three-year prison term. The workers, in Pio's absence, organized themselves into workers' associations and trade unions, and in 1875 there were thirty trade unions in Copenhagen. When Pio was released from prison in 1875 and found the changed conditions, he accepted a payment of money and migrated to the United States.[37] The Social Democrats continued to function in politics and gained adherents among both urban and rural workers, eventually joining the Radical party to form a government in 1929. Many Socialists migrated to America, where they continued to support Socialist programs in the United States.

As Denmark changed in the last half of the century and reforms were instituted affecting both rural and urban citizens, the interest in migration diminished. Shortly thereafter World War I discouraged migration, and that event was followed by strong restrictions on immigration during the 1920s.

CHAPTER 2

# *The Migration*

According to the records kept by the United States, 366,000 Danes migrated between 1820, when the government began counting the people who entered the country, and 1970. Very few Danes migrated during the four decades of the nation's history prior to 1820, so the absence of statistics is not significant, but many Danes who disembarked at Quebec and crossed the Canadian border into the United States were not counted until 1908. The number of Danish immigrants would therefore be higher than the official records indicate. A comparison of the Danish numbers with other Scandinavians for the period from 1820 to 1975 shows that the migration from Norway was more than double that from Denmark, with a total of 855,000, while that for Sweden was still greater, with 1,270,000.

The following table shows the number of migrants by decade:

*Danish Migration by Decades*[1]

| | |
|---|---|
| 1821–1830 | 189 |
| 1831–1840 | 1,063 |
| 1841–1850 | 539 |
| 1851–1860 | 3,749 |
| 1861–1870 | 17,094 |
| 1871–1880 | 31,770 |
| 1881–1890 | 88,132 |
| 1891–1900 | 50,231 |
| 1901–1910 | 65,285 |
| 1911–1920 | 41,983 |
| 1921–1930 | 32,430 |
| 1931–1940 | 2,559 |
| 1941–1950 | 5,393 |
| 1951–1960 | 13,706 |
| 1961–1970 | 11,771 |

The first year during which more than 1,000 Danes migrated was 1857 and the first year in which the number exceeded 10,000 was 1882, when 11,618 came to America. That same year, 1882, was also the peak migration year and after that the number declined gradually until the 1920s when the quota system forced a more rapid drop in migration. Following World War II the migration gained momentum so that each year until 1969 more than 1,000 Danes entered the country.

The most thorough work describing the Danes who left Denmark for America has been done by Kristian Hvidt.[2] Using the registers kept by the Copenhagen police on 172,000 migrants who left Denmark between 1868 and 1900, Hvidt examined the nature of Danish migration.

According to a numerical distribution, approximately two-fifths of the migrants came from Jutland, one-fifth from the city of Copenhagen, and two-fifths from the islands of Funen, Lolland-Falster, Bornholm, and Zealand (excluding Copenhagen). Out of every 100 migrants, 41 came from Jutland, 19 from Copenhagen, and 40 from the islands. The geographical distribution in these large units was not even, and that aspect becomes even more evident when the number of migrants from each of the nineteen counties is compared to the resident population of that county. Such a comparison shows that the largest percentage of the population to migrate was from Bornholm and Lolland-Falster, with the smallest percentage in the center of Jutland and the northern part of Zealand (see map). A simple numerical total also indicates that the majority of migrants came from the rural areas of Denmark, but a comparison of the rural-urban residents with population distribution shows that the highest rate of migration came from the cities and provincial towns. Many rural migrants departed directly for America, but others, especially those who lived near towns, migrated first to the neighboring towns. When an urban area could not provide employment for the domestic migrants, America became an alternative destination. Copenhagen was more successful in absorbing the workers than the other cities of the nation.[3]

The migrants were generally young. Fifty-five percent were between the ages of fifteen and twenty-nine. Because fourteen was the age for confirmation the usual practice was to remain at

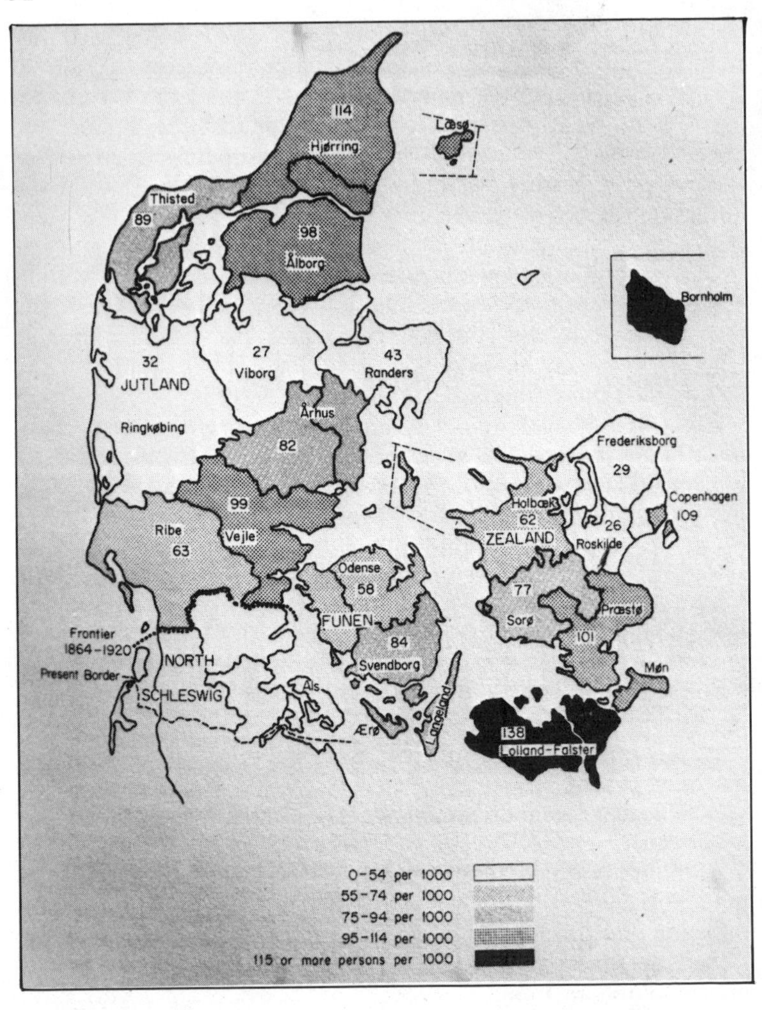


**Sources of Danish migration, 1868–1900, in the 19 Danish counties** (average of census figures for 1870 and 1901).

*Credit*: Kristian Hvidt, *Flight to America: The Social Background of 300,000 Danish Emigrants* (New York: Academic Press, 1975), p. 41.

home until religious education was completed, whereupon the youths could become full-fledged members of society. Marriage, on the other hand, was most commonly entered into after age twenty-nine, so prospective migrants beyond that age were restrained by a wife and children. Life between confirmation and marriage, therefore, was the simplest and the most ideal time to leave for a new country. Urban migrants were generally older at the time of migration than rural people. This age difference probably indicates the attempt of some rural persons to look for work in the towns first and then, after several years of failure, to migrate to America. Parents who were interested in migrating often would do so before the children reached school age so that the children could adjust to the new country before they entered an American school. If, on the other hand, the children had begun school in Denmark, parents generally preferred to remain in Denmark until the schooling had been completed.[4] Even though rural Danes migrated at a younger age than urban migrants, the oldest migrants came from the rural population. Probably the older persons went to live with children who had migrated earlier when they could remain with them on the farm and when there was room and opportunity to help with the work.[5]

Fewer women (60,000) than men (96,000) migrated, and their numbers were smallest in the fifteen-to-twenty-nine age category, where the total migration formed the largest amount. Instead of venturing to America for employment, women looked for jobs in Denmark as milkmaids or domestics. In the two decades prior to the turn of the century the migration of young women increased because of the growing demand for servants in America and the large number of single men who urged their migration with proposals of marriage. Another encouragement was the improved transportation accommodations and cheaper fares that were made available at the end of the century. The following is a letter written in 1907 to Katrine by a Danish immigrant who had been in America for fourteen years and who made a practical proposal:

If you are unwed, you can find a good home with me. I own my house in town and I earn more than 10 Crowns per day. It's been about 20

years since we saw each other, and you probably wonder who I am. My name is Ejner who worked in Halsted for Adolf Jensen when you were at the Andersens, and you were my first love. If you cannot come, ask somebody else who is willing to become a good housewife. My address is. . . .
I shall write some words in English: I am Loved uoy of all my Hart j have bin driming af bort uoy y hoppes dat uoy vill bi my wife.
Respechtifulli Good Bye
I am sand uoy one worm kiss.[6]

Women constituted a large portion of the thirty-to-forty age group because people in that category were generally married. In the early 1870s 43 percent of the Danish emigrants were members of a family group and in the 1890s that statistic had fallen to 29 percent. The males generally migrated in March and April and their wives followed in the late summer. This system permitted the male to earn money and find a suitable place to live. Transportation again was a factor because the improved safety and comfort of the voyage made it possible for the wives and children to travel alone.[7]

Danish artisans and professionals constituted a larger part of the migration during the periods before 1850 and after 1891, while farmers and laborers dominated the time between those dates.[8] The most significant aspect of the migration nevertheless was the predominance of the working class. Sixty-nine percent were members of the proletariat. The largest single portion of the migrants, 43 percent, were rural laborers. These men were interested in owning their own land, and the possibility of obtaining a farm in Denmark was limited. Peasant bondage had been terminated already in the 1770s, and by the nineteenth century the peasants had learned the advantages of local migrations. Land in Denmark was most readily obtainable in central and western Jutland, where the moorlands were being placed under cultivation, and not until after 1884 did migration out of that area rise significantly. The heaviest migration was from Langeland and Falster, where the land was much more fertile. Farms there were priced prohibitively and the parcels were so large that the possibility for obtaining land was remote. Rural laborers left not only because they saw few chances of becoming landowners, but also because of low wages and seasonal employment.

On Funen and Lolland-Falster the owners, in the 1870s, introduced sugar beets as a major crop. Work in the beet fields was necessary for only a portion of the season; consequently Polish and Swedish women were brought in for a limited period. The Danish farm laborer could not exist on such a restricted source of income.[9]

The second-largest category of migrants, also from the lower class, was composed of the domestic and industrial workers. These people could well have been agricultural workers earlier and migrated from the rural areas to the cities in search of a livelihood. They constituted about 25 percent of the total migration. The third major group included craftsmen such as smiths, joiners, bricklayers, carpenters, and bakers. This group was both socially and economically on a higher scale than the rural and urban laborers but constituted only 18 percent of the migrating group.[10]

Although the motivation compelling these people to leave their homes for another continent may be given with a degree of certainty on an aggregate level, an analysis of the thought processes in order to identify the causes for a single migrant is most difficult. The reasons varied from unrequited love to search for adventure, escape from economic hardship, and many others. Some decisions may have been spur of the moment, while others were the result of cautious analysis and thought. Peter Nicolaisen, a New York tailor and later an Iowa preacher, wrote that the guilds, the corporations, the civil service, the aristocracy, conscription, and the caste system all argued for his migration. Only the Christian faith practiced in Denmark encouraged him to remain.[11] There is even a possibility that people unlike Nicolaisen may never have sorted out their own feelings to explain their migration, but some broad generalizations explaining the most obvious and overriding motivations are valuable, as long as one does not forget the interaction of a variety of stimuli among individuals within the group.

The religious motive, so dear to the hearts of many Americans, was indeed a factor in the Danish migration, primarily for the Mormons and the Baptists. Political freedom, another popular theme, was a concern for some of the Socialists, who were nudged out of the country by the conservative government.

Politics was also an important consideration for those Danes who became German citizens with the transfer of Slesvig to Prussia and Austria, but who did not care to serve in the German army or undergo Germanization.

The most pervading factor, nevertheless, was economic—a prosaic reason. The economic motivation may have varied from unemployment and poverty to a general pessimism about future possibilities. In many instances the migrant first moved around Denmark in search of a farm or better employment, and if that failed, migration to America followed. Kristian Gade, for example, found the farmland on Mors to be expensive and purchased some heath land near the sea. That plot was not satisfactory, so he accepted the invitation from his brother to follow him to Washington. The same was true of Boy Jessen, in the twentieth century, who lost the farm in a depression and, unable to find another he could afford, migrated to America. Both Gade and Jessen expressed reservations about leaving familiar Denmark and their beloved country, but concern for the future of their children encouraged them to migrate.[12]

Between 1800 and 1840 Denmark's population grew by 39 percent, and the country could not absorb that many people and provide satisfactory economic opportunities. Economics may even have figured in the migration of Danes from Slesvig. Danish farmers in North Slesvig were forced to compete with German agricultural goods that were produced on the large estates, and towns in the area failed to develop industrially because of the competition from other German cities.[13]

Information of the economic advantages in America spread rapidly. "America letters" told about the conditions in the New World and were read, reread, passed from hand to hand, and published in newspapers. Most were favorable because conditions were good. One immigrant wrote, "I make 60 Danish rixdollars a month on which I naturally do well because food is much cheaper here than in Denmark."[14] Those who did not do well hated to admit defeat, or waited until they had more positive things to say. The letters were important because they reported conditions and gave directions for those who wished to follow. Many women were probably like Mrs. Ane Marie Strandskov, who left her Danish home because so many of her family were going and she would be lonely without them, but most went for economic reasons.[15]

The German poet Goethe, who also recognized the economic advantages of America, summed it up with, "Amerika, du hast es besser." But how much better did America have it? The Bureau of Statistics made a study of labor in Europe and the United States and the report supports the analysis of the Danish migrant and of Goethe.

**Wages in Illinois and Denmark**

| *Nonfarm*[16] | *Illinois 1874* | *Helsingør 1873* | *Percentage Increase in Illinois* |
|---|---|---|---|
| Bricklayers or masons (day) | $ 3.69 | $ .80 | 361 |
| Wheelwrights (day) | 3.75 | .85 | 341 |
| Plasterers (day) | 3.38 | .80 | 322 |
| Stonecutters (day) | 3.50 | .85 | 312 |
| Female servants—cooks and maids (monthly average with board) | 10.18 | 2.50 | 307 |
| Carpenters (day) | 2.87 | .80 | 258 |
| Cabinetmakers (day) | 2.83 | .85 | 233 |
| Blacksmiths (day) | 2.81 | .85 | 230 |
| Coopers (day) | 2.75 | .85 | 224 |
| Painters (day) | 2.56 | .80 | 220 |
| Tanners (day) | 2.50 | .80 | 212 |
| Tinsmiths (day) | 2.25 | .80 | 181 |
| Common laborers (day) | 1.58 | .60 | 163 |
| Tailors (daily piecework average in Denmark) | 2.33 | 1.25 | 86 |
| Shoemakers (daily piecework average in Denmark) | 2.31 | 1.25 | 85 |
| *Farm*[17] | | | |
| Ordinary hands, summer, with board (day) | 1.06 | .36 | 194 |
| Experienced hands, summer, with board (day) | 1.33 | .54 | 146 |
| Experienced hands, winter, with board (day) | .97 | .40 | 142 |

The Danish city used in the report on economic conditions was Helsingør, primarily because the United States stationed a consul in that port and not necessarily because it was a representative city in Denmark. In all probability, the smallness of the country would tend to equalize the wages throughout the nation, and Helsingør would therefore be typical. The usual daily wage for skilled craftsmen and artisans was approximately 80 cents and there was little fluctuation among occupations. The farm wages were probably those paid in the neighborhood of Helsingør.

The information about the United States is given by states rather than by cities, but the wages cited in Illinois are influenced largely by Chicago rather than other parts of the state. The farm statistics, on the other hand, are more for the entire state. There is greater variation among occupations in Illinois than in Denmark: a wheelwright in Chicago received $3.75 per day while a tinsmith was paid only $2.25. The construction workers and builders were especially well paid, undoubtedly because of labor demands following the Chicago fire.

A comparison of wages shows that in every occupation wages were higher in Illinois and in most instances the increase was considerable. Building trades paid well in the growing state, and the wage differential for female servants showed a sharp increase because the pay in Denmark was abysmally low. The farm laborers more than doubled their income in America but the increase was not as high as that for the tradesmen. Agricultural activity in Denmark, however, was disrupted during this period because of the flood of American grain into Europe and the appeal of the Homestead Act, which promised free farms and more than offset the relatively small increase.

An important question was the cost of living. Little advantage would be achieved if the worker received more wages in America but paid more for his expenses. How much more in real wages would an immigrant receive? An accurate comparison of costs between goods in Denmark and the United States is difficult to make because different families used varying amounts of food items, and could accommodate their diet to take advantage of lower costs on certain items. The consul at Helsingør reported that the laboring classes in Denmark did live differently from those in America in that the Danish worker's diet included es-

**Prices in Illinois and Helsingør, Denmark**[18]

| | *Illinois 1874* | *Helsingør 1872* | *Percentage Increase or Decrease in Illinois* |
|---|---|---|---|
| Flour, wheat, superfine (barrel*) | $ 6.60 | $16.66 | − 60 |
| Flour, rye (barrel*) | 6.05 | 13.72 | − 56 |
| Beef, fresh roasting pieces (pound) | .11½ | .12 | − 4 |
| Beef, fresh soup-pieces (pound) | .08 | .10 | − 20 |
| Veal, hind quarters (pound) | .13 | .11 | + 18 |
| Mutton, chops (pound) | .13 | .12 | + 8 |
| Pork, fresh (pound) | .12¼ | .11 | + 11 |
| Pork, corned or salted (pound) | .12 | .12 | — |
| Pork, bacon (pound) | .15 | .14 | + 7 |
| Pork, ham, smoked (pound) | .16 | .18 | − 11 |
| Pork, sausages (pound) | .13 | .16 | − 19 |
| Lard (pound) | .15½ | .16 | − 3 |
| Butter (pound) | .28½ | .27 | + 5 |
| Cheese (pound) | .18½ | .12 | + 54 |
| Milk (quart) | .06½ | .03 | +116 |
| Eggs (dozen) | .20 | .16 | + 25 |
| Tea (pound) | 1.00 | .63 | + 59 |
| Coffee (pound) | .27 | .25 | + 8 |
| Sugar, yellow C (pound) | .11 | .12 | + 8 |
| Soap (pound) | .08 | .06 | + 33 |
| Fuel, coal (ton) | 6.73 | 7.50 | − 10 |
| Fuel, wood, hard (cubic foot) | .04½ | .11 | − 59 |
| Shirtings, brown (yard) | .12½ | .18 | − 30 |
| Sheetings, bleached (yard) | .20¾ | .22 | − 6 |
| Boots, men's heavy | 5.51 | 5.00 | + 10 |
| Four-roomed tenements (month) | 10.60 | 4.50 | +136 |
| Six-roomed tenements (month) | 15.82 | 7.50 | +111 |
| Board, men (week) | 4.25 | 2.50 | + 70 |

* U.S. barrel weighed 196 pounds, while the Danish barrel was 100 pounds. The adjustment was made in calculations.

pecially "Milk-porridge, rye-bread, salt or fresh fish, with an occasional piece of smoked bacon." The common drinks were coffee with chicory and beer. The worker in Denmark lived more frugally than his counterpart in the United States and ate less "animal food."

Flour and fuel were cheaper in Illinois but dairy products and rents were much cheaper in Helsingør. Pork prices were approximately equivalent and there are no statistics for fish, beer, or fowl. Even though precise differences would be difficult to define, the cost of living for the essentials was lower in Denmark than in Illinois, but the amount was small in comparison to the increase in wages.

Additional information collected by the consul in Denmark came from reports prepared by the Danish government. These findings for 1872 can also be tabulated.[19]

**Laboring Classes in Denmark**

| *Location* | *Earnings per year* | *Expenses per year* |
|---|---|---|
| Copenhagen[1] | \$187–\$215 | \$133–\$322 |
| Provincial towns[2] | \$157–\$187 | \$110–\$191 |
| Country[3] | \$105–\$116 | \$ 99–\$137 |

1. The employers believed the earnings were sufficient while the employees contended they were not. Some workers spent money on the education of their children. Many, especially the young, participated in public amusements.

2. The earnings were generally sufficient, but there was some indebtedness.

3. Large numbers were in debt. Nothing was spent on education and few workers engaged in public amusements.

In all three categories the greatest expenses per year exceeded the greatest earnings per year, so there must have been indebtedness in all three categories. The consul reported that the expenses of the laboring classes varied according to earnings, but if there were any savings at all, the amounts were small.[20]

Similar statistics are not available for Chicago, but an estimate was made of the annual expenses and earnings of a laborer in Burlington, Iowa, who theoretically headed a family with two adults and four children. Food, rent, clothing, and taxes cost the typical laborer $622 per year while his income was $884. Annual savings in America, therefore, amounted to $261 or about 30 percent of his income.[21]

When a similar study and report by the Danish government was made twelve years later in 1885, the Danish American Socialist Louis Pio reported the findings from his perspective, and in more human terms. He believed that the Danish laborer's life was more bleak than the report indicated because the statistics were collected by the Danish government and the officials hoped to make Denmark look like a progressive country. Wages in Denmark, Pio admitted, had improved considerably since 1870 as a result of trade union efforts, but Pio agreed with the consular report of the Danish study that conditions were not good. The income of a laboring man in 1885 ranged from $188–$214 while his expenses were $183–$210. The lower-grade artisan received $240–$268 and was confronted with expenses of $227–$254. The earnings compare closely with those of 1873, although the maximum costs were greatly reduced.

Pio also highlighted a deficiency in the report because it failed to include costs of medical care, increase in family size, or lack of income through unemployment. These accidental costs would raise the total expenses by 20 percent, and could only be met through work by the wife or children or through starvation. If the worker received any kind of poor relief he lost his voting franchise. Twenty percent of the people in Copenhagen lived in a single room, and the "hovels" of the agricultural workers were unventilated and damp. The consul reported that the Danish worker saved little but spent his small surplus on beer, and further criticized the worker for his lack of ambition and energy. Pio objected to the charges because there was little motivation for thrift and the beer was only an occasional glass to wash down a sandwich brought from home. Neither could Pio accept a report which charged the worker for moving slowly in his work. Employment did not motivate him or promise advancement.[22]

The examination of the living conditions in Denmark and the comparison to those in the United States show that making a living in Denmark was difficult and that, given a place to go where the economic rewards were greater, there would be migration. Even though all workers would theoretically benefit by migration, some occupations promised greater rewards than others. One could question if the Danish worker was aware of the wages commanded by his trade in America and if that reward attracted him. A glance at the list of wages shows that bricklayers enjoyed a 361 percent increase in pay as a result of migration and that a house painter's increase was a lower 220 percent. Hvidt included an examination of migration according to trades that can be used in a tentative way to provide some insights into the migration.

While the comparison of wages was based on pay during 1873 and 1874, Hvidt's statistics are drawn from 1880 and he presents only six trades for comparison. Comparing the number of men in each trade to the number who left, Hvidt found that smiths left most frequently, followed by housepainters, bakers, carpenters, joiners, and bricklayers. The difference between Hvidt's listing and that of the wage list is great enough to discount the degree of economic reward in America as being the major selector. A more reasonable explanation would be the working conditions in Denmark. The smith's trade, for example, was being jeopardized by industrialization, while bricklayers were finding jobs in Copenhagen as its suburbs were developing. In all probability the Danish worker was influenced most by the working and living conditions in Denmark. His knowledge of America was not precise, but limited to the general impression of improved economic possibilities.[23]

To a small number of Danes "the land of the free" promised something more than political freedom because they were convicts and paupers who were given their freedom provided that they would leave the country. Evidently most European governments were exporting undesirables even though the United States objected. On several occasions the United States consul in Denmark was instructed to protest the actions and all efforts were made to intercept such persons in New York in order to return them to Denmark.[24]

While economic opportunity beckoned to the Danes, there were many facilitators that helped shake the Dane from his inertia and hurry him across the ocean. One of the important recruiters of migrants in the United States was the state immigration commission. Those American states with unsettled land hoped to hasten their development and established commissions with representatives from ethnic groups the states wished to attract. Commissioners discussed ways of advertising their states, but within the limits of a tight budget set by the legislatures. In most instances each state grouped the Scandinavian nations under a single person and assigned him the responsibility of drafting a brochure that would be printed and distributed in Europe.

In 1871 Nebraska, for example, authorized C. F. Walther to write a booklet describing Nebraska's soils, flora, fauna, products, directions for acquiring a homestead, and a map of the Burlington Railroad with its connections from coast to coast. The booklet was published in Copenhagen and identified H. C. Dührsen as the agent, with his address as St. Annaeplads and the Guion Line as the authorized carrier.[25] Most commissions existed only for a short time and in most states the funds were small so that an extensive program was not possible. Only Minnesota sent agents to Europe.[26]

Very closely related to the state commissions were some railroads which often advertised in the state pamphlets or issued some of their own. These railroads, recognizing the potential for rapid financial rewards, frequently sent men to Europe to carry on personal recruitment. The corporations such as the Chicago and Northwestern, the Illinois Central, and the Great Northern held lands that they had received from the government in support of railway construction, and they hoped to sell these lands as soon as possible. The new settlers would then develop farms along the railroad routes so that additional profits could be obtained from shipping commodities.[27]

Still another part of the recruitment network was the steamship business whose profits were directly tied to the ticket sales. In the early days before the Civil War the migrants generally traveled to America on ships whose primary function was to carry cotton and wheat to Europe and which were modified in minor ways to accommodate passengers for the westward voyage. In the later period when the Danish migration became heavy, the vessels were designed primarily for passengers, and although the cost was higher, the conditions were better. The sailing ships traveled slowly so that the Atlantic crossing from Liverpool to New York took approximately four to five weeks, but as the steam-and-sail ship was developed, and then the steamer, the trip was reduced to a period of ten to thirteen days. Denmark had no steamship line until 1879, when the Thingvalla Line was established.[28] Prior to that the Danes traveled primarily on such lines as the Hamburg-American, Red Star, Cunard, Inman, and Guion.[29] In 1890 the Thingvalla Line merged with the United Steamship Company and the new line was called the Scandinavian-American Line. During its existence the steamers of the Thingvalla Line exploited Denmark's location and carried migrants primarily from Russia and the Scandinavian countries, but it was under constant and sharp competition from the older, larger, European lines. The line also suffered several disasters that hurt its profits, including the sinking of the *Hekla* in Oslo Fiord in 1883 and the collision in the mid-Atlantic of the *Thingvalla* and *Geyser,* both ships belonging to the same line, in 1888.[30]

The first agents associated with shipping companies went to work in Denmark in 1860, generally on a part-time basis and as employees of German lines. The full-time professionals began appearing in 1867 with the change from sailing vessels to steam-powered ships. By 1868 there were eight chief agents in Copenhagen who located their offices at Nyhavn and, in cooperation with the Transportation of Emigrations Act of 1868, obtained authorization from the police by posting a 10,000 rix-dollar guarantee.[31] The agencies also sold items for the journey such as mattresses, jugs, and kitchen utensils, and exchanged American dollars for Danish currency.[32]

The agents in turn had subagents, who spread all over Denmark. In the 1880s the subagents numbered more than 1,000. Generally they were employed in other occupations, and worked for the steamship companies as a sideline, but the commissions were high—ten kroner per emigrant—the equivalent of a rural worker's monthly pay.[33]

Another type of person who did much to influence the migration was the returning Danish American. Although the Dane, unlike many Italians, looked upon America as a permanent home, many Danes returned to Denmark for visits with relatives or in some instances to find a wife. Invariably the community was impressed with the material prosperity the Yankee displayed and listened with trust to the information he gave. A word from one they trusted was more convincing than the promises of the agents, and many Danes began thinking about the United States. Others also joined the Yankee on his return and he quickly discovered that shipping companies gave him a free return passage if he could drum up a party of emigrants. Other Danish Americans who could not return for a visit wrote letters to friends and relatives and included prepaid tickets that made the decision much easier.[34]

Most of the Danes landed at New York, and those who entered the United States between 1855 and 1892 landed at Castle Garden, on the tip of Manhattan Island. After 1892 the newer and larger facilities were opened on Ellis Island. At either of these places the migrant could change money, purchase rail tickets to other locations, and buy a meal at the restaurant.[35] Here was also the opportunity to meet representatives of churches, and the Danish Church, operating through Our Savior Lutheran Church of Brooklyn, welcomed the Danish immigrant. The church provided the migrant with a list of Danish pastors and the locations of churches and high schools, and offered the help of the pastor of Our Savior Church to needy Danes. The pamphlet also included the following suggestion: "When you come to a place where there is a Danish pastor, go and consult with him on both religious and other matters, and he will give reliable information."[36]

The destination of the Danish migrant varied throughout the last century, and the Danes distributed themselves widely, but a pattern does emerge from a listing of states possessing the largest and second-largest Danish population.

**Two States With the Largest Danish-Born Population by Decades**

| | | | | |
|---|---|---|---|---|
| 1850 | New York | 429 | Louisiana | 288 |
| 1860 | Utah | 1,824 | California | 1,328 |
| 1870 | Wisconsin | 5,212 | Utah | 4,957 |
| 1880 | Wisconsin | 8,797 | Utah | 7,791 |
| 1890 | Iowa | 15,519 | Nebraska | 14,345 |

| | | | | |
|---|---|---|---|---|
| 1900 | Iowa | 17,102 | Minnesota | 16,299 |
| 1910 | Iowa | 17,961 | Illinois | 17,369 |
| 1920 | California | 18,721 | Iowa | 18,020 |
| 1930 | California | 23,175 | Illinois | 18,945 |
| 1940 | California | 19,726 | New York | 14,304 |
| 1950 | California | 18,053 | New York | 11,627 |
| 1960 | California | 17,503 | New York | 9,462 |

The first Danes remained in the port cities as they learned about the United States. Then came the Mormon migration and the California gold rush. The large migration beginning in the late 1860s headed for the farmlands in the Midwest and later for California farms and cities. Then, as the earlier migrants died, population in the former leading states declined and New York held on to many of the recent immigrants and became the state with the second-largest Danish population.[37]

The Danes are not one of the large ethnic groups to settle in America, and the percentage of the total population has always been small. The following table shows the size of the Danish community.

**Danish-Born Americans and Americans with One or Both Danish Parents[38]**

| *Year* | *Danish-Born* | *Americans with 1 or 2 Danish Parents* |
|---|---|---|
| 1850 | 1,838 | |
| 1860 | 9,962 | |
| 1870 | 30,107 | |
| 1880 | 64,196 | |
| 1890 | 132,543 | |
| 1900 | 153,690 | 187,844 |
| 1910 | 181,649 | 256,175 |
| 1920 | 189,154 | 320,410 |
| 1930 | 179,474 | 349,668 |
| 1940 | 138,175 | 305,640 |
| 1950 | 107,897 | 318,710 |
| 1960 | 85,060 | 314,290 |
| 1970 | 61,410 | 264,151 |

The largest number of Danes in America at one time was in 1920 when 189,154 were present, and the largest number in the Danish tradition was in 1930, when 529,142 people could trace their heritage to Denmark.

## CHAPTER 3

# *From American Exploration to the Early Republic*

THE Danes were interested in North America well before the nineteenth-century migration began, and in 1619, when Jamestown was only twelve years old, King Christian IV commissioned one of his subjects, Jens Munk of Norway, to find the Northwest Passage to the Orient. Munk, with two ships and sixty-five men, sailed from Copenhagen on May 9, 1619, and made his way past the southern tip of Greenland through Hudson Strait and into Hudson Bay. There he took possession of the country in the name of King Christian and called the region Novia Dania, but after extensive search failed to find the passage. Instead the expedition was confronted with a bleak winter, so Munk sailed south to what is now the Churchill River and prepared for the season. They built huts, cut wood, and killed wild fowl to compensate for their lack of equipment and provisions. They survived the autumn months well and the chaplain, Rasmus Jensen, led the celebration of Christmas in the traditional Lutheran way. But in January the winter became severe and exposure to the elements, shortage of food, and scurvy led to ill health and death. One man after another died, including Chaplain Jensen, until only Jens Munk and two men remained alive. Finally the temperatures warmed and by June they regained their strength, and sailing the smaller of the two ships, returned to Denmark arriving on Christmas day.[1]

Munk was one of many who searched for the Northwest Passage. Henry Hudson, an Englishman sailing for the Dutch nation, had explored the east coast of America ten years before Munk's disastrous expedition. The Dutch hired an Englishman as captain, but there were also Danes on board the *Half-moon* as she sailed up the Hudson River in 1609.[2] More Dutch ships followed Hudson's lead, and two of the ships were commanded by Danes, Adrian Block and Henrich Christiansen. Christiansen sailed his ship up and down the Hudson trading with the Indians for furs and corn and bringing supplies to stations on shore. He also constructed a little fort on Castle Island which he called Ft. Nassau, now part of Albany. Although Block carried on similar trading activity he is best known for his exploration around Manhattan Island, and even today his name is assigned to Block Island Sound, south of the present state of Connecticut. In 1614 he drew a remarkably accurate map of the entire New England and New Netherlands area.[3]

There were also Danish settlers among the Dutch who came to colonize the new domain. The presence of Danish sailors on Dutch ships and settlers in Dutch colonies should not be surprising because the two nations had much in common. Geographic nearness brought them together, and for centuries their citizens had enjoyed trade and commercial exchange. Commodities from Denmark, including cattle, herring, and wheat, moved from Ribe on the west coast of Jutland to Holland's ports. The aggressive Dutch traders also sailed their ships into the Baltic through the Sound, where they traded with the Danes, repaired their ships, and paid the Sound dues. Dutch citizens also went to Denmark for work and even Danish architecture was strongly influenced by the Dutch building styles.

In the seventeenth century the Dutch were sailing and trading all over the world, and the population of Holland was not large enough to support its growing empire. Consequently, there was a demand, not only for sailors but also for laborers in Dutch cities and domestics in Dutch homes. A Dane coming to Amsterdam in the 1660s found a Danish colony with a Danish church supported by the Danish government. The majority of the people were sea folk, but there were many others who left Denmark with permission to accept positions with the Dutch trading company.[4]

The first Danish family to migrate to the New World was that of Jan Jansen Van Breestede in 1636. Jan Jansen came from Bredsted in southern Slesvig but his name was modified in the Dutch setting and soon the family name became Van Breestede.

Jørgen Thomsen, from Ribe, was called Jurian Thomassen Van Ripen, and Laurens Andriessen, who lived by the bushes (*buskene*) by the church (*kirken*), became Laurens Van Buskirk. Jan Jansen and the others who followed came from various places in Denmark, but the majority came from the southern Jutland area. The reason for their migration was economic. The Dutch West India Company needed to develop the settlement in order to make a profit, so it encouraged settlers to migrate. Citizens from other nations migrated as well, and besides the Calvinists and Lutherans there were also Catholics and Baptists. Approximately 50 of the 1,000 people in New Netherlands in 1642 were Danes and by 1664 there were approximately 100.[5]

Two of the more famous Danes, Jonas Bronck and Jochem Pietersen Kuyter, arrived in 1639 on Bronck's ship *Conflagration of Troy*. Bronck, whose name remains with us to identify the Borough of the Bronx, purchased 500 acres from the Indians for two rifles, two kettles, two overcoats, two axes, two shirts, one barrel of apple cider, and six gold coins. He could not have made the settlement without the consent of the company, but his desire to gain the Indians' approval was wise. He won their trust, and later in 1642 he played the role of peacemaker between the Indians and Governor William Kieft. Bronck also brought with him farming equipment, seeds, and livestock and hired two of the Danes who arrived on his ship to begin clearing the land. The primary agricultural products were maize and tobacco, both Indian crops. He also built a house which he called "Emmaus," reflecting his religious attachment, and furnished the home with good furniture and books from Europe.[6]

Kuyter, Bronck's friend and brother-in-law, may not have been quite as wealthy, but he also bought land and in addition participated in the politics of the settlement. Kuyter received 400 acres from the company and became the first settler of Harlem. For a time he served as a member of the Board of Twelve Men, an advisory body of Governor Kieft. As a political leader he eventually became embroiled in a disagreement with the company leaders and Governor Peter Stuyvesant fined him 150 guilders and banished him for three years. Kuyter almost drowned on his way back to Holland when his ship was wrecked on the English coast, but he salvaged his possessions and records so he could appeal his case in the Dutch courts. He later returned to New Amsterdam and made peace with Stuyvesant, but was killed by the Indians in 1654.[7]

Although the Danes adapted their names and their economic activity to the Dutch way, not all of them chose to give up their faith. By law they were required to participate in the Reformed worship services and could be punished if they held services in their homes. In 1648, however, they joined some Norwegians and Germans to form a Lutheran congregation and met in homes to read Scriptures, sing hymns, and discuss their problems. Finally in 1654 they sent a call to Ernestus Goetwasser, a Lutheran pastor. With the blessing of the Lutheran Church Council in Amsterdam, Goetwasser left to answer the wishes of the new congregation. Stuyvesant, however, chose to order his return because Goetwasser was not a Dutchman or a Calvinist. Twenty-five men signed a petition protesting the decision, but Stuyvesant held firm. Pastor Goetwasser, however, did not leave on the appointed ship, but hid out with a Lutheran farmer and spent the entire winter in the colony, ministering to the colonists. Eventually he was captured and deported, so the congregation remained without a shepherd until 1669, five years after the English took New Amsterdam. The English called it New York and placed no restrictions against the Lutheran pastor.[8]

Following the British capture of New Netherlands, Danish migration declined, probably because the Dutch West India Company lost its trading position. Nevertheless, during Dutch rule, Danes settled not only in New Amsterdam, but also in Albany and in New Jersey. By 1704 the Danish community in New York was not only intact but large and prosperous enough to construct a stone church on the corner of Broadway and Rector streets.[9]

The next contact the Danes had with America came half a century later through the association of some Danes with the Moravian Brethren (Unitas Fratrum). Although the Brethren trace their history back to the times of John Huss, the brotherhood which developed in the eighteenth century was more a result of the work of Nicholas Louis Count von Zinzendorf. Zinzendorf's family had prevented him from becoming a clergyman, but that did not stifle his interest in religious matters. In 1727 he gathered like-minded believers to his estate at Herrnhut, Saxony, and created a religious community whose practices were heavily pietistic and ecumenical, and whose beliefs, though not extensively defined, were Calvinist. His hope was to bring about the unification of the various faiths.

Count Zinzendorf realized the need of working with the political leaders of the time, and while he was attending the coronation of Christian VI, in 1731, he learned from a West Indies Negro servant about the conditions of the slaves in that region. Zinzendorf was struck not only by the plight of the slaves in the West Indies but also by the problems of the Eskimos in Greenland and made both areas mission fields for the Brethren. In 1732 the first two Moravian missionaries were dispatched to St. Thomas and the Moravians had taken the first step into the New World. Eighteen more missionaries were sent over, both men and women, and they established missionary posts throughout the Danish West Indies. The Brethren experienced hostility from some local planters who were not interested in the education of their slaves, but they enjoyed some support from a few planters with a more humane view of their workers, and from King Christian.[10]

The Moravians then introduced their teachings into Denmark in 1737 and many Danes throughout the nation were won over, especially in the southern Jutland area. Adherence to the faith and its practice were illegal, however, so many converts spent some time in Herrnhut, Saxony, and some joined the Moravian settlements being founded in the American colonies.[11] Finally, in 1771, Christian VII repealed the existing restrictions that hampered the Moravians and they established a community at Christiansfeld in Slesvig.[12]

The Danish converts began the migration in 1742, when Christian Werner joined the colonists at Bethlehem, Pennsylvania, then a settlement barely a year old. Other Danes followed from Jutland towns such as Tønder and Ribe, but also from Copenhagen and Helsingør. The Brethren found it more economical to provide transportation on their own ships and many migrated on the ship *Irene*, commanded by a Danish captain and manned by a Danish crew. The Danes who migrated came from various walks of life, but some were Lutheran pastors who continued their profession in the New World. Other Danes were teachers, innkeepers, or missionaries to the Indians, and one produced bells for the Moravian communities.[13]

There were no separate and distinct Danish communities among the Moravians, and the orientation was strongly German. Many of the migrants were single men who married German spouses, and all references indicate that they adopted the German language and were absorbed into the German culture. This immediate assimilation of Danes further complicates the task of obtaining an estimate of the number that migrated. One source, a list of a cemetery in Bethlehem from 1742 to 1897, includes thirty Danish and Norwegian names, but there were Danes in other settlements as well.[14]

During the British colonial period close ties existed between the Danish West Indies and the colonies. There were business connections and Danish planters sent their children to the English colonies, especially Philadelphia, for their education. The American Revolution brought some Danish volunteers to the Rebel side, including naval officers and sons of upper-class people.[15]

An individual who illustrates both the connection with the West Indies and the American military was Christian Febiger. He accompanied his uncle, the newly appointed governor to St. Croix, but in 1772 he traveled extensively in the colonies from Cape Fear, North Carolina, to Penobscot, Maine, studying the economic activities and the business potential. He then settled in Boston and dealt in lumber, fish, and horses. He had enjoyed some previous military training, so during the battle of Bunker Hill he participated in the action and performed well. He also fought in major battles such as Brandywine, Monmouth, and Yorktown and was known by his men as "Old Denmark."[16]

In the days of the young republic, isolated Danes migrated to the United States. They were generally seamen, businessmen, artisans, doctors, teachers, and adventurers. Most settled in the cities and were rapidly assimilated.[17] One of these was Christian Guldager, a painter who at the age of seventeen won the gold medal in competition at Copenhagen. The award also provided for three years of study in a foreign country, but instead of following the beaten path to Italy, he was attracted to America because of Benjamin Franklin's blanket invitation in 1783 to European artists. Guldager married an American woman, made a good living painting portraits, and was rapidly assimilated. He is best known for his portrait of George Washington, and tradition identifies him as the creator of the symbol depicting a defiant eagle standing on a shield and clutching three arrows.[18]

The migration from Denmark continued to be small throughout the first half of the nineteenth century in spite of the large influx from other European countries. Those few who came generally found homes in the major cities both on the coast and inland. New York received the majority, and in 1844 the first Scandinavian society in America was founded in that city. Danes were included among the founders and early members, but in general these were not the ones who stimulated the large migration that followed.[19]

# Part II. *The Religious Dimension*

CHAPTER 4

# *Danish Mormons*

THE involvement of the Mormons with the Danes was a significant association because the migration of Danes to Utah was the first large wave of migration from Denmark to the United States. In the 1850s 2,898 of the 3,749 Danes who migrated were Mormons. In the next decade, 13,011 Danes migrated, and included in that number were 4,942 Mormons.[1] Hence Utah, which did not become a state until 1896, had acquired by 1860 the largest Danish population in the United States.

The first Dane who joined the Mormon church was Peter Clemmensen, who at that time lived in Boston. Although Clemmensen soon renounced his faith, he had converted a Danish sailor, Hans Christian Hansen, whose ship had docked at Boston. Hansen returned to England with his ship and was baptized at Liverpool, but he could not get to Denmark to tell of his new faith. Instead he wrote a letter to his brother, Peter, and returned to America. At Nauvoo, Illinois, he worked on the temple project. In 1844 he traveled to meet his brother, who had landed at Boston, and while he was away the Mormon leader, Joseph Smith, was murdered. Brigham Young, Smith's successor, met Peter and asked the new convert to begin the translation of the *Book of Mormon* into Danish. Young also made plans for the trek to the Great Salt Lake, and Hans was in the 1847 vanguard of Mormons which established the settlement.[2]

In October 1849 the church leadership decided to send missionaries to Europe and selected Peter Hansen and Erastus Snow, who spoke no Danish, to carry the Mormon message to Denmark. The missionaries, including Hansen and Snow, crossed the mountains and plains late in the year and arrived in Europe in spring 1850. Snow remained in England for several weeks while Hansen went ahead to convert his father and old friends. Unsuccessful with other members of his family, Hansen, joined by Snow and a third missionary, George P. Dykes, concentrated their efforts on the citizens of Copenhagen. Their first converts were won from a Baptist congregation headed by Peter C. Mønster, who earlier had welcomed them warmly because they too were dissenters from the established church. Mønster soon realized that his own flock was more receptive to the Mormon message than to his and he withdrew his support. By August 1850, some Baptists had affiliated with the new faith and the Mormons had established their base. One of the missionaries, Dykes, went to Aalborg, where he followed the Copenhagen procedure and won over some recent Baptist converts.[3]

Most of the witnessing was carried on quietly in the homes of interested people. Sections of Hansen's translation of the *Book of Mormon,* though unpublished until 1851, were read, and that material, along with several tracts, provided the source for discussion and study. Snow's tract, "A Voice of Truth to the Honest Heart" (En Sandheds Røst til de Oprigtige af Hjertet), was the most successful one and 140,000 copies were printed by 1882. The appeal was to biblical truths and sharp criticism was directed to the state church with its allegedly indifferent clergy. The gains were impressive. In six months there was a congregation of fifty members, and within the first year there were 300 converts.[4]

The Mormon missionaries had arrived at an opportune time for the propagation of their faith. The new Danish constitution written in 1849 granted religious liberty and the missionaries to Denmark did not experience the restraints by the state encountered by the missionaries in Norway and Sweden. Religious life in Denmark also was undergoing upheaval, and people were questioning the ineffective Lutheran church. Baptists, Methodists, and religious dissenters appeared on the scene and sowed the seeds of religious debate. The Mormons, therefore, were protected against government intervention and found an audience attuned to new religious approaches.[5]

Even though the constitution of Denmark guaranteed religious freedom there were no laws supporting that right. As a result some religious and political leaders attempted to place restrictions on the Mormons, but they were not successful. The Mormons also suffered harassment from the populace. At Aalborg, for example, a crowd of 1,000 who had come to witness a Mormon baptism by immersion in the Limfjord, was antagonized by the Mormon speaker when he told them that their church and clergy were of the devil. The crowd stoned the Mormons and broke windows in Mormon homes. More personal violence and property damage took place in small towns, where converts were more easily identified, than in the large cities. In the cities hostility was directed to the religious services by unruly elements who disturbed the services and interfered with the speaker. But the government would not prohibit the assembly of the Mormons, and after ten years, as the Mormons became more commonplace, harassment declined. The actual loss in converts is hard to estimate, but as in most other instances, the victims probably gained from the publicity and attention.[6]

Much of the opposition that was not violent and disruptive originated from the Lutheran clergy. Mormons were denounced from the pulpit and through pamphlets. An extensive attack of ninety-two pages was written by C. B. Garde, "The Errors of Mormonism" (Om de mormonske Vildfarelser Til mine Menigheder). The attacks focused heavily on the polygamy issue, associating it with adultery. Many letters written by apostates from Utah were published in the Danish press and made reference to polygamy. Mormonism was called unchristian, the leaders devious, and the followers ignorant. The charges of polygamy were not generally applicable, and a study of Ephraim, a Danish community in Utah, shows that slightly less than 10 percent of Danish families contained multiple wives. The Mormon migration, on the other hand, was different from the general migration of Danes because it contained 7 percent more women than men while the general migration in the last portion of the nineteenth century was 60 percent male. Polygamy may explain part of the difference, but the emphasis on family migration and the security within group migration must also be considered.[7]

Mormonism gained in spite of the opposition, partially because the Mormons did not rely on a trained clergy but took converts, instructed them briefly, and sent them out in pairs to witness. Twenty-five of the first 300 left their homes and became missionaries in various parts of Denmark. Many converts were journeymen who bore testimony of their new faith as they traveled in the country practicing their trade.[8]

The missionaries were most successful in the little villages around Aalborg, Aarhus, and Fredericia, and 53 percent of the converts were from Jutland. The largest proportion of the population to join Mormonism was in the northern province of Vendsyssel, the area beyond the Limfjord. In 1861 there were 662 members of the Vendsyssel Conference, with 115 married couples, 9 widowers, 36 widows, 18 betrothed men, 62 betrothed women, 2 divorced men, 8 divorced women, 58 youths over fifteen, 131 girls over fifteen, 46 boys between eight and fifteen, and 62 girls between eight and fifteen. Judging from the Mormons who migrated to America, converts were from every type of occupation, although generally they were on the lower economic level. Farmers and their families made up one-half of the migrants in the 1850s and artisans and unskilled laborers dominated in the 1860s.[9]

Later many of the Danes who had migrated to Utah, as well as their children, returned to Denmark as missionaries. Prior to 1900, 516 Danish-born missionaries took the journey back. The missionaries from Utah were assigned by the church leaders and went without pay for two or three years. Their families, in the meantime, had to struggle on their own although the Mormon community came to the aid of the "missionary widow." Christian Hansen solved the problem of his absence by marrying a second wife who was a "big, strong Danish woman" and took his place in the fields.[10]

The Mormons were interested not only in converting Danes for life in the hereafter, but also for the purpose of strengthening their community in Utah. At the time of the initial migration from Nauvoo, the Mormons hoped to escape from the United States and establish their Zion in Mexico, but Zion became part of the United States following the conclusion of the Mexican War, and Brigham Young's revised goal was to establish a state within the United States called Deseret. In order to create a state, however, settlers were needed and Young looked forward to the time when Utah could escape from the territorial status with officials appointed by the President of the United States to the status of a state where officials were elected by the people—Mormons.

Certainly the Danes were aware of the American connection with the Mormon faith and it undoubtedly aided in the conversion efforts. Danish newspapers had earlier carried the report of Joseph Smith's discovery of the *Book of Mormon* and other accounts that dealt with aspects of Mormon life, especially polygamy. Many Danes also had become interested in America and they had heard about the discovery of gold in California. Conversion was tied to migration and to a brighter future. Europe was decadent, poor, and plagued with wars, while Zion, like the United States, was the land of the future where their children could prosper. Danish interest in America was stimulated by the Mormon biweekly periodical *Skandinaviens Stjerne*, published in Copenhagen beginning in 1851. It served to stimulate conversion but also raised interest in Utah by talking about the price of land, the construction of the railroad, the nature of the harvest, and the social activity in Zion. Frequent letters from America were printed, and prospective migrants scrutinized the pages for travel advice.[11]

Migration, however, did not take place immediately because the base in Denmark had to be enlarged to support missionary activity. Not until 1852, a year and one-half after Hansen's arrival, did any converts leave for America, and then only a group of twenty-eight. The peak year for the Scandinavian mission was 1862 when 1,977 Danes, Norwegians, and Swedes were baptized. Conversions declined after that, probably because of continued opposition by the Lutherans and critical letters from earlier migrants who were unhappy. By 1905, 23,509 Danes had been converted and 12,696 migrated.[12]

Every significant aspect of the migration was planned and supervised by the experienced Mormon leaders. Each Mormon congregation was asked for migrants, who then assembled at collecting areas such as Aalborg, Aarhus, Fredericia, and Copenhagen. Those migrants who could not pay their own way could borrow money from the Perpetual Emigrating Fund and signed promissory notes. All of the money was then pooled and the Mormon agent signed a contract with a shipping firm. Because of the large number of people in each party, the leader was able to secure a cheaper rate. The cost per person amounted to approximately $26 on sailing vessels, and $30 following the advent of the steamship. The ships then went from Copenhagen to Kiel, and there the migrants crossed Germany for Altona and Hamburg. The next leg of the journey was across the North Sea to Grimsby or Hull, where they boarded a train for transit to Liverpool. Cholera raged in Liverpool in the early years, and more than twenty children from the 1853 group died of that disease.[13]

At Liverpool they boarded a ship for the long trip across the Atlantic. Prior to 1855 the migrants landed at New Orleans and then proceeded up the Mississippi River to Iowa, but because of disease and the heat they changed their route and landed in eastern ports, generally New York, and took the railroad to staging areas in Iowa. The route in 1859 was from New York to Albany by boat, then by train to Niagara; Windsor, Canada; Detroit; Quincy, Illinois; and St. Joseph, Missouri. There they took a river boat for Florence, Nebraska, near Omaha.[14] The staging areas in the Midwest varied. In 1854 it was at Westport, Missouri, where 180 out of 680 died, primarily of cholera.[15] In 1857 it was Iowa City, but from there they had to cross 300 miles of primitive and generally muddy roads, to Nebraska. That trip took as long as twenty days. The railroad was not completed to Utah until 1869, so from 1852 to 1869 the Danish Mormons walked, pulled and pushed handcarts, or traveled by ox-drawn wagons. A handcart party would include fifty handcarts with four to six people assigned to each cart. The carts carried mostly baggage while a few wagons drawn by oxen followed with provisions and room for the sick or exhausted. In 1859 the overland trip cost about $75 by handcart and approximately $100 by wagon, even though that leg of the trip was usually taken care of by Mormons from Utah who had come east to meet the migrants. When the Union Pacific reached Laramie, Wyoming, the charge for the remaining distance was only $29. The first steamship crossing of the Atlantic Ocean by the Mormons was made in 1867, and the time of travel when both the steamship and the steam locomotive were used in 1869 was twenty-seven days.[16]

No exclusively Danish colonies or churches existed among the Mormons, although there were concentrations of Danes. A section of Salt Lake City was called "Little Denmark" and it was home for the first group of Danes who arrived in 1852 and for some who followed later. Other Danish concentrations were Sanpete and Sevier counties, south of Salt Lake and Box Elder and Cache counties to the north. Many also settled in Mormon communities in Idaho. Even with the Danish concentrations in specific places, Danes were represented in most communities.

Instead of establishing isolated homesteads, the Mormons adopted a settlement pattern based on a village system familiar to most Danes. Irrigation, the basis for Utah farming, required cooperation, an activity not radically different from the later cooperatives in Denmark. The first dairy cooperative was organized by a Dane in Brigham City when he gained the use of 400 cows in exchange for shares in the operation. Group action was also necessary for fort-building and for Indian defense. Some Slesvig-Holstein veterans, for example, living at Sanpete organized themselves into the Silver Grays to protect their community against attack. The town system was especially important to those Danish tradesmen who could give up farming and return to the practice of an earlier trade.[17]

Initially most Danes practiced agriculture and for the first few years lived in dugouts and adobe houses. Later some built half-timbered houses with thatched roofs. Danish centers such as Sanpete County produced grain, dairy products, and eggs which were generally sold in Salt Lake City or to the workers in the mining camps. The farm wife molded butter into one-pound squares and then packed it in wooden boxes. The farmer then placed the boxes in the bottom of the wagon and covered them with sacks of flour to retain the coolness. The flour in turn was covered with grain. Eggs were shipped in boxes of oats to prevent cracking on the bumpy journey.[18]

The Danish language and culture were not consciously preserved in the Mormon church as they were in the Danish Church in America. English, in the view of the leadership, was the Lord's favored language and it was the language of Utah. Already in Denmark and on board ship the Danes learned English from the missionaries. Because there were no exclusive Danish communities in Utah, there were no Danish church services. The Mormon leadership, however, was tolerant of the Danish tongue and acknowledged that it was necessary to communicate the Mormon message in a language Danes could understand until they learned English. The leaders nevertheless promoted the collective Scandinavian concept rather than the specific Danish, Norwegian, or Swedish nationality. The Scandinavian meetings were held in sizable settlements and used for the purpose of religious instruction, and also as a rallying point for Danes. They sponsored plays, choirs, and social events. There were other ties as well that helped maintain the language and interest in Denmark. The missionary who returned to Denmark would visit his relatives and search out those Danes related to his Utah neighbors. His neighbors also sent him letters asking about their families, and he sent back answers and newspapers from Europe. Upon his return he was met by the community brass band and given many opportunities to talk about his experiences in Denmark.[19]

The only newspaper in the Danish language in the early days of the Utah settlement was *Skandinaviens Stjerne* and that was published in Copenhagen. In 1873 the *Utah Posten* was published for the Dano-Norwegian community, but it suspended publication after only thirty-six weeks. It was succeeded by the *Utah Skandinav,* which included columns in Swedish and English. The editor, however, held views not appreciated by the church leaders, so Anders W. Winberg began the publication of *Bikuben* in 1876 to respond to the *Utah Skandinav. Bikuben* proved to be highly popular and continued publication until 1935. Another publication was *Morgenstjernen,* a monthly journal dedicated to the history of the Scandinavian mission. It published biographies, excerpts from daybooks and journals, and European news items. The editor, Andrew Jenson, on one occasion also tried his hand with a newspaper and revived the *Utah Posten.* Jenson was unhappy with the folksy style of *Bikuben* and attempted to produce a more literary paper. He did not succeed financially, and later joined forces with the paper he disliked.[20]

Not all of the Mormons who crossed the Atlantic settled in Utah. Many of them left the fold and occupied land in western Iowa and eastern Nebraska. Others, called backtrailers, went on to Utah, but did not like Zion and returned to gentile areas. The Danish community in Douglas County, Nebraska (Omaha) included many backsliding Mormons. During the 1880s, when groups in the United States took up the cause against polygamy, some of the Protestant churches sent missionaries to the Mormon strongholds. The Methodists enjoyed some success with the Danes and used the Danish Methodist hymnal in church services. Another medium in circulation was *Vidnesbyrdet,* a Dano-Norwegian church paper. The Lutheran church came into the field later and concentrated its efforts in the urban areas. In spite of the large Scandinavian population this denomination experienced little success. In 1906 a Danish missionary society sponsored Pastor Harald Jensen of the Blair church in founding a congregation in Utah. The society also helped pay for the construction of a house of worship, but the flock remained small.[21] Once safely a part of the Utah community, not many Danes wished to leave and join other Danish settlements in America. At the same time, Mormons sent missionaries to Denmark to convert Danes, but they neglected to send missionaries to convert the Danes already in America.

Ironically, in the 1870s, when steam travel removed the serious hardships of travel to Utah, the Mormon migration declined, although 472 migrated in 1873. The obvious reason for the decline in migration was the dropping off of conversions in Europe. The newer generation in Denmark did not concern itself with scriptural literalism, so much a part of the Mormon meetings, and the improvement in social and economic conditions in Denmark did not drive the Danes to look to the Mormons as a source for new opportunities. By that time also Utah had built up a population sufficient for its needs, and Mormons with limited resources were not encouraged to migrate.[22]

The adaptive capacity of the Danish Mormons was boundless. They changed their religion; they broke loose from the quiet, predictable life in Europe and became frontiersmen in a rugged environment in the American West. The life of one of these, Jens Nielson, provides some insights into the experiences of the 12,000 who migrated.

Jens and his wife, Elsie Rasmussen, were converted in the fall of 1852 when two Mormon elders came to the neighborhood near Aarhus. Jens had married Elsie in 1850, at age thirty, and then bought about five acres of land on which he built a house. All the reports he had heard about the Mormons had been negative, but out of curiosity he accepted an invitation to attend a meeting where the two Mormons were present. He was impressed with their appearance and with their testimony and bought some of their tracts for further study. One and one-half years later, in March 1854, he and Elsie were baptized. Their former friends became enemies and his only desire was to sell the property and leave for Zion. He had almost completed the sale of his property when the president of the Mormon conference instructed him to become a missionary and carry the message in Denmark. He obeyed and together with a young man went out and baptized some converts. Finally, after one and one-half years, he received permission to migrate.

In the spring of 1856 he sold his property and with his wife and son traveled to Copenhagen. Nothing is said about traveling with a group of fellow believers, so they may have traveled alone to New York. From New York they took the railroad to the end of the line in Iowa, where they lost five precious weeks waiting for the construction of handcarts. The entire party numbered about 500 people, and they traveled with 125 handcarts and five wagons. Unfortunately the handcarts were poorly constructed and began to break, thereby causing further delays. Another problem was the harassment from a group of men who followed them through Iowa, threatening them with violence and frightening seventy-five converts from the train.

After crossing Iowa they rested for one week on the Missouri River while they gathered supplies for the thousand-mile trip to Utah. They estimated that the trip would be completed in seventy days, but since it took ninety, the food supply was inadequate. Then, in early September, as they were crossing Nebraska, half of the oxen stampeded and could not be located, so flour had to be taken out of the wagons and one hundred pounds added to each handcart. With all of the delays and the slower progress resulting from the heavier loads, the brigade encountered the chilling fall winds. In October they began reducing the rations, and on the twentieth a storm hit, dropping two inches of snow. Five hundred miles separated them from Utah when another snowstorm passed, leaving drifts two feet deep. Each night the migrants pitched their tents, which sheltered five men and fifteen women and children, but the loss of life was so great that soon Jens was the only man left in his tent, and he needed help from strong women to raise it. Also at this time their only son died. Finally Nielson's own feet froze and he could walk no farther. Elsie loaded him onto the cart and pulled him mile after mile until his strength and spirit returned and they reached Ft. Bridger, where wagons from Utah met them.

They arrived at Salt Lake City on November 9, 1856, and settled in Iron County in southwestern Utah. Elsie consented to Jens's suggestion of polygamy, so Jens married Kirsten Jensen, a woman he had baptized in Denmark, and later Katherine Johnson became his third wife. He helped establish five different communities in Utah, and in 1879 he was called on to found a colony in Navajo country in southeastern Utah. It was isolated and rugged country, and after an exhausting five-month ordeal the party, with eighty wagons, settled the town of Bluff on the San Juan River. The couple from the sandy, flat land of Jutland had become the persevering settlers on the mountainous Utah frontier. Jens, although handicapped by twisted feet from the handcart expedition, showed leadership in dealing with the Indians and renegade whites who stole horses and cattle, as well as endurance in maintaining irrigation systems requiring constant attention and frequent repairs. Faithful Elsie managed the house and garden, tended bee hives, wove carpets from old rags, raised silkworms, and found time to cover baseballs with buckskin.

Jens built a brick home on the northwest corner of the block for Elsie and himself, and a rock house on the southwest corner of the block for Kirsten, where he ate his midday meal. He died a respected man, two days short of his eighty-sixth birthday.[23]

Even if most Danes did not become Mormons and even though the large Danish migration was not the direct result of the Mormon migration, the Danes who went to Zion took the strangeness out of migrating to America and their stories expanded the horizons of those who remained in Denmark.

CHAPTER 5

# The Religious Divisions of the Danish Americans

## I *The Lutheran Church in Denmark*

DURING the time of the major migration movement, there were three distinct factions under the umbrella of the Danish church. The first of these was called the *Centrum*, a high-church party that followed the leadership of Jacob Peter Mynster. He did not encourage lay participation in the church and preached no awakening or repentance. Instead this eloquent preacher stressed personal piety and building a Christian faith. He also advocated the necessity of the institutional church, with its dignified ritual and administrative procedure. Mynster's influence was especially felt after 1811, when he became the pastor of the cathedral in Copenhagen, and on into the 1830s, when he became the bishop of the Zealand diocese. The *Centrum*, recognizing the contributions of both rationalism and romanticism, was nevertheless skeptical toward new movements in the church and softened the extreme trends as they became evident in the body of the church.[1]

The man who led a second segment within the Danish church was Nikolaj Frederik Severin Grundtvig (1783–1872). This famous Dane left his mark on other aspects of Danish life as well. He had attended the University of Copenhagen in the tradition of rationalism, a philosophy that stressed the use of the mind and the improvement of society. In its religious aspects it placed the Bible under scrutiny of reason and found it full of errors. Reason replaced faith, and a greater emphasis was placed on the gentle teachings of Christ than on doctrine and dogma. The church's mission, the Rationalists held, was to solve social problems, and on one occasion a leader in the movement maintained that pastors preparing for service in rural parishes should study physics, chemistry, and agricultural economics instead of Greek and Hebrew so they could serve the farmer's body as well as his soul.[2]

Grundtvig's first religious crisis took place in the autumn of 1810 when he realized that his optimism about man's goodness was without foundation, and that only through Christ could man be saved. Furthermore he viewed the Bible as the foundation of faith because it was God's revelation of the Savior. In time, however, he realized that this traditional Lutheran position did not refute the Rationalists' criticisms of the Bible, but merely brushed those views aside. After several years of study and contemplation he experienced a second religious crisis, which in 1825 led to his "matchless discovery": he would give up the Bible as the basis for faith and instead substitute the living and confessing church.[3]

The church was older than the Scriptures, he held, and had already existed in the days of the Apostles. When the congregation gathers for the sacraments of Baptism and the Lord's Supper and recites the Apostles' Creed, then Christ is present. Grundtvig also maintained that Jesus gave the Creed to the Apostles in the forty days between the Resurrection and the Ascension. The Scriptures, therefore, may contain contradictions and errors, and differing factions may all appeal to the same Bible for support, without damage to faith, because Scripture is not the basis for faith. While Scripture contains the Word of God, it is not itself the Word of God.[4] Grundtvig's answer, however, was in conflict with the orthodox Lutheran position, which maintained that the Old and New Testaments were the only norm and source of Christian faith and life, and that the creeds, including the Apostles' Creed, were based on the Bible.[5]

In addition to providing an answer to the Rationalists that satisfied himself and many others, Grundtvig influenced Danish life in other ways. He was a highly gifted hymnist, and more than a third of the hymns of the 1954 Danish hymnbook are ascribed to him as either composer or adaptor.[6] He composed more than 1,600 hymns in his lifetime, including "Built on a Rock the Church Doth Stand." Nevertheless many of his most impressive hymns have not become part of American religious worship. The beauty of the language and the meaningful images are frequently lost in the translation.[7]

Grundtvig was also an ardent nationalist who in his early years had witnessed Denmark's suffering from the British attacks on Copenhagen in 1801 and 1807, as well as the economic depression during the Napoleonic period. He was also serving in Parliament when Prussia annexed Slesvig.[8] Throughout his life he took pride in Denmark's language and not only studied the ancient sagas but published *Nordic Mythology* and other works that brought him acclaim as a leading scholar of the subject. He combined his nationalism, his interest in history, and his religious orientation with support of the Folk High School movement. Although he shares the limelight with Christen Kold, and although the schools did not develop precisely as he envisioned them, Grundtvig's name is always associated with the underlying philosophy of that educational movement.[9]

While the Mynster aspect of the church, the *Centrum,* was not influential outside of Denmark, Grundtvig influenced a large segment of the Danish community in America. That group which eventually became known as the Danish Church or "Happy Danes" is in debt to him for its inspiration and strong loyalty toward Denmark. Their attachment to the Danish language and the Folk High School movement in the United States show his impact.

Coinciding with Grundtvig's theological leadership was the disastrous conflict over Slesvig. In the hope of unifying the Danish people, Frederik VII promised a free and democratic constitution. The constitution, officially enacted on June 5, 1849, gave the Danes religious freedom. Even though the state was neutral in religious matters, the Evangelical Lutheran Church was the folk church (*Folkekirken*), and because practically the whole nation belonged to it, the church received financial support from the state. Grundtvig and his followers did not withdraw from the church, nor were they removed, even though Grundtvig and Mynster never became friends.[10]

The third segment of the church, the Inner Mission movement, can be traced to 1850 when Jens Larsen, a blacksmith, became a lay preacher. Larsen had been influenced by Grundtvig, but chose his own course when support for his mission was less than he expected. Instead he created his own Society of Inner Mission, composed of a group of laymen who sponsored him as their missionary to the people of Denmark. Conflicts arose within the group, however, and some members realized that what was needed was leadership from the clergy. At the annual meeting in 1861, when the problem was discussed, Larsen resigned, and the group, rather than disbanding, followed the leadership of Vilhelm Beck, who had preached the main sermon. Beck, a pastor's son, had completed his university training for the ministry, but struggled with a weak faith. He questioned the value of the ministry of his father and of Bishop Mynster, his father's mentor. Beck saw no changes in people's lives and no conversion and spiritual renewal. Beck wished for the church to make an impact on every aspect of daily life and saw the value in the direction Larsen had taken. The organization was reconstituted and called the Church Society for Inner Mission in Denmark, to indicate that its objective was revitalization of the faith within Denmark as a group belonging to the mother church. Beck became the editor of the society's "Inner Mission Tidings" and dominated the organization until his death in 1901.[11]

The purpose of the Inner Mission was to reawaken the religious life of the people, both rural and urban, and to oppose the different sects arising in Denmark. Initially only colporteurs selling approved publications were sent out, but soon many of them were commissioned as lay preachers. Local groups organized themselves into branches for the support of the Inner Mission, and often built mission houses that served as meeting places or hostels. In their personal life, the Inner Mission people emphasized personal faith and piety and renounced certain worldly acts such as dancing, drinking of alcohol, gambling, immorality, and Sunday labor. In contrast to Grundtvig, Beck and his followers believed in the depravity of man and worked for a conversion. They also insisted on a literal interpretation of the Bible.[12]

The Inner Mission movement, like the Grundtvigian, influenced the religious thinking of the Danish migrants in America. Its presence had a significant effect on such groups as the United Evangelical Lutheran Church or the "Pious [or Holy] Danes."

The terms "Happy Danes" and "Pious Danes," like most stereotypes, are not accurate, but their use in America was widespread.

The Danish church, therefore, was made up of three parts, the *Centrum*, the Grundtvigian, and the Inner Mission. All three groups existed in the latter half of the nineteenth century at the time of the large Danish migration, and although there were theological differences, all three claimed adherence to the Lutheran confessions.

## II *The Establishment of Danish Lutheran Congregations in America*

The migration of Danes to America during the first decades of the nineteenth century was insignificant, and those Danes who made the journey were scattered and assimilated rapidly. Even during the decade of the 1840s only 539 Danes migrated, but they located in the areas where future Danish newcomers would concentrate. In 1846 some Danes settled at Hartland, Wisconsin, and two years later Danes made their homes in other Wisconsin locations including Brown County, Neenah, and Racine. Their motivation was primarily economic; although they were Lutheran, the perpetuation of their faith was not the chief priority.[13]

Those Danes who were concerned with religion either joined other denominations or were ministered to by Norwegian Lutheran pastors. The Norwegian language was easily understood by Danes and the orders of service were similar. In 1851, for example, the Scandinavian congregation in Racine organized and it eventually became purely Danish.[14] Not until 1870, however, did the Rev. Claus Laurits Clausen, a Dane serving the Norwegian Lutherans, help organize the "Conference of the Norwegian-Danish Evangelical Lutheran Church in America." The inclusion of the word "Danish" as part of the name was a recognition that Danish congregations were being served by Norwegian pastors, but it was also an appeal to the Danish nationality. Danish young men were encouraged to enroll at the Norwegian Augsburg Seminary, and between 1872 and 1884 ten Danes graduated from the Minneapolis school and were ordained by the conference. Although few in number, these men would play an important part in one branch of Danish Lutheranism.[15]

**Danish Lutheran Denominations in America***

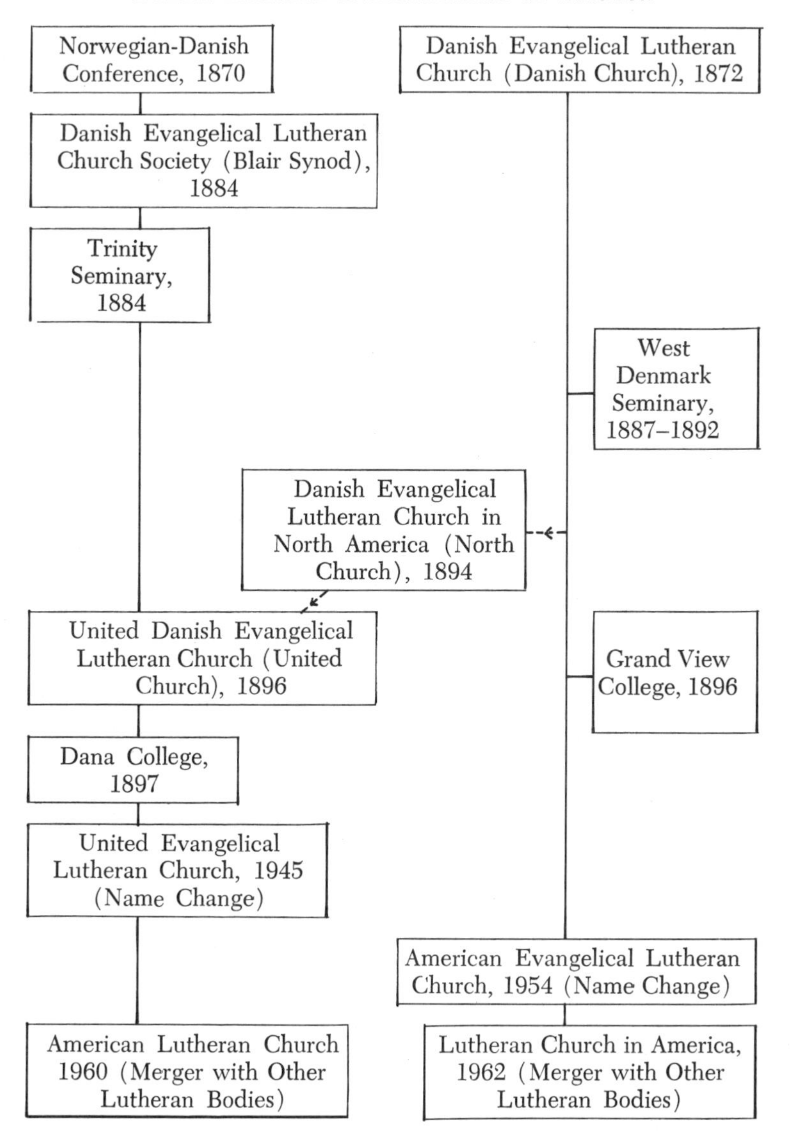


*Adapted from Thorvald Hansen, *School in the Woods: The Story of an Immigrant Seminary* (Askov, Minnesota, 1977), p. 135.

While there was doctrinal agreement, the Danes at the seminary, and those who later served as pastors in the conference, formed a special fellowship and were often referred to by the Norwegians as "our Danish Brethren."[16] The association with the orthodox Lutheran Norwegians was significant because it unified the opposition to Grundtvigianism in the conference and also because it oriented the group toward America instead of Denmark.[17]

On a visit to Europe in 1867, Pastor Clausen encouraged the religious leaders of Denmark to send Danish pastors to America. In response some men of the church, in 1869, formed the "Commission to Further the Preaching of the Gospel among Danes in North America." Finally in 1871 the commission sent two missionaries, Anders S. Nielsen and Rasmus Andersen, to America, but because they were not graduates of the University of Copenhagen, they were not ordained.

The commission in 1872 established preparatory and theological courses for prospective Danish American ministers at the Folk High School at Askov and later at other schools. After the completion of their course of study, the committee paid the traveling expenses of the pastors, gave them ministerial robes, and otherwise helped them financially, but they were ordained in the United States. Later in the century several pastors trained at the University of Copenhagen and ordained in Denmark also accepted calls to parishes in the United States. At approximately the same time that Nielsen and Andersen arrived, Niels Thomsen, a former missionary to India, took a pastorate with a Danish congregation in Indianapolis and Adam Dan, a teacher in the Jerusalem mission, accepted a call to Racine, and was there ordained by a pastor of the Norwegian-Danish Conference.[18]

In May 1872 the secretary of the Norwegian-Danish Conference wrote to the three Danish pastors, Dan, Nielsen, and Thomsen, inviting them to attend a meeting to discuss a Danish church in America. Adam Dan, responding for the others, replied that they preferred to work with the mother church of Denmark. Dan's refusal evidently was made because of Danish nationalism and also in opposition to the Norwegian pastors' antagonism toward Grundtvigianism.[19]

All four of these men met collectively at Waupaca, Wisconsin, on June 26, 1872, for Andersen's ordination and in all probability discussed the wisdom of founding an organization of their own. Three months later, when Dan and Andersen met again at Neenah, Wisconsin, an agreement was reached, and they formed the Church Mission Society (Kirkelig Missionsforening) that would function as a ministerial association. Although the organization would eventually become the first Danish denomination in the United States, the founders hoped to duplicate conditions in Denmark and chose to organize a society within the Danish Folk Church even though they were now living in America.[20] In 1874 they changed the name to the Danish Evangelical Lutheran Church in America (hereafter called the Danish Church), and then in 1878 they became an independent body by writing a constitution for their new denomination. The pastors maintained their loyalty to the mother church in Denmark even though it continued to refuse ordination to the pastors and provided minimal financial support.[21]

Unlike the mother church, the Danish Church in America exerted little power over the congregations. Matters of general interest and concern were dealt with at an annual meeting. Neither did the new denomination establish an ecclesiastical hierarchy or the post of bishop. It even divided the bishop's functions between two men, so that the president was the administrator and the ordainer admitted new clergymen. The confessional basis, however, was the same as that of the mother church.[22]

As a result two separate Lutheran organizations existed to minister to the Danes. The issue that soon surfaced and that would perpetuate the division was Grundtvigianism. Pastor Dan, although ordained by the Norwegian-Danish Conference and claiming that he was not a Grundtvigian, articulated Grundtvig's teaching and defended the Grundtvigians as good Lutherans.[23] The conference in turn decided to maintain friendly relations with the congregations served by the Grundtvigian pastors, but to oppose Dan's views and warn the congregations of the Grundtvigian teachings.[24] By 1877 the Danes within the conference founded their own newspaper and called it the *Dansk lutersk Kirkeblad* while the Danish Church called theirs the *Kirkelig Samler* (Church Gatherer) and chose Adam Dan as the editor.

In the first issue of the *Kirkeblad* the editor, Anton M. Andersen, interpreted the work of the pastors in the conference as being in the cause of true Lutheranism and claimed that the Danish Church was turning Danes toward Grundtvigianism. While the debate between the two editors was not intense, it nevertheless pointed out a division in doctrine, and soon several congregations split over the Grundtvigian question.[25]

The Danish Church was the larger of the two groups, and by 1878 included seventeen pastors serving 5,174 baptized members in sixty-eight congregations. But the pastors were not all Grundtvigians and held divergent views that would later lead to schism. The conference, on the other hand, had smaller numbers but was doctrinally of one mind.

## III *Conflict among Danish Lutherans*

An opportunity for Danish Lutheran unity appeared in 1884 when the Danes of the conference withdrew from the association with the Norwegians. Although the Norwegian-Danish association had been a happy one, some Danes believed that more effective work among the ever increasing number of Danish immigrants could be carried on by a Danish synod. It was a friendly parting of the ways by the two nationalities. Theoretically at least, they could have joined the Danish Church to create a single denomination for the Danes in America. At the time of the division, Pastor Andersen, editor of the *Kirkeblad* and a graduate of Augsburg, attended the Inner Mission convention in Denmark and also conversed with Beck and other church leaders. The advice given on all sides was to join with the Danish Church. Andersen agreed, but only on the condition that the Bible be accepted as the Word of God and that the confessions of the mother church be upheld.[26] Although the Danish Church did invite the group to attend the annual convention in September 1884, it took a critical stand and called the group "The Seceders." Andersen declined the invitation because no provision had been made to discuss the conditions of unity. John M. Jensen, the historian of the emerging church body, believes that the decision in favor of an independent organization was made even before Andersen's journey to Denmark.[27]

No one was interested in merger, so in 1884 the "Seceders" formed the Danish Lutheran Church Association in America. The headquarters of the new group was in Blair, Nebraska, and the nine pastors and the nineteen congregations were adherents of the teachings of Beck and the Inner Mission. Once the new association was formed and identified as a separate organization, tensions and controversy arose to further harden the division between the two Danish bodies. The Danish Church, or the "Happy Danes," on the one hand, viewed life in a relaxed way which stressed the enjoyment of God's creation, but at the same time zealously supported perpetuation of the Danish culture and language. A common Grundtvigian practice, for example, was for the pastor to meet and speak with the young people, usually in the parsonage. The meetings, however, were not strictly religious, but dealt with Danish culture, literature, and songs. The Blair church, or "Holy Danes," stressed conversion, sanctification, Bible study, Christian fellowship, and evangelism and was not greatly concerned with Danish culture and folk life.[28]

The Danish Church considered the Blair church a threat and feared that it might win over some members of the Danish Church by claiming to be both Lutheran and in harmony with the views of the Inner Mission. Further ill will developed when the Blair church opened a seminary in that Nebraska town in 1884. The conflict between the two Danish synods distressed men on both sides, but the differing concepts of the Bible prevented unity, and the hostility continued into the middle of the twentieth century.[29]

Although smaller than the Danish Church, the Blair church experienced the greater growth. An important part of that growth was the establishment of the seminary. It served as a symbol for the Danish immigrant and provided a rallying place for pastors and laymen. Even more important was the fact that it provided forty-two pastors for the denomination who were trained in evangelism.[30] The method of spreading the Gospel was patterned to a large extent after the techniques used by the Inner Mission in Denmark, where pastors gathered the people into mission houses and halls to preach repentance. In America the pastor, upon locating a Danish settlement, held a series of revival meetings. The goal was to convert enough people to begin a congregation. The members of the congregation were required to describe a conversion experience and then lead pious lives. Other Danes who were not members of the church could ask the pastors to officiate at baptisms, weddings, and funerals. Danes from the cities or upper classes tended to keep the church at arm's length, while the lower social levels and rural people usually made the commitment to the church. The rigid demands set forth by the Blair church discouraged membership for some people, but by 1893 there were thirty pastors serving thirty-nine congregations.[31] This emphasis on conversion gave way to the concept of church with Word and Sacraments. As children grew up and received Christian instruction they became members of the church without the conversion experience. Sunday schools received a greater emphasis and eventually as the Danish congregations turned to the community for members, pietism gave way to the formal church service. The concept of gathering holy people into holy congregations gradually declined during the first quarter of the twentieth century. Some leaders of the church such as P. S. Vig and N. P. Jensen believed that the revival meetings and prayer meetings were Methodistic and not part of the Lutheran heritage, and did not object to the change in emphasis.[32]

The Danish Church, from the days of its formation in 1872, had not been in close doctrinal agreement, but patterned itself after the church of Denmark, which permitted a variety of theological views. In the context of the United States, however, where competition between denominations existed, delineation of theological and doctrinal boundary lines was often necessary. When the Danish Church was labeled Grundtvigian by both the Norwegians and the Blair synod, those pastors and members who subscribed to the Inner Mission view objected to the charge and polarization began within the Danish Church.[33]

Several issues brought this conflict to the surface and schism resulted. One of the primary issues was the controversy at the newly created seminary of the Danish Church at West Denmark, Wisconsin. Initially in 1887 Pastor Theodore Helveg, a graduate of the University of Copenhagen, was the president and only professor, but the next year P. S. Vig, who sided with the Inner Mission, was added to the staff. Helveg was Grundtvigian and had supported Vig's appointment to quiet the factionalism in the church. But controversy arose from the doctrinal issues and intensified personal differences. Helveg had received his degree from the university and had enjoyed a comfortable upper-class life, while Vig had grown up in the lower class and attended a folk school. Before long the thirteen students also took sides and shattered the harmony of the small seminary. Pastors in the Danish Church also became involved and as a consequence the seminary was closed in 1892.[34]

Another divisive issue that arose unexpectedly was the question of the secret societies. The Danish Brotherhood, a secular society, was founded in 1872 and many pastors opposed it along with the Freemasons because of secrecy and the use of religion in the rituals. The Brotherhood denied any opposition to churches, but refused to change its ritual.[35] One of the churchmen hostile to the Brotherhood was Pastor F. L. Grundtvig, son of N. F. S. Grundtvig. Frederik Lange Grundtvig had graduated from the University of Copenhagen and embarked on a journey in 1881 with his new bride. The trip was to be a honeymoon as well as a visit to some of the Danish settlements in the United States.

At Neenah, Wisconsin, he met Pastor Helveg, who encouraged him to study for the ministry. He accepted the advice, studied informally, and in 1883 was ordained and installed as the pastor in Clinton, Iowa.[36] In an attempt to present an alternative to the Brotherhood, Grundtvig organized the Danish Folk Society (*Dansk Folkesamfund*) in 1887. It would support Danish culture, language, and folk high schools in America, and serve as a nonreligious fraternal society.[37] Although twelve pastors were charter members, the organization aroused opposition from some pastors in the denomination and they charged the society with being irreligious and that Grundtvig was trying to establish a faction within the denomination. The Inner Mission people in the Danish church feared this was a way of organizing a Grundtvigian bloc in the congregations through the local chapters that would tip the balance against the Inner Mission group.[38]

Two independent periodicals also appeared that participated in the debate. The older, *Dannevirke*, published at Cedar Falls, had Grundtvigian leanings, while *Danskeren*, published at Neenah, supported the Inner Mission views. The lay people were confused over the controversy and disillusioned with their pastors. Apathy was widespread. No church could continue under those conditions, and attention was given to solutions. Dissolution was discussed, but not accepted. The solution seemed to lie in writing a constitution that required the acceptance of all members. Vig and *Danskeren* maintained that the Danish Church was Lutheran in name only and that its position on Holy Scriptures was in error. The 1893 convention, held at Racine, ratified the constitution and set February 15, 1894, as the deadline for signatures by congregation and pastors. This requirement gave the advantage to the Inner Mission people, because they could miss the deadline and then claim they had been expelled. When the deadline had passed only forty of the 119 congregations and thirty-six of the fifty-seven pastors had signed. Some of the non-signing congregations continued to carry on an affiliation with the Danish Church, but the majority formed a new body that would eventually be called the Danish Evangelical Lutheran Church of North America, or more simply the North Church. The Danish Church continued to exist, but its membership was small and its growth slow. When it joined the Lutheran Church in America in 1962 its membership stood at 24,000 baptized members.[39]

The division did not bring peace, but the North Church had to defend its action and the Danish Church had to explain its position. There was conflict not only in the church papers and between the pastors, but also on the congregational level. Many congregations divided and often one group brought a civil suit against the other to obtain possession of church property. As a result many Danish communities had two small congregations where only one was needed. The life-styles of the two were also different. The North Church, being Inner Mission, insisted on a more devout life, while the Danish Church, being Grundtvigian, found nothing wrong with dancing and participating in the joys of life. The North Church, like the Blair synod, also relied on revival meetings and the conversion experience.[40]

## IV *The Growth of Two Danish Synods*

With such obvious similarities between the Blair and North churches, it was only a matter of time until a union of the two would be accomplished. Even before the division, the Inner Mission people in the Danish Church liked and used the Blair gospel hymnal, the *Sangeren,* and the Blair church had also opposed the Danish Folk Society.[41] A joint committee was established, and during 1895 and 1896 it worked on the details of the merger. Both conventions accepted the recommendations and on October 1, 1896, the merger convention was held and a constitution was accepted. The new church body, called the United Danish Evangelical Lutheran Church, had sixty-three pastors in 127 congregations and served 14,000 people.[42] The geographical distribution was also advantageous because the strength of the Blair church was in Nebraska, while the North church predominated in Iowa and Wisconsin.[43]

The Blair church had established a seminary, Trinity, and the North church had bought the folk school at Elk Horn, Iowa, for its seminary. With the merger of the two bodies, Professor A. M. Andersen moved to Elk Horn and joined P. S. Vig to form a single seminary and faculty. The next year, however, both men moved to Blair and Trinity Seminary served as the seminary for the United Church until recently. Through its early years, a certain tension remained from the heritage of the Blair church that stressed conversion and Christian living—the subjective Christian life—while the heritage of the North church, with its struggle for the Lutheran doctrine of Holy Scripture, represented the objective side.[44] Dana College, begun in 1899, had always been closely associated with the seminary. Most of the seminary students spent four years as proseminary students at Dana, and then three years in the seminary. Very often they studied under the same men for the entire period. Another problem was the Danish emphasis. The goal in the early years was to prepare an individual to preach Danish to Danes, and therefore little attention was given to preparation in English for work with Americans. The seminary enrollment was never high and averaged only ten students per year in the first two decades of the twentieth century. The enrollment at Dana College during the first two decades was on the average slightly over 100.[45]

Even though the Danish Church was seriously damaged by the secession of one-third of the pastors and congregations, the denomination, at its next convention in 1894, laid plans for its own seminary. Des Moines was selected as the location, which at that time was a growing city of 75,000 people. An offer had been made by a real-estate developer of the Grand View Land Company, David H. Kooker, and the tract he was promoting consisted of fifteen blocks located two miles north of the Iowa capitol. Kooker was willing to contribute one block of land and 60,000 bricks for the first building and to sell 100 lots at $100 profit for the church. In return the college would be ready for occupancy in 1895. One of the staunch supporters of the school was Mikkel Lauritsen, a realtor and owner of the Iowa House. He had long been a proponent of a religious school in Des Moines and had tried unsuccessfully to found a Danish congregation in the city. When finally the synod agreed to begin the construction of the college, Lauritsen bought a lot next to the school site, where he later extended his hospitality to many students. He also realized his dream of founding a congregation, and proved to be most helpful in raising money from Des Moines businessmen.[46]

The first building, which was to become the east wing of the main hall, was completed in 1895, but not until September 1896 was the school opened.[47] During the first year thirty-four students enrolled, three of whom were theological students. Grand View College, like Dana, became a symbol and a rallying point and served as a seminary until that function was ended in 1959. Grand View's other function, that of an educational institution for younger people, was subject to debate. One group hoped to make it a folk school, while the other argued for a religious school as an alternative to secular institutions. It never became a folk school, but it contained features of the folk school such as daily inspirational lectures in Danish, gymnastics, and needlework for girls. Many recent immigrants interested in learning English attended the winter term that was heaviest in the folk school tradition. The winter term offered no exams and enjoyed the biggest enrollment.[48]

The second president, Benedict Nordentoft, who later went to Solvang, California, stressed the more academic aspects and was criticized by those who preferred a folk-school orientation. Finally, in 1912, Thorvald Knudsen, who had been at the folk school in Tyler, Minnesota, became the president. The expectations of the folk-school adherents were not fulfilled, however, because he was responsible for winning state accreditation of the high school. He set up four departments: one was for English teachers, one was for Danish teachers, the third was a high-school department comparable to the public school, and the fourth was the folk high school, open from December to March. That organization seemed a reasonable solution. Grand View was accredited as a junior college in 1938 and operates today as a four-year college.[49]

Hostility between the two synods did not disappear until the 1920s. For most laymen, however, the theological differences were not always significant or even understandable. Often they moved from one community to another and changed from one synod to the other without experiencing problems. The language, hymnal, and liturgy were identical.[50] In 1921 the two synods met for the first time and agreed to translate into English the forms of worship for baptism, confirmation, and communion as well as the hymnal. The book of rituals was published in 1924 and the hymnal in 1927. Pastors and laymen supported union between the two bodies, or at least closer cooperation, but union was never achieved. The high point in the merger movement was attained in 1946, when an agreement was reached on all doctrinal items except the statement on the Word of God.

Following the failure to resolve that difference, the two denominations looked elsewhere, and the United Church merged with the American Lutheran Church and the Danish Church with the Lutheran Church in America.[51] Trinity Seminary was incorporated with Wartburg Seminary and the Grand View Seminary became part of the Lutheran School of Theology at Chicago.[52]

The two Danish denominations were significant not only to those who attended church but also to those who spoke Danish, because the church was a primary conservator of the Danish language. All schools teaching Danish—folk schools, parochial schools, or colleges—were started by Danish American Lutherans.[53]

The church and the Danish Folk Society also took part in the establishment of Danish colonies that became the last outposts of Danish culture and language. Realizing that the scattered Danes could not support a pastor and were soon separated from the Danish faith and culture, both Danish denominations, especially the Danish Church, encouraged the establishment of colonies that would attract Danes from Europe as well as Danish Americans. The focus of the community would be the Lutheran Church and the Danish language and culture. The first colony was founded in 1885 at Tyler, Minnesota, by the Danish Church and others planted by either the church or the Dansk Folkesamfund were located at Withee, Wisconsin; Danevang, Texas; Larimore, North Dakota; Dagmar, Montana; Askov, Minnesota; Wilbur, Enumclaw, and St. Andrews, Washington; Junction City, Oregon; and Fresno and Solvang, California. The last colony was established at Granly, Mississippi, in 1935. The United Church founded settlements at Kenmare and Daneville, North Dakota; Dane Valley, Montana; Fresno, California; and Eugene, Oregon.[54]

## V *Americanization of the Lutheran Synods*

Loyalty to the Danish language was strong, and the mission of the church at first was not to all nations but only to Danish-speaking Americans. As late as 1913, President Vig of Trinity Seminary reported to the annual convention that the goal of the faculty was to graduate pastors capable of preaching in Danish.[55] The American church service was almost identical to the one in Denmark. The pastor wore vestments with the ruff collar; the bell was tolled in the same manner as in Denmark; Scripture readings, sermon texts, rituals, and hymns were the same. Women and men sat separately in church.[56]

Nevertheless Danish would eventually be replaced by English. The Danish Church was slower to adjust, but it never lagged too far behind in making necessary changes. The first step was the creation of seminaries in the United States so that Danish Americans could receive their training in this country rather than journeying to Denmark. Danish was used exclusively in Trinity Seminary until 1895, when English was added, albeit minimally and sporadically. English was more common in the proseminary at Blair and had already been introduced in 1892. Grand View remained primarily Danish into the 1930s.[57]

Other indications of change included the translation of Luther's Small Catechism from Danish to English in 1904 and the use of English at the church convention in 1912.[58] After the United States entered World War I against the Germans, a great deal of opposition arose in the Middle West against the use of foreign languages by any immigrant community, including the Danish. To demonstrate his patriotism Governor W. L. Harding of Iowa, in his Language Proclamation, prohibited the use of foreign languages at any public gathering including schools, trains, telephone conversations, speeches, and sermons. The Danes resented being classified as enemies of the United States and reminded anyone who listened that they had suffered from the Germans and that the prohibition of Danish in Slesvig had been unsuccessful. The people at Fredsville, where two-thirds of the congregation originated from Slesvig, asked for a modification of the proclamation and observed that they had left their homes years ago in order to preserve their language. To make matters worse, Governor Harding, in an address on the Fourth of July, supposedly referred to those Danes who protested his proclamation as "the filth of Denmark."[59]

Some congregations consulted with the county attorney and held Danish services, and Harding soon modified his proclamation to permit foreign-language church services.[60] The Danes showed their loyalty by buying war bonds, and Vig estimated that by July 1918 there were 30,000 Danish Americans in the armed forces. The major impact, however, was the acceleration in the change from Danish to English. Vig, who five years earlier had upheld the necessity of a pastor preaching in Danish, in 1918 insisted on the skill of preaching in English. The Danish Church, in that same year, declared that congregations always had the right to use either Danish or English.[61] The mission of the church from 1900 to 1925 was directed primarily toward Danish immigrants, but with the decline of immigration during the war and the 1920s, the church had to turn to English-speaking Americans for membership.[62]

Even with the realization that English needed greater attention, the transition to that language was more a generational process than a rapid adjustment. Those children born during the war were taught English, so during the 1920s Sunday schools and confirmation classes were taught in English. An English hymnal containing translated Danish hymns appeared in 1927, as did the *Ansgar Lutheran*, an English weekly for the United Church.[63] Trinity Seminary in 1927 treated the two languages evenly, but by 1931 most seminarians recognized the future needs and preferred to study only in English. The word "Danish" was dropped from the title of the United Church in 1945 and from the Danish Church in 1953.[64]

A comparison of the number of Danish immigrants with the membership in the Danish denominations indicates that a very small percentage of the Danes remained true to the Lutheran Church. The Danes as a group were the least faithful of any of the Lutheran nationalities. In 1920 the United Church had approximately 26,000 members and the Danish Church 21,000, which amounts to approximately 25 percent of Danes in the United States.[65] But the membership total for the churches includes children born in America, so if a comparison is made to the Danish Americans plus the children born to one or both Danish parents the membership is reduced to 9 percent.

Even when one considers the membership in other denominations, the number of Danes within all churches was small. Christensen estimated that at least 10,000 Danes in 1920 were members of denominations other than the Danish Lutheran, and many Danes were associated with the Norwegian Lutherans.[66] Because this type of appraisal is highly speculative, any estimates of the percentage of Danes in denominations vary considerably. Olof Nelson claimed that only 8 percent joined any denomination, while Paul Nyholm estimated about 35 percent did, and Enok Mortensen made the number even higher.[67]

Even though scholars disagree on the actual amount of Danish involvement in the church, there is a consensus that the degree of affiliation with either of the Danish churches was low. Several reasons can be given that help explain this aspect of Danish life, but no single reason is truly verifiable. Already in Denmark the state church was not an integral part of the life of many Danes, and when the Danes migrated the mother church took practically no interest in former members. Another reason was that economics, not religion, was the primary motive for migration. In America the church was dependent on contributions from the members and was not the beneficiary of a subsidy from the state, so church membership became an expense that in the early days in America would interfere with the primary goal of migration. There was also an absence of religious leaders who could inspire the immigrants, and, instead, the leaders became involved in energy-consuming conflicts among each other. The conflict and the wide geographical distribution of the Danes led to an inefficient use of clergymen. Often two congregations existed in a Danish settlement where one would have been sufficient and at the same time there were small, marginal settlements that could not support a pastor at all. The period of migration may also have had an impact, because the Danes migrated later in the nineteenth century than the Swedes and Norwegians, and by that time European society had become more industrial, and much less interested in religious life.[68]

Even so, there was a distinct disparity in the religious involvement of the various groups. The rural Danes were more receptive than the urban Danes. Danes in country parishes lived more isolated lives and associated less with "worldly" people. Sunday services were important social events as well, and people gathered after service for conversation. Because of the distance from church and the poor transportation, families often dedicated the day to church and spent Sunday afternoons with friends and neighbors. Many homes had pianos or reed organs, and the devout gathered for singing and devotions. In the city there was less dependence on the church to fill social needs so the loyalty was not as great. The urban Danes also assimilated more readily and disapproved of the pastor's insistence on the use of Danish, especially for confirmation.[69]

The social welfare function of the church must also be considered, because the Danish denominations established orphanages in places like Chicago, Racine, Tyler, and Perth Amboy, and retirement homes in various locations. The two synods even cooperated in the support of a tuberculosis sanitarium in Brush, Colorado. All congregations sponsored Sunday schools, vacation schools, weekday schools, and Ladies' Aid Societies (*Kvindeforeninger*) that worked with children and the poor and distressed. In addition, acts of charity were performed by individual members of the congregation for needy fellow members.

Not only was there controversy between Danes in the Lutheran bodies, but also between the Danish Lutherans and the Danes in the "sects," as the Lutherans called Baptists, Adventists, and Methodists. Clergymen and members debated such topics as baptism, the second coming of Christ, resurrection, the eating of pork, and the keeping of the Sabbath. The conflict also broke into families when one or more members of a family would be "converted." A mother who became a Baptist would oppose infant baptism of her new child, while the Lutheran father would be horrified with the prospect of that child's death without the administration of the sacrament.[70]

Instead of providing a rallying point for Danish Americans, the church failed to attract most Danes and became instead a divisive element for the Danes who remained Lutheran and for those who became Baptists, Methodists, and Adventists.

## VI *Danish Baptists*

The Baptist faith gained its foothold in Denmark in 1839 when a Danish Jew, Julius Köbner, returned to Copenhagen from Hamburg, where he had been converted. Later that year, the man who converted Köbner, J. G. Oncken, also arrived in Denmark, and at Copenhagen and on Langeland he baptized people who through study had become interested in the Baptist teachings. At that time, however, the Danish government did not tolerate churches in the country other than the state church, so the Baptists endured persecution. Many converts were fined and suffered property confiscation if they had no money to pay the fines, while others such as Peter C. Mønster, who later helped the Mormons, were incarcerated. Many were encouraged to leave the country. While the Baptists did not encourage migration as the Mormons did, one scholar estimated that one Dane out of every three or four who had been converted migrated to the United States.[71]

The first Danish Baptist congregation in America was formed in 1854, when nine members from the Vandløse church in Zealand arrived in Potter County, Pennsylvania.[72] In all probability the Danes were attracted to Potter County by the publicity for Ole Bull's projected colony. This famed Norwegian violinist envisioned a colony for his countrymen, and although more than 1,000 Norwegians migrated, most drifted away when it became evident that Bull had been bilked by landsharks and the settlers could not get warranty deeds to the property.[73] Most of the Danish Baptists also went farther west and settled in Waushara County, Wisconsin. By 1858 the Pennsylvania church had disbanded.[74]

Other Danish Baptists migrated from the Zealand Church in 1853 and 1854 to Raymond Township near Racine, Wisconsin, and organized a church in 1856. The pastor, Soren Larsen, could not prevent a schism on the question of female participation in church matters and the Raymond congregation suffered a loss of all its members, save one. Lars Jørgensen Hauge, whose mother was one of the first Danes to convert to the Baptist faith, took over the remnant at Raymond in 1859 and began to rebuild it into an influential congregation. Soren Larsen, having abandoned Raymond, joined the Pennsylvania Baptists, who had settled at Waushara, and formed a church there in 1858. But controversy arose in that congregation as well, and the Adventists added to the confusion. Hauge took over the ministry there in 1859 and then went on to New Denmark, Brown County, Wisconsin, where he organized some Danes who had been converted after reading a tract, "The Blasphemers' Prayer." In later years these three Wisconsin settlements sent out settlers to the west. Waushara and Raymond members formed the church at Clarks Grove, Minnesota, in 1863 and many of the New Denmark people went to Shelby County, Iowa, causing the Wisconsin congregation to disband.[75]

Hauge also went to Chicago and gathered some Danish Baptists from Denmark and from Raymond and began a church in 1864.[76] Three hundred people out of the 1,500 population of Saelby migrated between 1855 and 1875, and most of them joined Chicago's Baptist community. The Chicago mission did not attain its potential growth, however, because of discord. One group split off from the congregation on the grounds that the original group was not spiritual enough for them.[77]

While the Danish Baptists were forming congregations, parallel efforts were underway among the Norwegians. The similarity in language made it possible for Norwegian and Danish pastors to preach in churches of either ethnic group. In addition there were often representatives of both Norwegians and Danes in most congregations, and on occasion even some Swedes. To coordinate the effort, the Danish-Norwegian Baptist Conference for the North-Western States was formed at Raymond in 1864 with Hauge as the first president. From that time until 1910, when the division was made on ethnic lines, the work of the Baptists with both Danes and Norwegians was unified. In 1876 there were twenty congregations in the conference, with a membership of approximately 1,000. Ten of the churches were in Wisconsin and the largest congregation was at Clarks Grove, Minnesota, with a membership of 156. Some of the twenty congregations were specifically Norwegian, or Danish, or Swedish, but most were blends of Scandinavians.[78]

The pastors who served the Danes were trained at a seminary founded in Chicago in 1871. It began under the name of the Scandinavian Seminary but in 1884 it was called the Danish-Norwegian Seminary. Most of its existence was in Morgan Park. During the first twenty years more Danes than Norwegians studied for the ministry, but from the 1890s on there were more Norwegians. Some European students intent on returning to Europe for their ministry also enrolled for their theological training. The seminary closed in 1912, shortly after the separation of the two ethnic groups, and the Danes decided to establish a seminary in connection with Des Moines College, a Baptist school in Iowa.[79]

Worship in the Danish language was the main reason for the existence of the Danish-Norwegian Conference as a separate branch in the Baptist church, and initially Danish was used exclusively. The conference also published church papers such as *Oliebladet* (The Olive Leaf) and its successor *Vaegteren* (The Watchman) in Danish. Discussions over the use of the language, however, had appeared already in 1898. One criticism expressed at the annual meeting was that excessive utilization of English would destroy the unique character of the conference, while another criticism expressed the fear that not enough English was used to meet the spiritual needs of the members. Worship services in English increased in number, nevertheless, and by 1924 no congregation in Iowa relied on Danish exclusively. Both languages were used, with Danish in the morning service and English in the evening service. As English became the dominant language in a congregation, the members would affiliate with the local Baptist church.[80]

The Baptists exerted strong church discipline on the members, especially in matters of the Sabbath. There could be no ball games on that day, no trading at the stores, no work, including duties at the cooperative creameries to which they belonged. The Baptists opposed the use of intoxicating drinks and celebrated the Eucharist with grape juice, but the homemade nonalcoholic beer brewed by the Danish housewife was not forbidden.[81]

The number of the Danes in the Baptist church is impossible to state in precise terms because the statistics include Norwegians and Swedes as well. The fact that Danish comes before Norwegian in the title of the conference indicates that there were more Danes, especially in the early days of the conference. Another problem was the Americanization of the members. As a family or a congregation became more accustomed to English, it would affiliate with an American church and thereby reduce the size of the Danish-Norwegian Conference. The membership given for 1900 was 4,805 in ninety churches. Statistics for 1909, including Norwegians, show a total of 6,217.[82] Even without removing the 1,000 or so Norwegians the number is not impressive. The Danish Baptist Conference, however, was an important agency in the lives of many Danes and in many Danish settlements, and did much in hastening the assimilation of the Dane into American society.

## VII *Danish Methodism*

Another one of the religions to find willing adherents among the Danes was the Methodist church. While the Baptist church in Denmark preceded the congregations in America, the Methodists first converted Danes who had migrated to America and eventually sent back converts to establish Methodist missions in Denmark.

One of the first Danes to be converted became one of the most ardent and effective missionaries for his newfound faith.

Christian Willerup came to Savannah, Georgia, in 1832 as a schoolteacher, and there he was converted to Methodism. He returned to Denmark for a time in 1846 and then migrated once again to the United States and found a home in Pennsylvania. There he was licensed to preach and in 1850 he went to Dane County, Wisconsin, as a missionary to some Norwegians.[83]

The Norwegian association with Methodism had taken place earlier. During the Napoleonic period, England, in its attempt to strangle French power by controlling shipping around Europe, had captured approximately 2,700 Danish and Norwegian sailors and brought them to England as prisoners. At that time Norway was part of Denmark, and Denmark was allied with France. Quaker missionaries visited the Scandinavian prisoners, and when the war ended, the men returned to their homes, some Norwegians remaining Quakers.

Opposition to Quakerism in Norway was oppressive, and as a consequence, in 1825 some Quakers left Stavanger on board a sloop, the *Restaurationen,* bound for New York. At first they settled on the shores of Lake Ontario in Orleans County, New York, but later migrated farther west to the Fox River in northern Illinois. In both settlements their neighbors were Methodists who treated them with friendship and welcomed them to their religious services. Although some Norwegians remained Quakers, most joined the Methodist faith.[84] The Norwegian-Americans became the mission prospects for the Methodists, and Billerup was sent to work with them. The Danish migration had not reached significant proportions at that time. In 1851 Willerup organized the Cambridge, Wisconsin, congregation, which was the first Norwegian-Danish congregation in the United States. From there he went to Racine, where his work met with success, and from 1855 to 1874 he lived in Denmark, working with the Methodist mission there.[85]

Another Dane to be converted was John C. Brown, who encountered Methodism at the Mariners' Bethel Chapel on the New York waterfront. Brown, born in Danish Slesvig but educated in Germany, became a sailor and eventually landed in New York. There he was exposed to Methodist tracts and services directed toward the sailors. After his conversion he also became a preacher and was sent to the Norwegians in Illinois on the Rock River.[86]

As the Danish migration gathered momentum, the Methodists began establishing congregations in the settlements. There were congregations in such locations as Racine; Chicago; Viborg, South Dakota; Neenah, Wisconsin; Ludington, Michigan; and Perth Amboy, New Jersey. Both the English speaking Methodists and the Norwegian-Danish Methodists established missions among the Mormons, but the response was marginal. In 1880 the Methodists organized a Norwegian-Danish Conference, which had its strength in Chicago and the Midwest.[87]

The seminary for the Norwegian-Danish church originated in 1870, when the president of Northwestern University of Evanston, Illinois, organized a Norwegian-Danish department within the university. Karl Schou, a Dane, who was both a student at Northwestern and at Garrett Biblical Institute, became the first teacher.[88]

The language question was crucial for this Methodist body because, like the Baptists, only the use of Danish justified its separate existence. The official journals of the conference were *Missionaeren* and its successor, *Den Kristelige Talsmand.* The question on the use of English in Sunday school was first raised in 1891, and the consensus was not to change, but to encourage the use of *Riksmaal,* the Danish-rooted language of Norway that the Danes could readily grasp. That way their branch of Methodism could exist for another generation. Even before World War I, however, English made inroads not only into Sunday school, but also into church services. Numerous congregations conducted one service a month in English. Those who hoped for the revival of *Riksmaal* would be disappointed because World War I and the declining migration from Denmark in the 1920s argued for the use of English. In many ways the debates over the language issue resembled those in the Lutheran and Baptist churches. The conference remained until 1943, when the congregations joined the English-speaking Methodist church.[89]

As the name indicates, the Norwegians dominated the fellowship. The Norwegian presence as well as the constant flow of Danish Methodists into the American Methodist churches makes it difficult to pinpoint the number of Danish Methodists. In 1910 the membership for the conference, including the Norwegians, was 4,984, and in 1931 membership was 6,360.[90] The Methodists, like the Baptists, may have been few in number, but their influence was present in the Danish community.

## VIII *Danish Seventh-Day Adventists*

The third non-Lutheran church to attract Danish members was the Seventh-Day Adventist group. The Adventists were especially successful in converting those Danes who had become Baptists. The best-known of the Danish Adventists was John G. Matteson, and his career illustrates many aspects of Danish Adventism. Matteson left Langeland with his parents in 1854 and settled at New Denmark, Wisconsin, where he was converted by the Baptists in 1859. The next year he entered the Baptist seminary in Chicago and soon began preaching for that denomination. He was converted, however, by the Adventists, and conducted revivals in Wisconsin, Michigan, Minnesota, and Illinois. He also edited a Danish language monthly, the *Advent Tidende*, which was directed to American readers but also had subscribers in Denmark. M. A. Sommer, critic of the establishment in Denmark, read the periodical, and although he was not converted asked Matteson for permission to extract articles for his own paper, in which he attacked the Danish church. Matteson himself returned to Denmark as a missionary in 1877 and the next year organized at Vendsyssel the first Adventist church in Denmark. He also compiled a songbook for the Danish Adventists. He returned to the United States and spent his last three years at Union College in Lincoln, Nebraska.[91] One of the Danish Baptists converted by Matteson was John F. Hansen. Hansen traveled widely among the Danish settlements and became the pastor of the congregation at Swan Lake (Viborg), South Dakota.

The Adventists established a seminary for the training of pastors in 1910 when they purchased the campus of a former Danish Lutheran institution in Hutchinson, Minnesota. There were no students on the college level until 1914, and the peak enrollment was sixty-eight in 1919. During that same year they changed the name of the Danish-Norwegian Seminary to the Hutchinson Theological Seminary because of the antiforeign sentiments of the World War period. The school closed its doors in 1928.[92]

Although the Adventists carried their message to the Danish settlements, the number of Danes who associated with the Adventists was minimal. Swan Lake, in 1876, for example, had only forty-five members, and judging from the small enrollment at the seminary, Danish support was marginal.[93] The membership in 1906, which did not differentiate between Danes and Norwegians, was 1,734, so assuming that one-half were Danes, the number of Danes in the denomination was perhaps 900.[94]

# Part III: *The Geographic Distribution of Danes in America*

## CHAPTER 6

# *Danes Settle the Woodland States*

### I *Wisconsin*

THE Danish migration into Wisconsin began in the late 1830s, although the numbers remained small for the following decade. John S. Bang, one of the first newcomers, migrated to Racine in 1839 or 1840 and worked there as a builder. He also helped found a Scandinavian congregation and served on the city council. By 1870 Wisconsin led the other states in the number of Danes, and held that distinction until 1890, when it yielded first place to Iowa.[1]

The Danes who settled in Wisconsin were significant in the migration because they were the first of the non-Mormon Danes who started a chain of migration. Information about Wisconsin from the writings of specific individuals led to an increase in the exodus, and the impact was felt not only on Wisconsin but also on other states. The first of these publicists was Claus Laurits Clausen, a Danish clergyman who became the pastor for some Norwegian settlers. He had migrated in 1843 and letters from both Pastor and Mrs. Clausen were printed in Danish newspapers.[2]

Another publicist was Lauritz Jacob Fribert, a Dane who migrated in 1842 and eventually settled at Watertown, Wisconsin. The year after his arrival he toured the United States and wrote a guidebook of 100 pages, *Haandbog for Emigranter til Amerikas Vest,* for Danes who wished to migrate to the new world. In it he included a roseate description of Wisconsin and a reference to Pastor Clausen.[3]

A third person influential in attracting settlers to Wisconsin was Rasmus M. Sorensen, who as a member of the Danish *Rigsdag*

(Lower House) had been a proponent of land reform and educational programs for peasants. He demonstrated his conviction by conducting evening school for peasants and establishing a folk school at Uldum, Denmark, in 1848. His dissatisfaction with Denmark also extended to the church and he participated in conventicles, or gatherings of a few faithful, as a protest against the rationalistic clergy. Frustrated with the difficulty of obtaining help from the state for the Danish peasant, he viewed migration to Wisconsin as an alternative. He had read not only Fribert's work, but his own son, Martin, had migrated to Waupaca, Wisconsin, in 1844. In 1852 Sorensen led a party of twenty persons including the remainder of his family to Waupaca, where he farmed, taught school, and helped his son as lay reader. Sorensen's son had become an Episcopal minister, but he preached to the Danes in Danish and used the old Danish order of worship. When Martin left for a parish in Illinois, the new Episcopal pastor could not preach Danish, so the Danes formed a Danish Lutheran congregation. They could have affiliated with a neighboring Norwegian congregation, but they harbored hard feelings from the earlier days when the Norwegians had admonished Sorensen for his association with the Episcopalians.[4]

In 1861 after the death of his wife, Rasmus Sorensen returned to Denmark for a visit and used the opportunity to lecture and write about Wisconsin. On the return trip he accompanied 150 emigrants who settled in that state. Again in 1863 he went back to Denmark and shortly thereafter returned with even more migrants.[5]

More attention was drawn to Wisconsin by some Danish Baptists who had migrated to Wisconsin in 1853. Three years later, in 1856, they were joined by some Danish Baptists who previously had settled in Pennsylvania. The man who drew them together and worked actively among the Danes in Wisconsin was Lars Jorgensen Hauge, who had migrated from Funen in the hope of becoming a missionary to the Indians. When he learned about the passage of the Homestead Act in 1862 he wrote a circular letter to fellow Baptists in Denmark about the advantages of the new legislation. The law impressed not only the Danish Baptists but made an enormous impact on the Danes in the next decades. "Our earthly conditions," reported Hauge, "are very good. The government is also very good and has recently passed a law by which each man can get 160 acres of land if he will settle on it."[6] After several years of service to the Danish Baptists, he returned to his initial objective and became a missionary to the Indians on the Sisseton Reservation in Dakota.[7]

Mogens Abraham Sommer, an early Danish Socialist, was also an emigrant leader in Wisconsin. As an agitator protesting social injustice and a dissenter within the church, he was not greatly appreciated by the Danish authorities. He was jailed on several occasions in Denmark, once for insulting the king, once for attacking the church, and ten years before his death for practicing medicine without a license. He migrated to New York in 1861 but soon returned to Denmark and opened an emigration office in Copenhagen. He conducted several groups of migrants to Wisconsin and to Chicago and in the course of his journeys crossed the Atlantic thirteen times.[8]

The first rural Danish settlement in Wisconsin was at Hartland, Waukesha County, west of Milwaukee. It was begun in 1846 by Christian Ludvig Christensen of Lolland and included settlers primarily from his home neighborhood. Migrating alone, Christensen had landed at New Orleans and made his way up the Mississippi River to Pine Lake, Wisconsin, where Fribert made his home. Nearby, at what became Hartland, Christensen obtained land and was soon joined by his family and neighbors. Although living in the primitive conditions of the dense forest, he collected and read books and entertained such European travelers as Fredrika Bremer and Rasmus Sorensen.[9]

In 1848 a group of fifty Danes arrived in Milwaukee and promptly divided into three groups to form three Danish settlements. This company, primarily from Zealand and Langeland, had hoped to travel with Rasmus Sorensen, but because of financial problems he remained in Denmark and instead sent a son with the group. The route they followed took them by sail to Hamburg, Hull, England, and New York; by canal boat to Buffalo; and by lake steamer to Milwaukee. The first settlement was near Green Bay in Brown County, the second at Neenah near Appleton, and the third at Racine.

Brown County attracted a Danish community because the Danes were looking for inexpensive federal lands. One of the most notable settlers of this community called New Denmark was Niels Godtfredsen. His physical strength as well as his leadership in the community and the willingness to assist his neighbors earned him the title of "King of New Denmark." It was not unusual for a leader in a Danish community in the United States to be called "King" and Godtfredsen was the first one.[10] The settlement in Brown County grew until about 1867, when 1,200 Danes lived there. In 1906 the Northwestern Railroad built a line through New Denmark and the new transportation connection made possible the construction of a milk condensery and a cheese box factory.[11] As the lands opened in the West most of the settlers left, and today only the name reminds anyone of Denmark.[12]

The second settlement, Neenah, was not a designated goal as New Denmark was, but rather a secondary settlement where Danes congregated after they tried other areas. Some of the Danes lived first with Norwegian communities and then went to Neenah, while others left Danish communities such as New Denmark for homes in Neenah. By December 1865, the Danish population included approximately seven Danish families and five single men.[13] The dense forest required the early settlers at New Denmark and Neenah to work prodigiously in order to clear the land for planting crops. For additional money they worked at sawmills, especially at Oconto, until the size of their farms was sufficient to provide their sole income.[14]

The third group went just a short distance south from Milwaukee along Lake Michigan to Racine County, where some Danes such as Pastor Clausen had already settled. After the 1848 group arrived migration continued slowly until after the Civil War, when Racine witnessed a heavy Danish influx. The J. I. Case Company, a manufacturer of farm implements, recruited in Denmark for woodworkers, and the Mitchell Company, a wagon factory, employed Danes almost exclusively. The number of Danes in the population continued to grow so that there were 2,815 Danes in 1900 and 3,494 in 1930. Racine never possessed the Danish population that Chicago did, but it claims to have the greatest per capita concentration of any city outside of Denmark. Even at the present time a section of West Racine is called

"Kringleville" and at the end of May the city celebrates its annual Kringle Festival. Racine continues to support an active Dania Society that began in 1867 as a fraternal society, a sponsor of social activities, and an agency to help immigrants learn English.[15]

The religious life of the Danes in Racine reflects a stronger concern for religion than in most urban areas. Included in the Danish community are Methodists, Adventists, Baptists, and Lutherans. In 1851 the Danes and Norwegians in Racine founded a church which they called a Scandinavian Lutheran church. The lay preachers and pastors who served the congregation in the early days were Norwegian and the congregation was predominantly Norwegian. During the pastorate of J. Muller-Eggen, a Norwegian, the congregation gained more Danish members because of the increased migration, so in 1871, when Pastor Muller-Eggen left, a call was sent out to a Dane, Adam Dan. After only one year a portion of the congregation objected to Dan's theology, which that group claimed was Grundtvigian. The matter eventually went to the Racine County Circuit Court and there the judge agreed with the findings of a theology faculty and several of the Norwegian pastors that Dan's teachings were not Lutheran and therefore heretical. At the same time the judge realized that the majority of the congregation sided with Dan, so he awarded the property to that group. The minority departed and formed a new congregation leaving Dan and the majority in the Danish Church. But in 1893 when the Danish Church divided and Dan was no longer in Racine, the congregation left the Danish Church and eventually affiliated with the United Church, the same denomination that opposed the teaching of Grundtvig.[16]

Five contemporary Lutheran congregations in Racine trace their history to the Danish migrants. Four of the churches earlier belonged to the United Church and in 1938 2,000 of the denomination's 30,000 members lived in Racine. The Lutherans at Racine even founded Luther College in 1902, but its enrollment always remained near 100, and after ten years, in 1912, it was closed.[17]

The largest rural settlement in Wisconsin was a cluster of

little villages in Polk County in the northwestern part of the state. The best-known locations in this area, which reminded the Danes of their homeland, are West Denmark, Luck, and Bone Lake. The Danish Baptists were the first to settle there in the early 1860s but there was little growth until the Lutheran Danes began the migration in 1869. The promoter of the settlement, Morten Christian Pedersen, was Lutheran, but he was motivated by neither religious nor economic reasons. His hope was to locate an area where the land was not prohibitively expensive so Danes with limited means could find homes. He had migrated to Neenah in 1863, but the cost of land there as well as the land in the open prairies of Iowa and Minnesota was excessive by his standards. He traveled widely through the Midwest and in the fall of 1868 found some suitable land where forty acres could be purchased for $50 or with a down payment of $13. The land, near Big Butternut and Little Butternut lakes, was wooded and not near a railroad, but it was beautiful and the St. Croix River was suitable for some transportation. Pedersen first notified his friends at Neenah and other places in Wisconsin of his project, but he also returned to Denmark several times in order to lead groups of settlers to the United States.[18]

The next spring, in 1869, the settlers arrived, some traveling by boat up the St. Croix and others overland by ox wagons. Economically the colony experienced a slow development. Clearing the land consumed an enormous amount of effort and then the soil was not highly fertile. The settlers supplemented their income by working in sawmills, hunting and fishing, and by producing craft items. Jes Smidt, an early resident, became widely known as a woodcarver. He had studied sketching at the folk school in Ashland, Michigan, and carved altar pieces, pulpits, and similar items for many places of worship. The establishment of a cooperative creamery in 1886 greatly contributed to economic stability and in 1901 a railroad was built through the settlement. In that year the larger, collective community had a Danish population of approximately 3,000.[19]

The first Polk County Lutheran congregation was formed in 1870, the year the settlers arrived, but the congregation at West Denmark remained so small, and the members so poor, that they worshiped in the community school for twenty years and postponed the construction of a church until 1900. In 1883 the pastor, Kristen Nørgaard, built a small building next to the parsonage on Little Butternut Lake in order to establish a folk school for the Danes of the county as well as residents from other parts of the United States. The local support, even though there were five congregations, was minimal and the eighteen miles separating the school from the railroad made it difficult to attract young people from other areas. Even though the folk-school idea died, the Danish Church used the building for its seminary from 1887 until 1892.[20]

The final major rural settlement in Wisconsin was established in 1893 at Withee, in Clark County. The owner of a lumber company, attempting to gain additional profit by selling some land from which timber had been cut, offered the Danish Church land at $8 to $12 per acre. In addition the lumber company would donate land for the church, construct a parsonage, and pay the pastor's salary for one year. The church leaders, meeting in convention at Waupaca, assigned a committee to examine the location and, following its approval, publicized the project in *Dannevirke*. The major obstacles to the development of an agricultural community were the absence of good roads and the removal of large pine stumps to make plowing possible.

Just when the settlers were taking hold of the overwhelming task, the Panic of 1893 gripped the nation and the prices for farm goods declined severely. With the colony on the verge of failure, Pastor A. S. Nielsen, who had been deeply interested in the project from the beginning and at the same time had been searching for a less demanding parish than the one he served in Chicago, offered to become the pastor at Withee and provide some leadership. Pastor Nielsen accepted the position without any commitment of support and in the knowledge that the bankrupt lumber company was unable to honor its pledge of paying the pastor's salary for the first year. He brought some Chicago families with him and the colony stabilized. Most of the settlers came from sections of Wisconsin, Minnesota, and from Chicago rather than from Denmark. By 1908 the Danish population was approximately 1,000. Financial stability was achieved through dairying and with the establishment of a cheese factory.[21]

## II *Michigan*

Although Wisconsin was farther west than Michigan, the early Danish settlers preferred that state, and there were only thirteen Danes in Michigan in 1850—primarily seamen working on the Great Lakes. The person who stimulated the migration to Michigan and especially to Montcalm County was Christian Jensen (Johnson), a Dane who arrived in 1853. His letters to Denmark captured the optimism of the frontier.

> Here is limitless forest land which can be bought for next to nothing. The Americans are honest people. The country is ruled by a president, elected for four years. There are good civil courts and many pretty girls. I shall marry one of them.

Unfortunately, when the Civil War in the United States broke out the veteran of the 1848 war with the Germans enlisted in the Union army and was killed in his first battle.[22]

Jensen's letters, however, attracted August Rasmussen, who migrated in 1856, and more relatives and friends in the following years. Rasmussen, who later wrote a history of the settlement, bought 80 acres at $2 per acre and paid for it by working for the landowner. The land had to be cleared before it could produce a crop, so he alternated between working on his own land and earning cash by working for others. He received $1.50 per day during the harvest season and reported that American farmers paid more in food and wages than "those long-fingered, proud noblemen in Denmark, who feed their harvest people on salt herring and barley pudding seven hundred and twenty times a year." Jobs, especially at the sawmills, were plentiful and wages were six times higher than in Denmark. Rasmussen built a log cabin, constructed the furniture, dug a cellar and a well, and grew corn, wheat, potatoes, and flowers. His wife tended the garden, milked the cow, and looked after the baby and on occasion received visits from the Indians. That idyllic picture would attract anyone, not only Danes, and he further reported that thousands of acres of good farm land could be acquired for almost nothing.[23]

More Danes came and other settlements were begun in the

county, resulting in seven Lutheran congregations. By 1914 the Danish population numbered 8,000, which included the largest concentrations near Gowen and Trufant. The early settlers worked in sawmills to earn money, but most eventually turned to farming and found the soil especially suitable for potatoes.[24]

From Montcalm County the Danes spread to Muskegon and Manistee counties and to places like Ashland, Ludington, Grand Rapids, and Grayling. In the late 1860s they were also attracted to Marquette County by the iron mines and to the lumber mills of Menominee County—both in the Upper Peninsula.[25] The Danes began arriving at Manistee in 1860, seeking jobs in the sawmills. By 1868 there were twenty-six sawmills and most of the Danes were single men living in shacks along the river or in boardinghouses. There were many other Scandinavians as well, and in 1869, when the Norwegian pastor W. H. Wald arrived, he formed a congregation with a membership of twenty Danes, twelve Norwegians, and eight Swedes. One of the wealthy Danes in Manistee, E. N. Salling, had joined another denomination, but he contributed frequently to the special needs of the Lutheran congregation. In 1873 the congregation started a Danish parochial school, but the transition to English was rapid, and already in 1911 the congregation worshiped in English on one Sunday a month.[26] At the turn of the century there were more Danes in Manistee than in any other town in Michigan. The Danish population was almost 1,000, and twenty-five of the businesses were owned by Danes.[27]

Through the efforts of Pastor H. J. Pedersen, Michigan also became the home of a Danish folk school. Pedersen, the product of a folk school in Denmark and the former president of the folk school at Elk Horn, Iowa, selected a site near Grant, a Danish community halfway between Montcalm County and Muskegon. In 1882 Pedersen bought forty acres of cleared land a few miles from Grant along the railroad line. The region had been cut over by lumbermen and there had been occasional forest fires killing some of the remaining trees. Pedersen called the place Ashland and began building the school. There were 3,500 Danes in Michigan, who were potential supporters of the school, and many more Danes lived in neighboring Wisconsin and Illinois. But the enrollments were never large and in the five and one-half years of Pedersen's leadership only 201 students attended, with most of those who did coming from Montcalm County. Even J. Christian Bay, best known for his position as director of the John Crerar Library in Chicago, was unable to succeed during his two-year term as leader, from 1900 to 1902.[28]

## CHAPTER 7

# *Danes in the Prairie States*

### I *Illinois*

WHEN Danes purchased their tickets for America, approximately one-third identified New York as their destination. New York was not the end of the travels for most immigrants, however, but only a temporary residence while they gained their bearings or earned money for the journey west. Chicago was also one of those landmarks for Danish immigrants, and 10 percent of the entire emigration listed Chicago as their goal.[1] In contrast to New York, however, Chicago became the home for many Danes, so that in 1900 there was a Danish population of 10,000, the largest Danish community in America.[2]

The United States census of 1850 indicated that up to that time, only ninety-three Danes had selected Chicago as a place of residence. Wisconsin farm land had been more appealing, and some of those ninety-three could well have been earning money to enable them to continue on to agricultural settlements. The Dane who attracted the most recognition during this early period was Andrew Jackson Miller, a producer of nonalcoholic beer and soft drinks. He bought and built some wooden shacks at Clark and Randolph streets in the Loop and Danish immigrants were advised by native Chicagoans to go to "Miller's Town." Unfortunately he lost it all in the Panic of 1857.[3]

Another center in these early years was at La Salle and Kinzie, about five blocks north of Miller's Town and just north of the Chicago River. Here was a low-rent area where the artisans found shelter and where the Dania Club in 1864 rented space for its meetings. The area soon took on a Danish appearance, with blooming plants on window sills, shiny knockers on doors, and white scoured steps.[4] A popular meeting place for the Danes was Wilken's Cellar, a German café one block west of Miller's Town at La Salle and Randolph.

The Danish settlement pattern in Chicago was similar to that of the other ethnic groups in that the first migrants gathered in or near the Loop, and then moved outward through a series of leaps into the less densely settled parts of the city.[5] The majority of the Danes remained in the initial locations throughout the 1870s, although by approximately 1870 a small number began to collect on the South Side. This small group first formed near Thirty-seventh and State, and in 1874 St. Michael church was located at Thirty-sixth, and St. Stephen on Thirty-seventh Street. In 1884 there were about 400 Danes in Wards 4 and 5 on the South Side. This small Danish community maintained its identity into the 1920s, but the members had relocated several times ahead of the advancing black neighborhoods. In 1899 St. Michael had moved to Ninety-eighth Street and St. Stephen to Sixty-fourth and Eberhart.[6]

Approximately in 1869 the majority of Chicago's 3,700 Danes began to move out of the Loop in a northwesterly direction. The new community was concentrated near Grand and Milwaukee avenues but extended as far south as Milwaukee and Des Plaines, and as far north as Milwaukee and Huron. The area was about seven blocks long and several wide. The approximate population of the Danish community during the 1880s was about 6,000 and the Milwaukee neighborhood included about two-thirds of Chicago's Danes. Among the Danish establishments were two Danish hotels, Dannevirke and Dannebrog, a Danish cigar store, a photography studio, a book store, and the new headquarters of Dania.[7]

Even though the Danes clustered around Milwaukee Avenue, at no time did they dominate the ethnic composition of any ward. Already in the 1880s they continued the migration toward the northwest and yielded their location to Poles and Jews. By 1892 the major Danish settlement was being formed east of Humboldt Park. It was not an immediate change, but gradual, so that by 1898 about 2,500 Danes continued to live in the Milwaukee Avenue area while about 4,000 Danes resided near Humboldt Park. At the turn of the century Chicago's Danish population

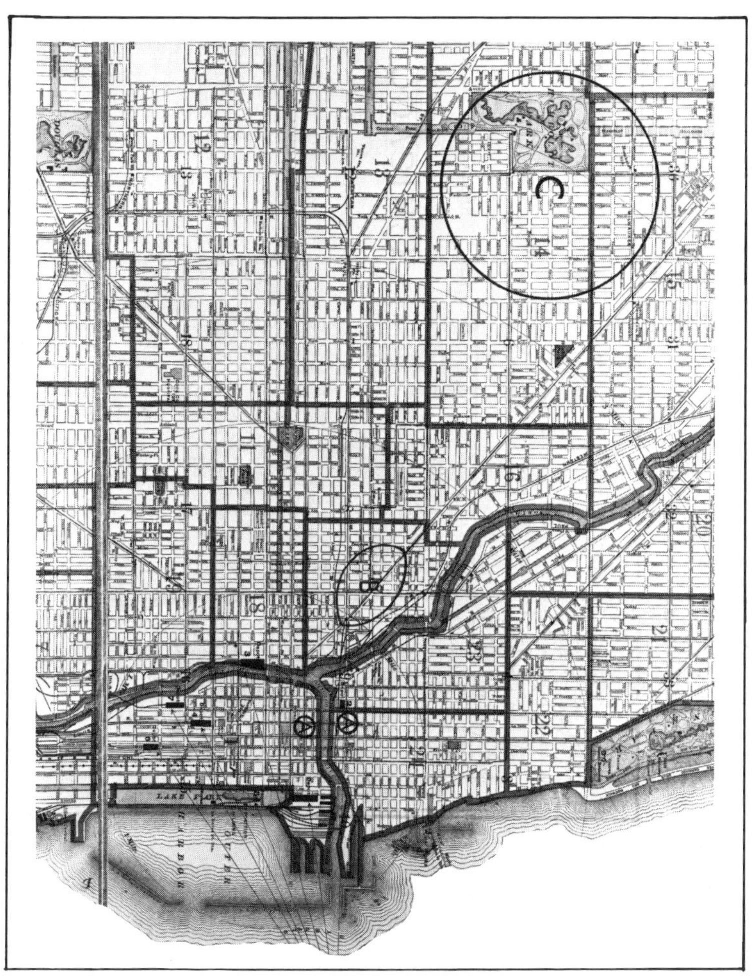


**Danish concentrations in Chicago, 1850–1929**
Circles added to show Danish locations:

A. 1850s–1870s
B. 1870s–1890s
C. 1880s–1920s

*Credit*: Chicago Historical Society

numbered 10,000, which meant that two-thirds were located between the Loop and Humboldt Park and the remainder scattered throughout the city. As the Danes moved northwestward toward Humboldt Park, they distributed themselves more widely and there was less of the concentration that had existed earlier on Milwaukee Avenue, so that the Danish area covered about twenty blocks in length and seven blocks in width. North Avenue between Western and California was referred to as the "Danish Broadway." After the turn of the century the Danes also settled the region north and west of Humboldt Park.[8]

The Danish migration to Humboldt Park was encouraged as early as 1872 by three Danes, Banker Ferdinand Winslow, Col. August Jacobsen, and Peter Madsen Lagoni. Winslow was a handsome, impressive individual who won the confidence of the Chicago Danes. Later, in association with Pastor Claus Clausen, he became involved with a land-development project in Virginia. It collapsed in 1872, about the same time that his bank did.[9] Jacobsen had served under General William Tecumseh Sherman during the Civil War and made a fortune in real estate afterwards, but he did not associate in the social life of the Danish community. Peter Lagoni got his start by taking families out to Humboldt Park in his carriage for Sunday inspections. Lagoni later built a saloon at Western and North and it became a favorite meeting place for Danes and Danish societies.[10] If a man were drinking excessively or spending beyond his means, Lagoni told him quietly to go home. He also refused to sell the 10-cent cigar to anyone who could not afford it and offered instead a 5-cent variety.[11]

The outward migration continued for the Danes after World War I, when they again gave way to the advancing Poles and Jews. In this instance, however, the Danes did not form another core community, but scattered through Chicago and the suburbs. After 1920 the older Milwaukee center had completely disappeared and the Humboldt community was well on its way to disintegration.[12]

An observer of the Chicago Danish community, Jean Figaro, in a weekly column, "Gennem Lorgnetten" (Through My Glasses), identified five kinds of Danes.

(1) Danish-Danes always wear a Danish society pin in their button hole. The Danish colors are on their walls at home and a picture of King Christian IX or Frederik VII. Most also have a picture of Peter Noer and Viggo Danielsen in full regalia. Over the lady's writing table you will generally find a picture of the Danish Old Peoples' Home.
(2) Danish-Americans are the politicians or would be politicians. They are well dressed and wear glasses. Their homes are without style. They never read Danish papers except during election time.
(3) The Cosmopolitans are made up of both rich and poor. They are very critical, but do not like to be criticized themselves. At present, they read a great many modern Danish books instead of Kipling, but it is only a question of time when it will be the other way around. They read Danish papers edited in Denmark and in the United States. All our prominent Jews belong to this group.
(4) The Monkeys consist of the spiritual lower class with higher aspirations. They want to play in our comedies, to speak at our festivals, and to write songs on all occasions. They often forget to finish the sentences they speak or write. They never read anything but Danish written by themselves, which does not enlighten them very much.
(5) The Common Mortals are the writer and the gentle reader who want to be left alone and to live their own lives.[13]

Figaro's five categories, although intentionally gross generalizations and written without claim to objectivity, furnish a realistic picture of social life in Chicago's Danish community. One should not consider, however, that the five categories were mutually exclusive, clearly delineated, or that they applied to all Danes. Even so, the sources available today do indicate the activity in some of these groups and serve to illustrate Danish life in an urban setting.

The first two categories, the Danish-Danes and the Danish Americans, can be combined for practical purposes. There were a few Danish-Danes whose attachment to their homeland eventually led them back to Denmark. General C. T. Christensen was one of these individuals. He had fought in the American Civil War and had lived in New York and Chicago for many years, but eventually he returned to Copenhagen.[14] Another person was Gorm Rasmussen, who was the founder and president of the National Tea Company. He could afford to keep his attachment to both nations and in 1924 purchased Sølust, a mansion near Copenhagen, for 500,000 Danish kroner.[15]

But the majority of these two groups were loyal Danes who would probably visit Denmark, only to return to their homes in Chicago, where they would eventually die and be buried in Chicago's Mt. Olive Cemetery. This group celebrated the king's birthday and organized activities to bring the Danish community together for Danish events. One such occasion was the ninetieth anniversary of Hans Christian Andersen's birth. To commemorate the occasion they proposed that a statue of the author be created and placed in Lincoln Park. There was considerable debate among the committee members as to whether or not the commission should go to Johannes Gelert, a Danish sculptor living in Chicago who had proposed the project, or if there should be an open competition. When the committee voted to award the commission to Gelert without a competition, the minority stalked out of the meeting.[16]

The committee also was divided on the location for the statue. Should it be situated in Humboldt Park in the Danish neighborhood, or the more prestigious Lincoln Park on the lake front? Eventually the statue was finished by Gelert, placed in Lincoln Park, and dedicated in 1896, with 10,000 people present.[17]

Another event sponsored and supported by this group of Danes was the celebration of the fiftieth anniversary of the 1849 Constitution. But even then there was controversy. The Central Committee that had been split over the Hans Christian Andersen statue still remained divided and some of the societies feared that participation of the committee members in the festivities would only splinter the colony further. In addition, most lodges were opposed to holding the celebration at all because the Danish governmental changes made in 1866 were so reactionary that the 1849 Constitution was practically abrogated. If there was to be a celebration at all, the lodge members preferred less divisive events to commemorate such as the victories of Denmark in the 1848 and 1850 wars with the Germans.[18]

But the anniversary was celebrated and the earlier misgivings proved groundless because more than 10,000 Danes gathered for the occasion. The chairman, nevertheless, had become disgusted with the petty jealousy and independence of the various leaders, so following the event he resigned and the committee disbanded.[19]

The need for a coordinating committee for Danish clubs and events was obvious. There were scores of lodges, clubs, and choruses, but none worked for the unity of the Danish community. So in 1906 another effort was made and the Central Committee of the United Danish Societies was founded, representing twenty-five different societies. Niels Juul, congressman and former collector of the customs, was chosen president. The goal was to coordinate the societies, to support the Old People's Home and the orphanage, and to sponsor an annual gathering that would convey to the Americans the size of the Danish community.[20]

This time the committee endured and laid plans for an annual celebration of Constitution Day at Riverview Park. The place was an amusement park where there was eating, dancing, and rides for those who wished to vary their activity from the speeches and singing. The first festival was held in 1909, and in 1910 more than 10,000 attended, many to hear the Socialist mayor of Milwaukee, Emil Seidel, speak about socialism. In 1920 there was a similar turnout to celebrate not only the Constitution, but also the return of Slesvig to Denmark. The festivities of that year also reflected a new era in America and began with a parade of 100 automobiles.[21]

The third group in Chicago's Danish community was the intellectual, or as Figaro put it, the cosmopolitan. Many of the cosmopolitans participated in the activities of the Danish-Danes and the Danish Americans, but there were distinctions. Very few concerned themselves with the church, some were Socialists, and Emil Dreier was an atheist. Others such as Max Henius and Morris Salmonsen were prominent Danish Jews and Henry Hertz had a Jewish heritage. The meeting place for this group, in the first two decades of the Danish community's existence, was Wilken's Cellar in the Loop, and the Round Table around which they gathered became its symbol. As the Danes moved west, other locations, such as the newspaper office of *Chicago Posten* or taverns, became replacements for Wilken's Cellar, but none gained the fame of the original meeting place.[22]

The moving force behind this group was Emil Dreier, who

migrated in 1854 and worked first for Miller in the Loop. He then opened a pharmacy on Milwaukee Avenue and in 1867 became the Danish consul in Chicago. He sported side whiskers and was corpulent, so his friends called him "The Turtle." The heat and gout bothered him and he was temperamental, but he had many friends. His appointment as consul had created some controversy because the Danish consul in New York asked the Dania Society of Chicago for nominations when the vacancy occurred. Anton Skov nominated George Bay and Ferdinand Winslow supported Dreier. In the discussion that took place in the presence of the two candidates, Skov spoke disparagingly of Dreier, and when Dreier received the support of Dania, Skov expressed these same feelings in a letter to the consul in New York. Dreier received the appointment, and Dania ordered Skov to apologize to Dreier for his attack, primarily because it was a breach of club rules. Skov did go to Dreier's residence, but the appointed witnesses and Dreier did not think it a suitable apology. Dreier was insulted by the actions of Skov and the lukewarm support from Dania, so he resigned, taking Winslow and other supporters along. Winslow then started the Scandinavian Society, which lasted until 1872, when his bank collapsed. Dreier returned to Dania that same year, primarily through the efforts of Henry Hertz.[23]

Wilken's Cellar, with its Round Table, was the place where Dreier and his friends met several times a week late in the afternoon.[24] The table was reserved for the Danes and guests, and generally writers, architects, sculptors, and intellectuals were "invited" to join. One of the regulars, Max Henius, described the experience:

> One went down eight steps and found oneself in a half-dark cellar, where it was necessary to use gaslight overhead to see anything. Tables and chairs were the cheapest kind—wood. Just beside the entrance stood the so-called "round-table." Its surface had never known a table cloth. The table was covered with a pattern of rings made by many wine glasses. The uninitiated called the place the "sewer." Promptly at five in the afternoon, the cellar stairwell was darkened by the Consul's gigantic frame and soon his red face was visible with his curious self-made glass cigar. His friends were waiting patiently as

the consul always led the conversation. Wilkens provided free lunch with a five-cent or ten-cent glass of wine.[25]

Other members of the circle included Niels C. Frederiksen, who was well known both in Denmark and in the Danish American community. He had received all the advantages of an upper-class upbringing in Denmark and had married the daughter of D. G. Monrad, the Danish prime minister. At one time he held a seat in the *Rigsdag* and a professorship in the University of Copenhagen, from which he had graduated. But in 1875 his investments became worthless when the empire in sugar and timber he had built collapsed and he resigned his posts and departed for the United States. Upon his arrival in 1877 he worked on Scandinavian papers for four years. He first purchased *Heimdal* from Fritz Frantzen along with his bookstore, and in an attempt to give the newspaper a better literary quality hired Clemens Petersen, Louis Pio, and Poul Geleff.[26]

Although Petersen was a literary critic and Pio and Geleff were intelligent and good writers, they were not trained for business, nor were they practical. Witty Danes, aware of the instability of these men, called the place "Frederiksen's Hospital," a pun on Frederiks Hospital in Copenhagen. But the new writers did not attract increased readership, and with Frederiksen also unable to attend to details, the paper closed in 1878.[27] Although the *Chicago Directory* identified Frederiksen as a boarder at 217 Milwaukee Avenue he showed ingenuity in improvising a place to sleep. Because he was the editor of the paper he obtained a pass on the Chicago, Milwaukee, and St. Paul railroad. Every evening he boarded a train leaving the city and made himself cozy in the warm car. After having traveled approximately 200 miles, he got off at a station and waited for a return train.[28] In 1881 he moved to Milwaukee, opened a land office, and sold land for the railroad company. After one year he returned to Chicago, where he began his speculation in western lands.[29] Before long his land speculation made him a millionare and he had illusions of winning a seat in the United States Senate. In 1889, however, he suffered another bankruptcy and he returned to Europe and lived at various places until his death in 1905.[30]

Henry Hertz was one of the members of the Round Table who, in contrast to Frederiksen, achieved political success in the United States. He was the son of Martin Hertz, the police inspector of Copenhagen, and had received an education at the university. He migrated to Chicago in 1869 and went to work in a bank until the fire of 1871, when he moved to a farm in Illinois for a year. After his attempt at farming he returned to Denmark as an agent for the Government Commission for British North America to recruit workers and farmers for Canada.[31] He soon returned to Chicago and, as a result of his association with the Republican party, held several positions, such as coroner, county recorder, and county clerk. His most prestigious achievement was a federal appointment as Internal Revenue Collector for the First Illinois District.[32] He was also a frequent speaker at the Constitution Day celebrations and at the testimonial dinners in the Danish community. A gregarious person, he joined many organizations, including Dania, which elected him president.[33]

Probably the most famous of the Chicago Danes was Max Henius, son of a Polish Jew who had migrated to Denmark and attained prosperity through blending and selling an Aalborg *snaps* (schnapps). The elder Henius sold the enterprise in 1881 and young Max, who had hoped to assume control of the operation, looked instead to a future in America. Even though he had just completed a doctorate at Marburg, when he arrived in America he was forced to try several jobs that did not suit him. He eventually opened a drug store and in 1886 outfitted a laboratory in the back of his shop. His specialty was brewing, and he wrote about the topic and taught students as well.[34]

One of his major contributions to Chicago was his solution of the mysterious spread of typhoid fever. He found that the children were infected by milk that had been diluted with contaminated water from Lake Michigan. Henius, like Hertz, was a spokesman for the Danish community in Chicago, and a frequent toastmaster and speaker at Danish meetings. He was also well known for the efforts he made toward the creation of Denmark's Rebild Hills National Park.[35]

Also in attendance at the Round Table were the artistic members of the Danish community, the architects, sculptors, and some painters. The architects were in demand for building up a growing city, and the sculptors could frequently get commissions following the Civil War for statues commemorating leaders and veterans of the war and for creating tomb monuments of deceased people. Painters were in lesser demand, a fact that generally compelled them to move either to the East or West coasts.

Two sculptors who were part of Dreier's circle were Carl Rohl-Smith and Johannes Gelert. Rohl-Smith had migrated in 1886 and practiced his artistic talents first at the Hecla Iron works and then at the terra-cotta factory at Perth Amboy, New Jersey. When he came to the Midwest he received commissions for sculptures that commemorated the Ft. Dearborn Massacre, an equestrian statue of General Sherman, and the veterans' monument for the capitol grounds in Des Moines. The more prudish Iowa citizens were dismayed with the veterans' monument, in which he pictured Mother Iowa as a generously endowed woman, and raised a few murmurs of objection.

The other sculptor, Gelert, was also well known, but was not as successful financially. One of his works that received public attention was a statue commemorating the policemen killed during the Haymarket Riot. Instead of being permitted to choose the means of presentation and to follow his creativity, he was instructed to do a statue of a policeman. The statue was criticized during Gelert's time as being an unimaginative piece of junk, and amidst the protests of the 1970s the statue, located at Haymarket Square, became a target for people resentful of the police. For the sake of its protection it now stands inside the police academy building. After doing the Hans Christian Andersen statue, Gelert went to New York in search of work, but prosperity eluded him. Unfortunately paralysis weakened his right hand and he entered the Danish Home for the Aged in Brooklyn. There he received little attention from the public, and only Pastor Rasmus Andersen spent time with him. He died in 1923 an embittered man who had received honors and gold medals for his work, but inadequate monetary compensation.[36]

The fourth group, the religious people, got shabby treatment from the journalist Figaro, probably because they bought church papers rather than *Revyen*, but the columnist was accurate about the desire of some members of this group to participate in Danish events. Pastor Adam Dan, for example, appeared at events such as Henius's reception for a visiting Danish poet to which eighteen local poets had been invited, and he also served on the Hans Christian Andersen statue committee. The church also sponsored a Children's Home in Chicago and supported the Old People's Home. These two institutions, especially the Old People's Home, provided a focal point for all the Chicago Danes, and the clergymen and church members received publicity for their humanitarian work. Both institutions frequently received financial support from clubs and societies whose profits from social events were directed to worthy causes.[37]

Both of the Danish Lutheran denominations were represented in Chicago and both opened and closed churches to keep up with the Danish community as it shifted its locations. No Danish congregation was established until 1872, and those Danes who were interested in religion either attended the Scandinavian congregations or the Danish Baptist congregation which had been established in 1866.

In March 1872 some Danes asked Adam Dan from Racine to help organize a congregation in Chicago. For several months he commuted weekly, but it soon became unsatisfactory for him and the arrangement had to be ended. By July, however, the congregation, Trinity, received a minister from Denmark and by 1874 it had a membership of 172.

Trinity was located at Superior and Bikerdike, just west of the Milwaukee Avenue colony, so, as the Danes moved west, it was not immediately influenced by the change. Soon, however, more members found homes near Humboldt Park and asked Trinity for religious services. No satisfactory arrangement could be made, so in 1890 former Trinity members built a new congregation, St. Ansgar, near Humboldt Park. It grew, and by 1920 it had a solid membership of 650. Trinity, on the other hand, continued to lose members, so in 1905 it also moved to the Humboldt Park area. But in 1927, when Danes were moving out again, St. Ansgar dissolved and Trinity remained the only Danish church in the area. These two congregations, in addition to St. Stephen and St. Michael on the South Side, were the congregations of the Danish Church in Chicago.[38]

The United Church had no congregation in Chicago until

1890, when Pastor P. C. Trandberg founded Siloam congregation. Trandberg taught in a Congregational seminary for a while, and from 1890 to 1893 conducted his own seminary. Eventually most of his students and his congregation affiliated with the United Church.[39] Siloam was located on Ada Street, south of the Danish community, and in 1909 it relocated on Cortland and Lowell, northwest of Humboldt Park. Siloam, however, sponsored a daughter church, Ebenezer, in 1895 and it had a more favorable location on Wabansia and Rockwell, close to Humboldt Park. During this same period Gethsemane was begun near Logan Square and Golgotha was established on the South Side.[40]

The religious groups furnished vital support to the Danish community in teaching the Danish language and Danish music. This activity, in addition to the church services, funerals, marriages, and lectures, helped to perpetuate the Danish heritage and brought the Danes together. In 1914, for example, the three congregations of the Danish Church reported an attendance of 284 children in Sunday school, 93 in vacation school, and 73 in Saturday school. All three types of schools stressed religion in the Danish language, while vacation school was held for eight weeks and taught the language in addition to religious subjects.[41]

Figaro, the journalist, did not elaborate on the identification of the last group, but it is the group that included the majority of Danes and probably the largest number of readers. The number of Danes in Chicago in 1890 was approximately 7,000 and, based on an examination of the Danes during that time, approximately one-half were in manufacturing and trade, one-fourth worked in personal and domestic service, and the remainder found employment in transport, communication, and clerical work.[42] According to an analysis by Philip Friedman, approximately 43 percent worked in manufacturing, mechanical, and building trades, 29 percent in domestic services, and 28 percent in commerce and professions.[43]

While Friedman examined the total number of Danish workers in Chicago in an attempt to identify the kind of jobs held by individuals in the work force, another study has attempted to measure the success or upward mobility of the Danes. Utilizing the census materials from the 14th Ward, which contained a large Danish and Scandinavian population, for the years 1880,

1890, and 1900, David Bunce identified those residents present in the ward for those census years and compared the occupational change and stability. The Danish upward mobility (or improved occupational positions) was 15.9 percent, greater than the 12.3 percent for the Norwegians and 9.2 percent for the Swedes. There were some Danes who suffered job-status decline, but the proportion was only 4.4 percent for the Danes, compared to 5.3 percent for the Swedes and 6.1 percent for the Norwegians. The Danes were also more geographically mobile and moved nearly three times over a twenty-year period, while the Norwegians and Swedes moved less than two times during the same period. Bunce's conclusion is that the Danes' occupational and residential pattern fit the American worker more closely than the pattern set by the Norwegians and Swedes.[44]

The Danishness of all the groups Figaro described was demonstrated through a variety of societies that were created and disbanded before and after the turn of the century. The oldest of the clubs was Dania, and its membership represented the entire spectrum of Chicago's Danish American society. It had been founded in 1862 by twelve Danish artisans who wished to formalize their association with each other, but it soon served as the major club and became the source of leadership in the Danish community for twenty years. The original purpose was to provide for "the entertainment [of the members] through reading, discussion and other useful means." To achieve this goal they rented a hall for meetings, looked after the provisioning of foods and drinks, bought books for their library, and sponsored annual masquerade balls. Later, in 1865, the bylaws expanded the scope of Dania "to occasionally provide lectures, recitals, and debates. . . ." The society provided services for its own members, including a sickness fund, but it also worked for the Danish community in general by helping Danes find employment, providing an English night school, and even serving as a missing-persons' bureau.[45]

The early meetings were held in the Kinzie and La Salle Street area and later, after the Chicago fire had destroyed the meeting hall, followed the Danish community to the Chicago and Milwaukee Avenue region.[46] Although there were times in the early period when the future looked bleak, the club grew, and by

1872, only ten years after its founding, it boasted a membership of 400.[47] But Dania's influence declined, first because of competition from other Danish societies and then from the dispersion of the Danish community. The initial competition came from the Danish veterans of the German wars. They organized in 1876 and carried on their recruitment efficiently and displayed impressive uniforms at the parades and public events.[48]

Other societies also arose with more particular, narrow purposes. The result was that Dania members withdrew because that club had lost its purpose and had no specialization with which to attract membership. The society also suffered when many of the Danes moved to the South Side and the meeting hall was located on Milwaukee Avenue. Dania eventually followed the Danes to the Humboldt Park neighborhood, but later, when the Danes scattered out from that location, there was no new concentration of Danes for Dania to move to, so it stayed and became surrounded by non-Danish groups.[49]

Among the various specialized groups that formed before the turn of the century there were the many singing societies. *Harmonien*, founded in 1886, was the oldest, and the *Dansk Arbejder Sangforening* (Danish Workers Singing Society) was the largest. In 1936, when *Harmonien* observed its fiftieth anniversary, it still had a membership of 200. Another focus of activity included the lodges and societies such as the *Vaabenbrødrerne* (Brothers in Arms or Veterans of the Danish Wars), founded in 1876, and the Danish Brotherhood, which began its first Chicago chapter in 1883. They provided mutual aid and also staged social activities such as masquerade balls. The athletic clubs also attracted Danish members and were formed after the turn of the century, thereby indicating the greater growth of leisure time and the increasing assimilation into the geographic environment. The groups included organizations for sharpshooting, football, hunting and fishing, cycling, and Danish gymnastics. The theater groups used local Danish talent as well as guest actors from Denmark, and they leased large theaters such as the Opera House and the Garrick Theater for their performances. Both Marguerite Hertz, daughter of Henry Hertz, and Gerda Henius, daughter of Max Henius, received favorable reviews from the people who knew them well. On the other hand, pettiness also existed, and on one occasion the profits of a play could not be distributed to Danish charities because one actor demanded more money than he received and threatened to sue.[50]

The proliferation of societies continued unabated, so that there were societies for youth and for people interested in reading and education. There was even a club called *Kaffekanden* (The Coffee Pot) that boasted no rules or bylaws and offered only amusement.[51]

In addition to Chicago, Danes settled in the northern Illinois communities of Dwight, McNabb, Sheffield, and Plano. These were basically agricultural settlements founded in the 1850s and 1860s, and made possible by the railroad. Many Danes initially worked for the railroads, while others farmed on rented land. Although some Danes remained in the communities and established Lutheran churches, large numbers migrated west for farm lands in the plains states.[52]

## II *Minnesota*

The initial Danish settlement in Minnesota was made in Freeborn County in 1861, along the southern border of the state. Lars Jorgensen Hauge, a Baptist pastor who had migrated to Wisconsin in 1858, led members of his flock to Clarks Grove in 1861.[53] By 1868 there were sixty people in the community and by 1889 there were 267. This settlement became the largest Baptist congregation among the Danes in the United States. Other Danes also were impressed with the area and established such communities as Alden (Grundtvigian), Geneva (Inner Mission), Albert Lea, Blooming Prairie, and Ellendale.[54]

The early settlers raised wheat, but in 1878, when wheat prices dropped with the increased wheat production in the plains, farmers looked for other products. Success with corn was unpredictable because of the threat of frost in the late spring or early fall, and that in turn meant that fattening of cattle was not an alternative. One solution, albeit not suited to limited acreage, was the development of pasture for the production of cattle for stocking the western ranges. Another possibility was dairying. That, however, could be done only on a small scale because a dozen cows kept the farmer's wife busy milking, skimming the cream, and churning it into butter.[55]

It was in 1884 that Hans Peter Jensen visited Denmark and witnessed the operation of the newly invented cream separator as well as the organization and management of a cooperative creamery. At that time cooperative creameries were beginning to gain popularity in America. In order further to consider that alternative, several men visited the creameries in Iowa and were especially impressed with a cooperative creamery at Oran, Iowa. The Baptist congregation, whose members had provided most of the support for the study and direction, also served as hosts for the meeting of interested persons. The decision was made to proceed, so they took the constitution and bylaws from Oran's creamery and translated the document into Danish. Membership was not limited to Baptists and soon eighty farmers had signed the document, giving the creamery milk from 500 cows. The organization then bought two separators, a boiler, an engine, two cream vats, a box churn, and other equipment. Religious attitudes, however, remained strong because no milk was received on Sunday and no work was carried on at the creamery on that day. The entire project worked so well that it not only brought sound economic growth to the community but encouraged the people to extend the cooperative concept to a general store, and the collective purchasing of implements, hardware, lumber, and fuel.[56] By 1897 Freeborn County was densely settled and the price of land had risen to $40 per acre, making it necessary for young men in search of inexpensive farms to leave the county.[57]

The second major settlement came as a result of a decision of the Danish Church at its annual convention in 1884 to appoint a committee of five, including Pastors Grundtvig and Kristian Anker, to locate some land where the scattered Danes could gather in a colony. The committee agreed to purchase 35,000 acres of land in Lincoln County from the Winona and St. Peter Railroad on the condition that only Danes would be permitted to buy farms for the first three years. The price per acre for the first year would be $7 and it would be restricted to a 50-cent yearly increase. If 12,000 acres could be sold within the specified time, the railroad promised to donate 240 acres for churches and schools. The sales of land were made by Adolph Boysen, the agent for the railroad.[58]

The first sale was held on June 27, 1885, with approximately seventy people assembled at Lake Benton. After an inspection of the designated land around the town of Tyler, east of Lake Benton, the land seekers made the purchase, totaling 3,000 acres. The next day, Sunday, the group took a steamboat to an island in the lake and celebrated the successful beginning with a church service and a picnic. Most of the land purchasers then went home to Clinton, Iowa; Elk Horn, Iowa; Clifton, Illinois; and Racine, to return with their families at a later time.[59]

The congregation was formed in 1886, and after a short period of being served by visiting pastors, the faithful extended a call to Pastor Grundtvig. He had encouraged the congregation to include a statement in the constitution forbidding membership in secret societies observing any form of divine worship. The congregation refused to make the addition, and Grundtvig charged that the railroad agent, Boysen, was excessively sympathetic to the Danish Brotherhood. Grundtvig returned the call with the understanding that he would not accept the position unless the restrictive clause were added to the constitution.[60] The congregation, in 1888, sent the call to H. J. Pedersen. Pedersen had migrated to the United States in 1875 and served several parishes in Michigan. Five years later he accepted the position of the presidency of Elk Horn Folk School and then in 1882 he returned to Michigan and opened a new folk school at Ashland. The Michigan school was not a success, so he readily accepted the position in Tyler, where he saw possibilities for yet another school.[61]

Pedersen soon carried out his dream and became the founder and first president of the folk school located on the south edge of Tyler. The Danes at Tyler agreed that a folk school was desirable, but they collected only $650 for the project. Pedersen's appeal in *Dannevirke* was more successful and people from all over the country contributed $1,167. The building was constructed by the Tyler citizens in four months and opened in December 1888 with nineteen students. Pedersen called the school Danebod, which means "One who saves the Danes."[62]

The purpose of the school was "to combine in its teachings [and] learning, morality and religion, giving special attention and effort to arouse and strengthen in the minds of its students, a love of the good, the true, and beautiful in literature, and especially Danish literature."[63]

Pedersen started optimistically, but like Ashland the school's existence in Tyler was tenuous, so he resigned in 1903. Thorvald Knudsen, from Nysted, Nebraska, was then called and under him the school enjoyed expansion of the facilities and an increased enrollment. The enrollment for the summer session generally stood at forty young women and the winter session at sixty-five young men. Knudsen was absent from 1912 to 1916, during which time he served as president of Grand View College, but then came the war, increased emphasis on English, and the decline. Even though efforts to revive the school continued into recent times, the folk school in its traditional sense ended in 1931.[64]

The community, on the other hand, continued to grow. By 1906 it had constructed a church, parochial school, a stone hall, gymnastic hall, and an orphanage in addition to the folk school, and by 1921 the congregation numbered 800 people, The settlers prospered economically as well. In 1894 they established a cooperative creamery and then followed with a fire-insurance society, an elevator, a bank, a telephone company, and an agency for selling farm animals.[65]

The third settlement in Minnesota was Askov, named after the location in Denmark of the folk high school. This settlement was begun in 1906 as the result of religious motives, but in this instance it was the Danish People's Society that made the arrangements and not the Danish Church. The location selected by a committee was on the Great Northern Railroad 100 miles northeast of St. Paul and fifty-seven miles southwest of Duluth. There the society obtained about 20,000 acres of land that cost $10 per acre but could be purchased with a 20 percent down payment. The People's Society members did not manage the sale of land, but they did help settlers move possessions to the farms.[66]

The purpose of the settlement was to help preserve the Danish heritage and to build a Lutheran congregation, so advertising appeared in *Julegranen* and church publications. Most of the settlers came from other states and not from Denmark. People from Chicago hoped to escape the city's poor living conditions and foul air and to secure instead a wholesome environment for their children. Many came who wished to be in a community where the Danish language, school, and church predominated. Askov appealed to others from North Dakota, where farmers had been frustrated by grasshoppers and drought and to people from Tyler because of the lower land prices. Most settlers had accumulated some wealth in their first years in America, so the pioneering period was short.[67]

The timber on the land had been harvested, and in 1894 the remainder was burned in a massive forest fire. By the time the Danes arrived the brush had grown back, and so the task was to remove the old white pine stumps and also the new growth. After World War I, 130,000 pounds of surplus explosives were sent to Askov for stump removal.[68] Another problem was the soil. The forest fire had burned the humus in the soil, leaving a stony, glacial loam and clay for farming. As an agent from the University Extension told the settlers, "To make a farm here, first you log the land, then you bush it, then you stump it, then you stone it, then you plow it, then you seed it."[69] The most productive cash crop was potatoes, with yields as high as 300 bushels an acre. The crop that soon took priority was the rutabaga. A cooperative creamery that opened in 1911 was highly successful. Even though many farmers received less than $1,000 from the dairy operation, it was a consistent source of funds that paid for basic farm expenses.[70]

By 1916 there were 1,000 people in Askov who were Danish or of Danish descent. The public school curriculum included Danish literature, language, and history until 1942. The Lutheran congregation also utilized Danish and although the congregation was affiliated with the Danish Church it included Danish people from the United denomination in its membership.[71]

## III *Iowa*

Although some Danes made their homes in Iowa as early as 1837, the number remained small until after the Civil War. The first settlement sufficiently large to support a Danish congregation was at Cedar Falls, in the northeastern part of the state. There Pastor C. L. Clausen, the Dane who served a Norwegian parish at St. Ansgar, Iowa, recognized the spiritual needs of his countrymen and in 1867 established the Scandinavian Church Society. He conducted periodic religious services in Cedar Falls, but a part-time ministry was not satisfactory, so when A. S. Nielsen arrived from Denmark, Clausen recommended that the congregation call him to become its pastor. Under Nielsen the congregation became the Danish Evangelical Lutheran Church, and it remained the only Danish church in Iowa until 1875.[72]

During the early 1870s more Danes, especially from North Slesvig, came into the Cedar Falls region, and the area eventually became the second-largest Danish community in Iowa. The rural location where many Danes settled was west of Cedar Falls at Fredsville, which means village of peace. There the Danes built a church, parsonage, a creamery, and several shops. Included in the residents of this community were Jeppe Slifsgaard and his son Truels. Truels had arrived at Cedar Falls in 1869 and rented some farm land. In the correspondence with his father he talked about agriculture and the creamery that had been established. The father in turn wrote to Truels about the cream separator being introduced in Denmark, and in 1882, when he also migrated to America, he brought with him a separator produced by Burmeister and Wain of Denmark and a person trained in making butter. This was the first cream separator in the United States and it required two months of deliberation by the customs officials to decide on the amount of tax. Finally, in 1883, Slifsgaard and his son started "The Danish Creamery," which they operated for several years and then sold to a group of farmers who made it into a cooperative creamery.[73]

The Danish settlement in western Iowa claiming to contain the largest rural concentration of Danes in the United States was located within the counties of Shelby and Audubon. Five Danes appeared in the Shelby County census in 1856, but because they did not remain it is generally assumed that they were either Mormons bound for Utah or migrant railroad or farm workers.[74] The first permanent Danish settlers were some Danish Baptists from Brown County, Wisconsin, who in 1865 established a community at Cuppy's Grove. More Baptists joined them from Racine, and in 1876 the Baptist church claimed a membership of 124.

The Danish Lutheran settlement began in 1869, four years later, when some Danes, working on the Rock Island line between Des Moines and Council Bluffs, bought a section of land near the present town of Harlan. They did not settle the land, however, until the fall of 1870, when Ole Jacobsen dug into a hillside and made a crude shelter. That dugout, ten feet by fifteen, became home for ten people for the following winter. Danes from other parts of the United States and Denmark continued to migrate into the area, and by 1895 there were 3,000 Danes in the two counties, and in 1900 P.S. Vig, the Danish Lutheran leader, estimated that 12,000 Danish speakers lived in the thirty square miles.[75]

The center of the Lutheran settlement was at Elk Horn, and a congregation was founded there in 1875. The Norwegian pastor, Olav Kirkeberg, a staunch Lutheran, not only ministered to the Lutherans, but worked zealously to regain apostates who had converted to the Baptist and Adventist faith. In 1878 the Danish Church established a folk school at Elk Horn with Kirkeberg as president, and in 1890 the local congregation opened an orphanage. Elk Horn became a Danish village and Danish was the common language, even for the children, unless an English-speaking person came to town. The population of the town was composed largely of retired farmers and approximately a dozen tradespeople who owned the businesses. Eventually the leaders in the community established cooperatives for insurance, a lumber yard, and several creameries.[76]

Some of the Danes who moved to Elk Horn did so because of the religious climate provided by the church and folk school, and both the community and the school enjoyed growth in the 1880s. But the town and the entire area were torn by the denominational schism of the Danish Church in 1894. After the division Elk Horn became the center of the Inner Mission group, while the Grundtvigians' strength lay in Kimballton, five miles north. For many years the two towns engaged in extensive bickering and rivalries, largely because of the religious division.[77] The religious controversy did not, however, prevent the continued cooperation on the economic level. In 1907 the two communities constructed a railroad spur line from their area to Atlantic, where a connection with a main line was made.[78]

Although other clusters of Danes had formed in various Iowa counties, the last major settlement was in Emmet County, in the northern part of the state. This county was sparsely settled in 1880, and it was through the work of Adolph Boysen and N. C. Frederiksen that Danes were attracted. Boysen's family was aristocratic. Following the German annexation of Slesvig, it sold its holdings in Haderslev and purchased an estate in Denmark. But Boysen was not satisfied, so in 1872 he migrated to Cedar Falls. Although his biography does not clearly describe his activities during this time, he may well have become interested in real estate while a resident of Cedar Falls. In 1880 he moved to Milwaukee, where he served as vice-consul from 1880 to 1883 and at the same time contracted with the Chicago and Milwaukee Railroad to publicize and sell land in Emmet County. He then moved his residence to Chicago, where he was a participant at Dreier's Round Table. His real-estate activity continued, however, and over a period of eighteen years he sold more than 1 million acres of southern Minnesota land to Danish and German farmers, including the Danish settlement in Lincoln County. His first financial loss was incurred in Kansas when a series of dry years brought disaster not only to the land developers but to the farmers, many of whom were Danes. He remained in the real-estate business, and while numerous Danes were taking land in Canada, Boysen decided that Canada was too far north and turned instead to Arkansas, where he sold land suitable for irrigation and the production of rice.[79]

The price for the land in Emmet County was inexpensive, only $5 per acre, and if the settler paid $5.50 immediately and then brought his acreage into cultivation within two years, he would receive a rebate of $2.50. The railroad also promised forty acres for a church, but in order to obtain a deed a congregation had to be chartered. The prospective settlers, therefore, many of them living in Clinton, chartered St. Ansgar Lutheran Church even before they had left for their new home.[80]

The first Danish settler arrived in 1881, although the major migration began in the spring of the next year. The land sales were sluggish at first and a correspondent to *Dannevirke* pointed out that the Danes going west could not get better land any cheaper. As the people increased in number, a township was organized and called Denmark and the village was called Ringsted, after the hometown of the postmaster's wife. In 1888 about forty families had homes in the township and by 1891 the congregation was stable enough to construct a church building. Not unlike many rural parishes, much of the work was done by donated labor. The building was not situated on the forty acres granted by the railroad, but two miles southwest, more in the center of the township. The forty acres instead was used for the cemetery and the parsonage.

Two years after the construction of the sanctuary the Danish Church passed a resolution establishing a new constitution and stipulating that those congregations refusing to sign within a time limit should be removed from the roster. The issues were not clear in the laymen's minds, so they neither signed nor did they affiliate with the North Church. The congregation remained independent until 1897, when it accepted the proposal to join either the Danish Church or the newly created United Church. The vote was twenty-seven to twenty-five to join the United Church. Because the vote was so close, they divided the property and did so with as little controversy as possible. The pastor favored the United Church, so the parsonage and the forty acres went with him, and his congregation was called St. Paul. The minority received the St. Ansgar building, but by earlier agreement could not retain the name, so the congregation became St. John instead.[81]

Ringsted was incorporated as a town in 1899, when the Chicago and Northwestern was built through the community. St. Paul congregation, during the same period, decided to build its new church in town. In spite of the differences over religion, the community exhibited signs of cooperation and organized a mutual-aid society that later became a member of the United Danish Societies. They also built the Denmark Creamery Company in 1892, a cooperative creamery, and the Ringsted Cooperative Creamery in 1915. There were about 1,000 Danes or children of Danish parents in the community in 1910.[82]

Farming in the prairie states of Illinois, Minnesota, and Iowa had an advantage over Wisconsin and Michigan because the enormous physical labor of cutting trees was not necessary. Turning the prairie sod, although it required extra oxen and a special plow, was much easier by comparison. But at the same time the shortage of timber or its total absence was a problem. Invariably the early settlers either dug into a hillside to create a home called a dugout or they brought with them enough lumber to construct a ten-foot-square shanty which served as a temporary shelter. The bed, table, and some household articles were kept inside, while the cookstove was outside, although sheltered under a roof.

Fortunately for the settlers, the railroads had crossed the Midwest, and during that period of settlement Wisconsin pine logs were floated down the Mississippi River to the Iowa river towns and cut into lumber. The lumber in turn was transported by rail to the point nearest a settler's new farm.[83] In certain localities, such as Emmet County, the land was poorly drained so it was necessary to dig ditches and lay tiles in order to drain the ponds and swamps. Although the work was backbreaking and tedious, some could be delayed for years while the farmer plowed the higher ground.[84] Other problems caused by both nature and man included blizzards in winter, droughts in summer, hailstones, grasshoppers, prairie fires, poor transportation, low prices for goods, and high interest rates for loans.

Subsistence farming was the usual beginning. The farmer purchased a cheap team of horses, a wagon, a plow, a cow, an old sow, and some chickens. The initial crop on the freshly turned sod was corn, and it was not highly productive as the corn plant tried to obtain nutriments from grass roots still not decomposed. But after the first year, the farmer's land produced more corn and he was able to add some acres of wheat. Initially the animals grazed on the native prairie, but as their number increased the farmer planted timothy, clover, and alfalfa to increase the production of fodder for each acre. In the early years, when the distance to the railroad was great, the farmer was limited to producing corn for the fattening of cattle and hogs, but as more lines were built he could produce more wheat and also diversify with dairy cattle and dairy products.[85]

## CHAPTER 8

# *Danish Settlements in the Plains States*

### I *Nebraska*

THE Danish population of Nebraska is scattered throughout the state, but there are two concentrations. The first and largest is along the Missouri River, including Douglas County (and the city of Omaha), and the counties to the north and west, Washington, Burt, and Dodge. The other center is along the Platte River in the central part of Nebraska in the counties of Kearney, Howard, Hamilton, and Nuckolls.

The non-Mormon Danes who settled in eastern Nebraska began arriving after the Civil War, in the mid-1860s, from the states of Iowa and Illinois. Some lived for a time in Omaha, working for the Union Pacific and related industries while others took land in the eastern counties to grow wheat, oats, and barley or to raise cattle and swine for the Omaha packing houses.[1]

Because of the tardy start by the Danish Lutherans in America, nothing was done to organize a congregation in Omaha until 1874, when Pastor H. Hansen of the Norwegian-Danish Conference began a ministry there. But in the ensuing conflict between Hansen and the Grundtvigians, the congregation, in 1878, voted by a count of 21 to 22 to dismiss Hansen and obtain a pastor from the Danish Church. As a result, Our Savior's church became the congregation of the Danish Church and later, in 1886, Pella was founded by the Blair synod.[2]

There was no Danish neighborhood in Omaha and the Danes generally were dispersed.[3] Very often occupation decided residence and included in the variety of employment were dairies at the fringe of the city which hired many Danes. Our Savior's church provided a rallying point for Danes on the south side and Pella did the same for the northsiders. Two major institutions that further helped the cohesion of the Danes in America were headquartered in Omaha—*Den Danske Pioneer* and the Danish Brotherhood.[4]

The western settlement was begun in Howard County through the efforts of some Danes from Waukesha County, Wisconsin, including N. J. Paul and Vice-Consul C. F. J. Moeller. In December 1870 these two men camped on the Loup River, which flows into the Platte, during a preliminary investigation of settlement sites. Even though it was intensely cold and they had to stay awake all night to keep from freezing, they found the land fertile and not far from the Union Pacific Railroad. They returned to Wisconsin and formed the Danish Land and Homestead Company, electing Lars Hannibal president.[5]

Hannibal and four others traveled to Nebraska in March 1871 to select a specific tract, and after twelve days of further search, they decided to file for the land on Oak Creek, about twenty-five miles northwest of Grand Island. Additional settlers arrived in May, and soon the colony of Dannebrog (the name of the Danish flag) was made up of people living in tents, shanties, dugouts, and sod houses. C. C. Schlytern, a Swede, bought several sections from the railroad and platted a town in 1873, which was also called Dannebrog.[6]

The village soon included a store, a blacksmith shop, and a shoemaker's shop. Most of the Danes wore wooden shoes not only around the farmyard, but also on trips to Grand Island, the nearest town. Lars Hannibal dammed up Oak Creek in 1874 and built a water-powered flour mill.[7]

The second settlement in Howard County was Dannevirke, an outgrowth of Dannebrog. Niels Hansen had come to the United States in 1871 and was working for the railroad in Arkansas when he read one of Hannibal's advertisements. By that time, 1873, all of the homesteads were taken at Dannebrog, so he moved to Munson Creek, eighteen miles northwest, and found good timber and a tract that had not been claimed. Hansen worked at Fort Hartsuff and hired a neighbor to break ten acres of prairie. Draft animals were in short supply in the early years, so often two neighbors supplied one ox each to make a team. The settlement grew in size, especially in 1877, when a group of settlers came from Lansingborough, near Troy, New York, and by 1879 most of the homesteads were taken.[8]

Four miles west and north of Dannebrog was the town of Nysted, founded in 1882. Danes had moved into the area as Dannebrog expanded and by 1879 the settlement was large enough to support a congregation. The community, first called Daneville and later Nysted, became important because it was more centrally located in the Danish community than Dannebrog, which was on the eastern edge.

A folk school was opened at Nysted in 1887 in a rundown frame building that at one time had been used as a store. In spite of the problems and small enrollment a new building was constructed the next year, and by 1894 fifty-nine students attended.[9] Under the leadership of men like Thorvald Knudsen and A. Th. Dorf, the Nysted school enjoyed a comparatively successful existence. With the emphasis on English during World War I and the restriction on immigration, enrollment declined, and in 1936 the weakened institution fell victim to the national depression and the Midwest drought.[10]

The Danes of Howard County, in contrast to many Danes, participated in local politics and several men became members of the state legislature. But at the same time, they fit the Danish pattern in their attempt at economic cooperation. Their first effort was made in 1874, when each farmer contributed $5 for a sorghum mill to make molasses.[11] But the collective idea did not last long. As Alfred C. Nielsen said, "The pioneers in our community were cultural individualists and economic collectivists. . . . As time went on these farmers tended to become cultural collectivists and economic individualists." By buying goods where prices were a bit lower, the Danes ruined their associations.[12]

The other county in central Nebraska with a large Danish population was Kearney County. This community was not developed through a land company but through communication by relatives and friends. Many of the settlers came from southern Wisconsin, northern Illinois, and places like Chicago and Plano. The settlers often took advantage of the railroad network and sent the wives ahead on the passenger train while the men rode with the animals and equipment on chartered cars. But as late as 1877 C. J. Jorgensen made the trip from Plano to Kearney County by covered wagon in thirty days.[13]

The settlement was begun in 1874 when A. C. Christensen filed a claim, and soon the largest concentration of Danes was in Cosmos Township, approximately five miles south of Minden. Many small churches, including the Baptist, were scattered through the countryside in the early days, but most soon closed and the farmers attended the churches in town. Many of the Danes also retired in Minden, and in 1920 an Old People's Home was founded in that town.[14]

The settlers on the plains followed familiar patterns of living from Kansas to Dakota. The first home was either a shanty, a dug out, or a sod house. The shanty, a familiar construction for settlers on the prairie, was suitable for a plains summer but inadequate for winter. The sides were single walls of boards nailed to a frame, and its advantage was its rapid construction and protection against the sun and rain.

The sod house was warmer in winter and cooler in summer than the shanty because it was made of strips of matted grass roots and soil. The sod was cut into pieces three inches thick, several feet long, and ten inches wide. The strips were simply stacked on top of each other until the desired height was reached for each wall, and then it was covered with a roof. A makeshift roof could be constructed of poles and grass, but a better roof could be made of boards covered with tar paper and then more sod. Proper material and construction were essential because a leaky roof in wet weather would make the house muddy and dank, and even in dry weather fine dust would sift down into the living area. Some homemakers attached muslin to the ceiling to catch the dust. Mice and snakes often made their homes in the walls and in summer of 1874 Nebraska experienced a grub-worm infestation that brought uninvited guests. Most farm wives hoped to move into a frame house as soon as possible, although in some instances residence in the sod house was prolonged or a second sod house was constructed with greater attention to comfort. In that event the roof was properly built, a floor of boards added, and the walls of the house plastered with clay and at times even papered. In Howard County the farmers were building frame houses in the 1880s, indicating a state of prosperity and proving that a decade in a sod house was enough.[15]

By the time the Danish settlers reached the plains, agricultural practices had been set and A. C. Nielsen observed that his father "began to unlearn Danish farming methods and to learn American ways."[16] The initial farm procedures of the plains also resembled those of the prairies and the first crop was usually sod corn that produced only about ten bushels per acre. The second year, when the roots had decayed completely, wheat became the widely grown crop.[17]

Initially in Howard County the grain was hauled to Grand Island by wagon, but with the construction of the railroad to St. Paul the distance was shortened, and eventually the tracks were laid to Dannebrog. Throughout the plains it was the railroad that made it possible for the farmers to exist at all, because the economy depended on the shipment of grains. Transportation costs reduced the profit, and at least one farmer thought the merchants in Grand Island cheated him because he did not know English. Even though he realized the value of knowing English, the opportunity for learning it was limited because Danish was generally spoken in the settlement.[18]

The diet of the Danes in Howard County and in the plains states was dependent on the production of the farm and garden. All farmers had gardens that produced a wide variety of vegetables, but especially kale for soup and potatoes of both the early and late variety. When times were difficult the Danes subsisted on corn meal mush, milk, sorghum molasses, parched wheat and rye for coffee, and biscuits made of "goose wheat" ground coarse in a coffee mill.[19]

Hardships on the plains also resembled those of the prairie and the procession seemed to be a never-ending one. In 1874 and 1875 there were grasshoppers; the winters were severe in 1873 and 1880; drought came in the 1890s along with the depression. Hail, prairie fires, and tornadoes were frequent threats, but less destructive over a large area. Many Danes, especially women, were unnerved by the loneliness and quietness of the plains. A Danish woman who had migrated to Dawson County in 1881 would on occasion climb up on a shed to see if another human might be passing by.[20]

But there were good times as well, especially in the late 1870s and 1880s. Farmers hired workmen to dig wells and erect windmills for an improved water supply. Barbed wire and grain binders simplified their labors in the 1880s and alfalfa and winter wheat increased yields and profit in the mid-1890s. Although many Danes would eventually continue on to California, the majority found the plains acceptable and settled south to Texas and north to Canada.[21]

## II *Kansas*

The first Dane in Kansas was John Nielsen, a former California gold miner, who, in 1855, chose a home in Marshall County along the Nebraska boundary. In 1869 some Slesvigers also settled there and together with some Swedes started a Scandinavian church. Another Danish community was founded in 1869 by some Grundtvigians in Lincoln County who called the place Denmark. This community was the only Danish settlement ever attacked by Indians, and on May 30, 1869, about sixty Indians raided the area and killed five people, three of whom were Danes. As the Danish population increased, it organized a congregation in 1877 and built a church in 1880. Another Grundtvigian group of about fifteen families settled at Lyndon in Osage County, but a colony projected for Logan County failed. The settlement was approximately seventy miles west of Hays, not far from where Louis Pio had staked out his Socialist colony eleven years earlier. A frequent problem in this western area was lack of rain. The Logan County failure damaged the reputation of the clergymen as colonizers and was largely responsible for the transfer of projects such as this to the Danish Folk Society.

By 1870 there were Danes in almost every county in Kansas and by 1910 2,759 Danes lived in the state. Many of the rural Danes later migrated to the cities and in 1920 Kansas City, Kansas, and Kansas City, Missouri, each had a Danish population of 400. The Danes there supported a Danish church, a lodge of the Danish Brotherhood, and organizations affiliated with the United Danish Societies.[22]

## III *Colorado*

Although Denver is now the community with the largest Danish population, the settlement at Brush, northeast of Denver on the South Platte River, was more significant at the turn of the century. In the 1880s some Danes had settled on homesteads at Harrisburg Flats, approximately thirty miles southeast of Brush. To supplement their income the men went to Brush in the fall of 1889 to work in the potato harvest and there realized the value of irrigation. Several families left the dry, sandy soil at Harrisburg Flats and moved to Brush immediately, while others soon followed. In 1892 church services were conducted in the Danish community and three years later they organized a congregation. The first constitution of the congregation established a free church that prohibited affiliation with any synod, and thereby avoided the denominational strife that was prevalent at that time.[23]

The man who made a significant contribution to Brush was Jens Madsen. He had started his training as a landscape architect in Denmark, but then went to England to complete his education. While in England he contracted typhoid fever and was taken to a deaconess hospital. After he recovered from his illness, he abandoned his studies in landscaping and migrated instead to the United States, where he studied theology first at Trinity Seminary at Blair, and later at the English Lutheran Seminary in Chicago. He became ill again in 1897, this time with tuberculosis, and, like many others afflicted with that disease, went west to regain his health. In Colorado he realized the need for hospitals and vowed to build a home for consumptives. He completed his studies at Blair, was ordained in 1902, and the next year accepted a call to Brush on the condition that he would be permitted to work on a sanitarium. In 1903 he started the Lutheran Deaconess Institute and Sanitarium Auxiliary with representatives from the two Danish synods and from the Swedes and Norwegians as well. The first buildings were dedicated in 1907 and the hospital was called Eben-Ezer Mercy Institute. Madsen designed the buildings himself and then, using his early training, chose for landscaping trees and shrubs that would grow in the dry prairie. When Madsen gave up the pulpit at St. Ansgar church, the congregation divided in two and both sections soon built their separate church buildings. Eben-Ezer, however, continued to serve Danes from both denominations.[24]

## IV *South Dakota*

Dakota Territory was established in 1861 and in 1869 the territorial government organized a board to encourage immigration to their region. A Norwegian, James M. Wahl, received the assignment to enlist Scandinavians and he traveled to Illinois, Iowa, and Wisconsin to proclaim the virtues of life in Dakota. The railroad barons were also eager to develop the settlements and to gain new customers, so they placed advertisements in such newspapers as *Dannevirke* for the years from 1879 to 1885. They encouraged the readers to join the excursion parties which left on special trains from Wisconsin and Iowa for the West. The round-trip fares were inexpensive and the ticketholders were given stopover privileges.[25]

Still other promotion was carried on by real-estate agents such as A. Boysen, the Dane who had sold land in Iowa and Minnesota. He established an office in Mitchell and advertised in *Dannevirke* about the productive land along the James River. He reminded the readers that the land he sold earlier in the prairie states for $6 had appreciated to $25 per acre and that good land was available in Dakota for $10 per acre. His hopes for the future were high and he fully expected that the Danish colony being planted west of Plankington in Aurora County would surpass the population of the Danish settlement in Lincoln County, Minnesota. Another land agent, Anthon Pederson of Kingsbury County, included an endorsement of the fertility of the soil from the Rev. H. J. Pedersen of Danebod. Dakota Territory appealed to the Danes because the land was either free under the Homestead Act or inexpensive in comparison to the land in the Midwest.[26]

Extremely effective were the letters and reports sent to the Danish American newspapers by the immigrants themselves. Comments dwelt on good crop prospects, rainfall, and the condition of wheat and corn. There must have been few hardships, or they went unreported, because the tone of the Dakota reports was optimistic. On October 28, 1891, *Dannevirke* reported that 14,085 acres of public land were still open under the existing federal land legislation.[27]

The population census indicated the growth of Danish settlements. Dakota Territory had 115 Danes in 1870 and 1,447 in 1880. But there were 4,369 in 1890 and 5,038 in 1900. The peak was reached in 1910 with 6,294 and declined in 1920 to 5,983.

The two general concentrations of Danes were in the southeast corner and in the east-central counties near Minnesota. The southeastern counties of Clay, Turner, and Yankton developed first, and already in 1864 some Danes resided at Yankton, including M. P. Ohlman, who established a cigar and liquor store. But the majority of Danes were farmers who settled close to the Missouri River at Gayville. Calle N. Johnson, for example, migrated from Slesvig in 1869 and built a log house on his homestead. The next spring he met the woman who was to become his wife at the Sioux City, Iowa, railroad terminus, and together they walked back to Gayville and were married by a Norwegian pastor.[28]

Another settlement, also made in 1869, was at Viborg. The initial Danish settlers took land in Swan Lake township and then were joined by more who migrated both from Denmark and from Racine. In the spring of 1874, more settlers arrived from Chicago. A land agent known as "Tykke" (Fat) Nielsen had recruited settlers for the founding of a Danish colony in Brule County. The party had made it as far as Yankton and was waiting for the river boat to complete the loading of its cargo so the journey would be continued. While they were waiting they met some Danes from Swan Lake who had come to Yankton on business. After some conversation, four Chicago Danes went for a quick visit to Swan Lake and were so impressed that they and the entire party settled in Turner County.

Viborg received a significant stimulus in 1893 when the Great Northern Railroad built its line through the area on its way from Sioux Falls to Yankton. The Rev. A. S. Hansen, who visited Swan Lake in 1884, considered it the most Danish settlement in America. The landscape evoked memories of the jutish heath, as did the houses with thatched roofs and the numerous outbuildings of stone. The widespread use of Danish further completed the image.[29]

The second major settlement was in the east-central counties of Kingsbury, Brookings, and Moody. The settlement took place approximately ten years later than that of the Viborg area. In 1877 Lars Christensen and Andreas Jensen left Sioux Falls in a prairie schooner and selected some land in Kingsbury County. These two men had worked in the copper mines in Upper Michigan for a while, and then settled on land near Sioux Falls.[30] Many of the Danes who followed them to Kingsbury County were from the Thy region in Denmark, and the lake near the settlement was called Lake Thisted. Their dialect was clearly different from the others and frequent comments were made about the group and its conservativism. Other pioneers in the general area were Jutlanders who settled in Moody County north of Dell Rapids and former residents of Vendsyssel who farmed near White in Brookings County. The settlers destined for Kingsbury County usually took the train to Luverne, Minnesota, and traveled the last 100 miles by wagon.[31]

The Danes of South Dakota followed closely the settlement patterns and the agricultural methods of the non-Danish community. In the flood plain of the Missouri River, their homes were generally log cabins because wood was available. The Danes, however, added a Danish touch and thatched many of their homes. The chinks in the walls were filled with clay, and often the entire walls, both outside and inside, were plastered with clay. Many of the young men after they had filed their claims went off to work in lumber camps in Wisconsin, in copper mines in Michigan, in machine shops in Moline and Chicago, on river boats at Yankton, or on the railroads in order to earn cash. Some of the earnings went to the neighbor who was hired to plow the land during the intervening months.

The Danes were among the first to give up sole dependence on grain and become diversified farmers. They generally grew grain crops, but they also raised hay, cattle, and hogs and some worked with dairy cattle. Cheese-making as a community venture was begun as early as 1872 in Turner county. Prosperity came to many of the immigrants, and Peter Aggergaard, "king" in Viborg, owned twenty-five sections of land.[32]

## V *North Dakota*

The two Danish concentrations in North Dakota are opposites in several ways. One location, the older settlement, is in the southeastern part of the state while the other is in the northwestern. A second difference is that the southeastern community, located primarily in Cass County, was completely separated from the Lutheran church, while the one in the northwest was the result of Lutheran church initiative.

The Danes who settled in Cass County came primarily from the Thy peninsula and from Slesvig. One of the first to migrate from the Thisted area was Christian Westergaard, who landed at Portland, Maine, in 1872. He eventually found a job as gardener in Waukegan, north of Chicago, at $25 per month. While there he met the Norwegian Fabian Socialist Marcus Thrane and became the typesetter and printer for the paper *Dagslyset* (The Light of Day). The financial support, however, was minimal, so Westergaard took the paper with him to Becker, Minnesota, where he continued as publisher. This arrangement lasted until 1878, when Westergaard's mother-in-law expressed her desire for larger land holdings, so Westergaard responded favorably when a subscriber offered to help him if he wished to settle in the Red River Valley. Westergaard and his brother made the move in May 1878, and the families followed in July.[33]

The Slesvig Danes originated in the Flensborg area and had earlier settled in Iowa. One of them, Thomas Nissen, from St. Ansgar, had traveled to Fargo in 1878 to invest money, and he was impressed by the area's potential. He encouraged some of his friends to go west, and they began arriving in 1879.[34]

Even though the people were religious there was no organized Danish church in the community. Anyone who cared could attend the English churches, and the Sunday schools were held in district schoolhouses. Danish religious books were brought over and religious activity in Danish was present on the family level. Most of the churches in the community were Baptist, Presbyterian, and Adventist; none was Lutheran. On several occasions Lutheran pastors tried to begin a congregation, but without success, probably because of the unwillingness to assume the financial responsibilities of constructing a building and paying a pastor.[35]

In contrast to the casual attitude toward religion, politics occupied the attention of the Cass County Danes. Those Danes who had migrated from Jutland and had belonged to the Venstre (Left) party became Democrats in the United States, while the Slesvig group brought with them the Republican views from Iowa.[36]

The settlements in the northwestern counties of Ward, Burke, and Renville can be called colonies because they were formed through collective effort. Yet there was no special organization for the settlement procedure. Land was homesteaded by individuals and the church only encouraged the people in search of new homes to join the new communities. The person who promoted this type of program was Pastor H. Hansen of Hutchinson, Minnesota. In 1895 at the convention of the Blair Church, the delegates decided to elect a Colonization Committee of one pastor and two laymen to study the possibility of founding such a colony.[37]

The committee decided to establish a colony in Ward County, where the Soo Line was encouraging settlers to build farms. Pastor Hansen consulted with the synodical president and they agreed it would be a suitable venture. Hansen spoke of the project to Danes in Minnesota congregations and many went to look over the land and take out homestead claims. The filing fees were $14 and no taxes would be collected for five years. The initial settlement was made near Kenmare, a stop on the railroad. There, on October 14, 1896, on a grassy hill, with the backdrop of a plains sunset, Hansen and a dozen homesteaders formed Trinity church. Other settlements followed at Flaxton, Norma, Bowbells, and Daneville, and by 1906 there were five congregations in the region.[38]

So many of the new settlers were young people, including some from Denmark, that Hansen became concerned with the problem of how they would occupy their time during the long winter months. Hansen, therefore, in 1902 turned his small home into a boardinghouse for twenty young men and hired a woman to manage it. With the assistance of two female instructors he began to teach religious and secular subjects. So satisfactory was his project for both the students and the community that he repeated the program the next winter. A board of directors was established and the school was called Brorson High School in honor of the Danish hymn writer. In 1905 the congregations built a three-story frame building which had the capacity for forty students and an apartment for the director. They also engaged one of the dynamic men in the community, Jens Dixen, as the director.

Dixen was a devout Christian and in 1903 he had traveled around the world at his own expense visiting mission stations and preaching. Upon his return he was asked to head the high school. Even though he had no formal training, he read widely and had a keen memory and a gift for eloquence. He became an inspirational preacher and teacher. In 1907 he again went on a world tour, returning to Brorson in 1909, where he remained until 1914.[39]

The high school enjoyed a successful existence for a time and its enrollment peaked in 1913 with an attendance of fifty-six. But as World War I neared, migration slackened, and with the entry of the United States into the war, young men were needed in the army. Brorson closed its doors and the building was sold, but twenty-five of those who participated entered into the work of the church. It was considered a folk high school by some, though it did not stress the Danish language and culture. Luther's *Catechism*, for example, was taught in English and considerable emphasis was placed on the use of English and elementary-school subjects.[40]

The majority of the Danes in North Dakota migrated from Minnesota and Iowa. The usual method of travel was by train. Rental for a boxcar was only $20, and that could be used for people, possessions, and animals. The men went first to file the claim, construct a house, and begin breaking the sod. The families followed the next spring.[41]

One of the large Danish communities, Kenmare, boasts a Danish mill. It was built by Christian C. Jensen on his homestead eleven miles north of Kenmare and had the capacity for grinding as much as 200 sacks of grain per day. When it was no longer used it was moved to Kenmare and enshrined in a park.[42]

## VI *Montana*

The Danish community in Montana, located in the northeastern part of the state, was largely a continuation of the North Dakota settlement. The political boundary did not change the natural environment and agricultural practices and crops were identical for both states. Clergymen, also from the two states, served congregations on either side of the boundary.

The settlement of Montana followed that of North Dakota by about ten years. The Montana settlers were generally people from North Dakota looking for new farms. A typical settlement pattern is illustrated by the Strandskov family. After migration from Denmark the Strandskovs had settled at Alden, Minnesota, but as the sons matured they went to North Dakota for their farms and then in 1910 continued on to Montana. The decisions were largely related to land prices. Minnesota land had become scarce and expensive, so North Dakota provided places for young men to begin their careers. Then after several years North Dakota land became more valuable and Laurits Strandskov received $4,200 for his North Dakota land and bought a farm in Montana for $1,600. Because the move from North Dakota to Montana was relatively short, the possessions were generally moved with a caravan of wagons, trailers, and hay racks. The tractor, having become part of the equipment in the fields, also was used for pulling the vehicles, along with a 500-gallon fuel tank.[43]

The first congregation was founded in July 1906 by members of the United Church who settled at Daneville near Westby. That same year the Danish Church founded a colony farther south, at Dagmar, and the next year, in 1907, formed a congregation. It was common practice for the pastor to take out a homestead claim in order to supplement his income from work on the land as well as from the increasing value of the property.[44]

By 1911 there were 300 Danes within a ten-mile radius of Dagmar, and judging from the large number of children, the settlers must have been comparatively young men and women.[45] Other Danish settlements were at Reserve, Antelope, McCabe, and Sidney.

## VII *Texas*

While the only sizable settlement of Danes in Texas is Danevang in Wharton County, there were several individual Danes who settled in Texas as well as several small clusters of Danes in certain parts of the state. Two of the individuals whose names deserve mentioning are Charles Zanco and Hans Peter Nielsen Gammel. Little is known about Zanco except that he was a young Dane of twenty-eight who died at the Alamo, while Gammel arrived later, in 1877, and became the owner of a large bookstore. It was Gammel who collected and published *Laws of Texas,* still considered as the standard reference work on Texas history.[46]

The settlement of Danevang (Danish Field) was initiated by the Danish People's Society in 1894. Other colonies such as the one in Tyler, Minnesota, had been established by the Danish Church, but this was the first one started by the society. The land committee went to investigate possibilities in Texas and found a tract of 25,000 acres in Wharton County that the Texas Land and Cattle Company was willing to sell. Although the location was 600 miles from the Danish centers in the Midwest, the tall grass reached the bottom of the wagons and the soil was fertile.[47] The price for the land was $9 per acre with $1 down and 7 percent interest on the remaining $8 to be paid over an eight-year period.[48]

The society, under the leadership of J. C. Evers, published brochures advertising the location and printed maps showing railroads connecting the area with the Midwest. The settlers who began arriving in 1894 were Danes originally from Slesvig, Funen, and Zealand who had settled in the Midwest earlier. They had learned some English and had earned money for the new venture, so by the end of 1895 more than 9,000 acres had been sold.[49]

The first few years were most difficult and many settlers left for other locations. They suffered loss of property from storms and heavy rains, and in 1897 anthrax killed seventy horses. Part of the problem was with the settlers themselves because they tried to apply their techniques of northern agriculture to the South. Wheat and oats were not suitable, however, and so unproductive were their efforts that they had to buy fodder for the cattle. The answer to the problem was to adopt southern crops and techniques and soon they were planting cotton. The thrift and hard work of the remaining settlers so impressed the agent representing the bank, whose task it was to evaluate the condition and explore the reasons why the Danes were not making the payments for the land, that he recommended extensions be arranged. Payments were resumed and completed when times improved.[50]

The Danes at Danevang became a tightly knit community because of their ethnic similarity, the difficult times, and a strong religious allegiance. The settlers called a pastor in August 1895 and set aside forty-five acres for church purposes. On that land they also built an assembly hall, a parsonage, and in 1909 a church building. Another factor in this social unity was the rural isolation in which they lived. The nearest town was El Campo, eleven miles away and connected only by a dirt road that was often impassable. The children attended a public school, but the community was so completely Danish that not until 1938 did the trustees hire a teacher who was not of Danish extraction.[51]

It was only natural that the previous experiences with cooperatives in the Midwest and the unity of the group committed the Texas settlement deeply to the cooperative way. In 1897 a mutual fire-insurance company was formed that required no capital but worked on the assessment plan. It was patterned after a plan established in Cedar Falls, Iowa, whereby each member signed a note for 3 percent of his insured property that was payable on demand. Only if a member suffered a loss of property through fire did the members contribute to the fund. By 1905 there were thirty-nine members with $30,827 of insured property. The heaviest assessment for a given year was $5.25 per $1,000 of insurance. In 1913 they organized a telephonc company which collected no dues or assessments until 1919 because each member paid for his own installation and the owner of the store served without charge as the switchboard operator. After 1919 there were occasional assessments for line repair and the formation of central service, which was added in 1929. Although neither of these cooperatives exists any longer, the contemporary Farmers' Cooperative Society was formed in 1920 for the purchase of items such as gasoline, fertilizer, and insecticides and for such service establishments as a cotton gin, a welding shop, and a grain drier.[52]

## CHAPTER 9

# *East and West Coast Settlements*

### I *The East Coast*

DURING the time of Danish migration to the Midwest, some of the Danes stopped in the eastern states. The process began as early as the 1850s and continues on into contemporary times. Some Danish farmers settled near Portland, Maine, a port for some immigrant ships, in approximately 1855. Others came later and found factory work in the city and also in the neighboring towns of Falmouth and Westbrook.

The Danes who came to Massachusetts first arrived in the 1880s and found homes and jobs in Woburn and Worcester, while the migrants who settled in Connecticut lived in the towns of Bridgeport, East Port Chester, New Haven, and Hartford. Many of these Danish communities at Portland, East Port Chester, Bridgeport, and Hartford were large enough to support Lutheran churches, and most began in the 1890s, although Portland's church was founded in 1875. In general terms, however, the Danes in these communities and in the congregations were few in number.[1]

The settlement in Perth Amboy, New Jersey, was significant because it became not only a Danish concentration, but also served as a clearinghouse for the Danes who worked temporarily in that city on their way west. The Danes who migrated there in the 1860s did so because of the nearness to New York and because of the employment opportunities in the brickyards. Initially the Danes suffered harassment and abuse from the Irish, already in the area, who resented competition in the job market. But in 1866 Christian Brun, a veteran of the Civil War who had served on the Union side freighting supplies to western forts, arrived in Perth Amboy. He had adopted western manners and clothes and discarded the timidity of the greenhorn Danes. He became the leader of the Danes and helped plan some retaliation against the Irish. Brun sent two Danes walking down a dark street, and when a gang of Irish attacked them, the Danes came out of hiding and fought off the Irish. From then on the Irish realized that the Danes would defend themselves, and the Danes had equal access to the jobs.[2]

In 1870 Pastor A. L. J. Søholm came to gather the Danes, and in 1872 they built a small church. Unfortunately many disagreements arose over the construction of the church and a split developed. The quarrel became so bad that part of the congregation left and joined the Norwegian Synod, while others held back from participation in the life of the church. When Søholm left for the West, the congregation was served by R. Andersen from Brooklyn. Finally in 1887 St. Stephan's received a pastor, Ole Jacobsen, and for twelve years he worked to draw the congregation together.[3]

At first the Danes were relatively poor, but some became successful in the factories in the area. Especially successful were Karl Mathiasen and Otto E. Hansen, who in 1888 formed a partnership to produce terra cotta. Many small companies were engaged in the production of terra cotta between 1850 and 1875, and Mathiasen and Hansen, along with other Danes, found jobs in the small plants. After 1875 the terra-cotta factories became larger in size and profits increased because of the building boom in metropolitan New York. In 1893 Eckardt V. Eskesen joined Mathiasen in the firm and they formed the New Jersey Terra Cotta Company. Practically all the employees were Danes.[4]

The remaining eastern state with a large Danish population is New York. One of the older settlements outside of the city was at Troy, on the Hudson, and in 1874 Pastor Søholm organized a congregation there. More significant, however, was the Danish population in New York City, that grew in size, especially in the twentieth century. In the early days of Danish migration only sailors, craftsmen, and domestics remained in the city, while almost everyone went west. The congregations in the New York area had many young married women who remained in the urban center to work in homes. After the turn of the century more businessmen, intellectuals, and middle-class Danes made their home in the city.

A cohesive Danish community never existed in metropolitan New York, although there were clusters that supported Danish churches in the Bronx and in Brooklyn. The Danes scattered through the metropolitan area and kept track of each other through the newspaper *Nordlyset* (The Northern Light, 1891–1953). Its circulation, however, never exceeded 5,000.[5]

As in Chicago there were many Danish clubs that were concerned with a wide variety of interests, but there was little cohesion between them, and the wide dispersal of the Danes kept the membership small.[6] One of the organizations based in New York was the Danish American Historical Society (Dansk-amerikansk historisk Forening), which held its first annual conference on December 29, 1931. The purpose was to publish Danish American history and to support the archives at Aalborg. Membership in the organization was by invitation but the carefully selected members produced little of lasting value. One of the reasons was a misunderstanding between the chairman, Charles H. Johnson, and the director of research, Baron Joost Dahlerup. Eckardt V. Eskesen attempted to revive and invigorate the declining organization, but without success.[7]

## II *The West Coast*

The Danes became aware of California even before the discovery of gold and four adventurous men figured prominently in that isolated community in the days when California was still part of Mexico. All four men, setting the pattern for later Danish migrants, entered California from the Pacific side, and three of the four illustrate Danish involvement in world-wide maritime activity.

The first Dane in California, Mathias Fellom, was born at the turn of the nineteenth century at Helsingør, a port on the shipping lane to the Baltic. He had gone to sea on a whaling ship and when that vessel ran low on provisions in the Bering Sea, the captain steered for Bodega Bay on the California coast to purchase supplies from the Russian outpost. There, in 1822, Fellom left the ship and traveled to Monterey, the capital of California, where he found employment as a soapmaker with John Gilroy, another former whaler. The primary export commodities from Mexican California in that period were hides and tallow, so Fellom eventually purchased his own ranch and imitated the practices of the Mexican cattlemen. He also married a native Californian and in 1845 became the alcalde, or mayor, of San Juan Bautista. He adopted the way of life of his new home and lived there until his death in 1868.[8]

The next Dane was a ship's carpenter, Peter T. Scherrebach, who landed at Yerba Buena (San Francisco). He had been born at Haderslev in 1813 and arrived in California twenty-two years later in 1835. After several years of working as a carpenter and operating a boat, he used his construction skill to build a home for himself and his new wife, Mary Sullivan, an American, who had migrated overland by wagon. After tension developed between the United States and Mexico, and the Bear Flag Revolt took place, Scherrebach joined Johann Sutter's staff at the Sacramento fort. After the war and the annexation of California by the United States, he served on the San Francisco town council and also as the collector of the port.[9]

An ardent supporter of the United States was William Alexander Leidesdorff, the third Dane. He had been born on St. Croix in 1810 to a Danish father and a Creole mother and received part of his education in the United States. After arriving in California in 1840 as captain of an American ship, he remained in San Francisco and became a Mexican citizen. He built a warehouse and the town's first hotel, and in addition received a grant of 35,000 acres of land from the Mexican government. The grant lay on the south side of the American River, next to Johann Sutter's holdings, but unlike Sutter he remained in San Francisco and concentrated on being a merchant.[10]

As a businessman conversant in six languages, he became an associate of Thomas O. Larkin, the American consul in Monterey, and in 1845 Larkin appointed him vice-consul. Although never officially confirmed in that position by the president, Leidesdorff functioned as vice-consul in the eight months prior to the Mexican War. Following the discovery of gold, Sutter notified his neighbor and business associate and asked if he wished to invest in a gold mine.[11]

Leidesdorff instead hired James Marshall, discoverer of gold at Sutter's mill, to search for gold on Leidesdorff's property. The report told of the presence of gold, but death on May 18, 1848, prevented Leidesdorff from claiming it.[12]

Peter Lassen also arrived in California by sea, but on a ship from Oregon. Born at Farum in 1800, the same year as Fellom, Lassen was trained as a blacksmith. In 1829 he took an English ship to Boston and worked in several eastern cities until he moved to Keytesville, Missouri, 100 miles east of Kansas City. Here he met Sutter bound for California, and in 1839 Lassen and ten friends also left for the West. After several days' travel, they joined seventeen Pacific-bound migrants including fur traders, settlers, two missionaries and their wives, and Frederick Wislizenus, a German-born doctor.[13]

The party of twenty-seven, however, was weakened by dissension and desertions, so that at Fort Hall Lassen and his friends decided to continue to Oregon with those who had remained. The following spring Lassen sailed to Bodega Bay and from there traveled overland to Sutter's Fort. After working as a blacksmith, he realized the need for construction timber in San Francisco and in 1841 or 1842 purchased 1,000 acres of forest near Santa Cruz, building the first sawmill in California. In 1844 he received a land grant of more than 22,000 acres on Deer Creek in the northern part of the Sacramento Valley. With the help of Indian labor, he built an adobe cabin, a blacksmith shop, and engaged in ranching and farming.[14] After annexation Lassen's good fortune turned and his activities in the gold fields and in ranching were unsuccessful. In 1850, after being forced to sell his ranch on Deer Creek to pay his debts, he moved eastward to Honey Lake and Susanville and in 1859 was killed, evidently by Indians, while on a gold-hunting expedition. An inactive volcano in northern California and a national park bear his name.[15]

While little is known about Fellom's participation in the revolt against Mexico, Leidesdorff and Lassen were drawn into direct participation through the activity of John C. Fremont. This famous explorer arrived at Sutter's Fort on December 1, 1845, on an expedition to Oregon. Fremont's presence, although officially scientific and peaceful, was significant because it helped crystallize the resentment of American settlers against the

Mexican government in California. Relations between Mexico and the United States had deteriorated over the borderlands ever since President James K. Polk began implementing his expansion policy and especially after the failure of the Slidell Mission in October 1845 to purchase parts of the Mexican Southwest.

After spending a month searching for the other members of his exploration party, Fremont returned to Sutter's Fort and on January 19, 1846, took Sutter's launch to San Francisco. He spent several days with Leidesdorff and then, accompanied by Leidesdorff, traveled to Monterey to visit Larkin.[16] In a report, Larkin described Leidesdorff as "decidedly partial to the United States." The Mexican officials doubted the peaceful claims of Fremont and ordered him out of the province. He complied, and slowly moved northward, arriving at Lassen's Ranch at the end of March 1846. From there he continued toward Oregon.[17] A messenger from Washington, Archibald H. Gillespie, landed at Monterey and Larkin sent a letter to Leidesdorff with instructions to provide Gillespie with money for the trip up the Sacramento River. Leidesdorff complied and on April 25, Gillespie was on his way.[18]

From Sacramento Gillespie traveled northward and arrived at Lassen's on May 1, one week after Fremont had left.[19] Lassen feared that Gillespie and his aide would encounter Indians, so he and three others joined Gillespie in pursuit of Fremont. Following his interview with Gillespie, Fremont returned to California to participate in the conflict with Mexico.[20]

The war with Mexico officially ended in 1848 with the cession of western lands, including California. The same year that the treaty was signed, gold was discovered on the American River. Danes in the United States as well as in Europe were not immune to the craving for sudden wealth. Those who had taken up residence in California were among the first to go to the gold fields. Most were seamen who earlier had left their ships and had taken up land-based occupations. Other Danes were those seamen who heard of the discovery when their ships were docked in San Francisco harbor. Still others were living in Denmark when the news arrived in Europe and they joined the European rush for California. Only a few Danes traveled to California on overland routes because by 1849 not many Danes, other than those who had joined the Mormons, had settled in the eastern states.

The behavior of Danish miners revealed no particular pattern, but demonstrated an independence and a freedom of movement. A few, such as P. G. Funck, struck it rich and returned to Denmark to buy a ship or a parcel of land.[21] Others invested their money in California, while still others bought farms in the Midwest. The majority found gold mining unprofitable or the hardships and sicknesses to which they were exposed bothersome, and returned to their familiar occupations in San Francisco. The most widespread activity for these Danish migrants centered on ships—building, sailing, or managing them.

One of the earliest ship builders was Mads Christian Holm, a Danish ship carpenter from Mors. He found employment on an American ship at Helsingør and arrived in Boston when the news of California became public. He immediately boarded a ship for California and upon landing in 1850 became a carpenter instead of a miner. With money from construction he established a shipbuilding operation at Oakland and soon attracted shipbuilders to the neighborhood. In 1855 he sold his holdings, sewed the money into vagabond clothes to avoid thieves, and crossed the continent. He then continued on to Denmark, where he married and resumed shipbuilding.[22]

Other employment opportunities included freighting inside the bay and on the river, along the coast, and on the ocean. The vessels generally used on the bay were flat-bottomed boats called scows, which transported cattle, gravel, stone, and lumber. Freighting proved so rewarding financially that many Danes arriving in the 1850s never joined the search for gold. Because of the large number of Danes and Scandinavians serving in the coastwise fleet it was called the Scandinavian Navy.[23]

Among those Danes who became notable in maritime shipping, especially of wood products, was Charles Hansen. Hansen, later called the lumber king, came to California in 1850 and started a sawmill and shingle factory at Redwood City. After first obtaining a sloop, Hansen and his partner soon owned ships that hauled timber to San Francisco and to the mines. In 1869 he expanded his market and built a plant in Tacoma on Commencement Bay. Thirty-three percent of that lumber went abroad to markets in South America and Australia. Even though Tacoma was initially not a good location because of its distance from the open sea, the Northern Pacific Railroad made it the line's western terminus and Hansen could sell to the domestic markets as well.[24]

As the San Francisco Bay region became occupied, Danes found homes throughout the area, but the greatest number settled in the city of San Francisco itself. They did not, however, congregate in specific districts of the city, as did some of the easily distinguished ethnic groups, but scattered throughout the American community. Nevertheless there were concentrations, such as Rincon Hill, where the rich Danes found homes, and in the North Beach district, where the seamen lived.[25] The poorer Danish craftsmen occupied the district "South of Market," while the largest concentrations of Danes were farther to the south and west in the "Mission" district. *Bien,* the Danish newspaper, for example, was located at Oak and Franklin, and the Scandinavian church, attended by many Danes, was at Howard and 13th Street. York Street between 21st and 22nd streets was called "Little Denmark" and served as the location for Danish churches and many Danish shops.[26]

The Danes of the city followed many kinds of occupations, but were frequently engaged in building trades, restaurants, bakeries, delivery services, and small cigar or jewelry shops. The Danes also patronized their numerous taprooms, pubs, and saloons that carried such names as "Holger Dansk," "Danmark Saloon," and "Copenhagen." Here they found the opportunity to converse in their mother tongue in a setting of paintings and decorations to remind them of Denmark.[27]

One who became a prominent citizen was Carl Gustav Larsen, a cabinetmaker, who arrived in San Francisco in 1869. After settling in Berkeley and working on some of the buildings of the university, he decided to open a coffee house near Market Street and called it Tivoli Café. It soon became a meeting place for Danish societies. In 1904 he began the construction of a seven-story building which would provide more space for the coffee shop and would also serve as a residence for two families. It was destroyed in the 1906 earthquake and fire, but, undaunted by the setback, he rebuilt it and added a small hotel over the restaurant. Earlier in 1888 Larsen had purchased some land that later became a residential area known as the Sunset District. On part of this land he raised hens that provided the restaurant with fresh eggs. It was from this farm that he gathered the eggs after the earthquake and took them to his friends and acquaintances as gifts. In the 1920s, when much of his land was made into a residential area, he presented several tracts of property to the city for parks. He also remembered his countrymen by providing them with jobs and food when they were in need.[28]

The first major agricultural settlement of Danes was in Sonoma County at Petaluma, seventy-nine miles north of San Francisco.[29] The locality has become famous for its egg production, and the Danes claim credit for its early development. Petaluma possesses a mild climate that made year-round farming possible, and was situated on a stream that simplified transportation by boat to the San Francisco markets. In the early years of supplying food for the city, the farmers noticed the consistent demand for eggs. Seeking a sure profit one farmer after another shifted his efforts to poultry-raising and egg production.

A Dane, Christopher Nisson (Nissen), leaving that part of Slesvig which became part of Prussia in 1864, arrived in Petaluma that same year. Although he initially worked as a nurseryman, he became interested in raising hens for egg production. Nisson's goal was to bring greater efficiency to egg production. Instead of permitting the hens to hatch the eggs and tend the chicks in the old, inefficient manner, Nisson gathered the eggs each day and purchased a small, experimental ten-egg incubator. His neighbors asked him to hatch chicks for them as well, and he established the first commercial hatchery in the United States. Within ten years, six hatcheries were located in Petaluma, as well as a factory producing incubators for the world market. Only a small investment was necessary for the establishment of a chicken ranch because an acre of land would support a thousand Leghorn hens, and because of the mild climate the shelters could be built simply and inexpensively. Petaluma became the center for egg production in California and in the 1930s it had over 3,000 chicken farms, with over 5 million hens.

Two hundred fifty of these farms belonged to Danes, including one of the largest, with 25,000 hens.[30]

One of the major concentrations of Danes in the state of California was at Fresno. Fresno attracted Danes not only in the days of colonization of the central valley, but as early as the 1850s. The earliest economic activity of that region, begun at the time of Spanish settlement, was ranching. Later, as the miners expanded their search for gold southward from the American River, they tried their luck near present-day Fresno and in 1850 located some gold at Millerton and Coarse Gulch.[31]

Millerton attracted George Greiersen from Falster, who opened a store in the mining community in the mid-1850s. Greiersen had arrived at San Francisco in 1852 to join his half-brother and partner, Gustav O'Hara Taaffe.[32] After operating the store a short time, Greiersen and Taaffe sold the business to a brother-in-law, Francisco Jensen, and another Dane, Otto Frølich.[33]

Taaffe, the most famous of these four men, was born in 1825 and received commercial training in Denmark. He left for California at the beginning of the gold rush, but remained in San Francisco as a businessman and insurance agent. In 1859 he became the Danish consul and later the consul for both Norway and Sweden. He was also active in the formation of the first Lutheran church in San Francisco and the Scandinavian Society. In 1869 he wrote a book that was published in Copenhagen in which he described California's opportunities and encouraged migration. Through Greiersen he became familiar with the Fresno area and in all probability considered a colonization project of that area as irrigation became a reality. He died, however, in 1874 before the settlement experienced its expansion.[34]

After the introduction of irrigation in 1871 the settlers grew wheat, barley, and hay. Leland Stanford was so impressed with the productivity of the land that he extended the Southern Pacific Railroad into the area in 1872. The agricultural success of the community was thereby insured, and within a short time the settlers introduced fruit trees, alfalfa, and grape vines. In 1874 the "Trespass Act" went into effect, which completed the transition from ranching to a farming community by requiring the livestock owners to fence their animals. Also in 1874 there were twenty-four business establishments and twenty-five houses in the town. Frølich had already recognized the significance of the railroad and in 1872 built his store in the townsite of Fresno, where his building also housed the telegraph office. Frølich later sold his business to become a partner in a bank and a producer of wine.[35]

Francisco Jensen also forsook Millerton, established a store and hotel at the crossing of Dry Creek, and in 1870 became its postmaster. He named his new town Copenhagen and promised a free town lot and free water to all prospective residents. By 1877 he realized that he could not compete with Fresno; he sold his property, planted fruit trees, and engaged in quartz-mining.[36]

The significant event for Fresno occurred in 1877, when, because of drought, muscat grapes dried on the vines before they could be picked. Some growers stemmed them, boxed them, and shipped the dried grapes to San Francisco, where they were sold as raisins from Peru. But the raisins were of high quality, and when the truth eventually came out as to the origins of the fruit, a new economic activity was established and raisins became synonymous with Fresno.[37]

The continuation of the settlement of the Fresno area was through the colony system that had been used successfully at Anaheim, near Los Angeles. A land company purchased a tract of land, channeled water to the area, and sold lots of twenty to forty acres in size. The settler then leveled the land and purchased water for irrigation. Alfalfa was planted for immediate profits, while vines and fruit trees produced fruit after several years.[38] The initial colony, Central Colony, was founded in 1875, while the first colony to appeal directly to Danes was the Scandinavian Home Colony, established in 1878 on 1,920 acres of land.[39]

A promotional meeting, held at Bonanza House in San Francisco, to evaluate the possibility of starting a settlement in the San Joaquin Valley attracted forty people. The owner of the hotel and one of the speakers was a Dane, Henry Saxtorph.[40] The primary speaker and the agent for the Southern Pacific, Charles A. Henry, offered twenty-acre lots with water rights for $350. A down payment of $110 was acceptable, with the remainder to be financed over the next five years. Although his ancestry was Scottish, Henry's association with the Danes was understandable because he had been born in Copenhagen and had not migrated to San Francisco until 1870. In 1880 he bought *Valkyrien*, a Danish newspaper, from Peter Freese, and used it for the promotion of sales in Fresno, Kern, and Tulare counties. He also opened an office in Copenhagen, from which he sent out prospectuses on the colonies.[41]

Although Danes settled in other Fresno colonies, including the Central Colony, land sales in the Scandinavian Colony were at first restricted to Scandinavians. Later other nationalities were accepted and by 1882 almost every lot in the colony had been sold. In less than five years the price of the lots had doubled.[42] Not only were the Danes active in tending vineyards and fruit orchards, but in 1893 some Danish raisin-growers also started a little dairy as a sideline. It quickly grew into a large business and was called the Danish Creamery.[43] Danish communities near Fresno include Selma, Reedley, Bowles, Easton, Caruthers, Burrel, Raisin, and Tranquility.[44]

Another concentration of Danes is to be found along the northern coast of California in Humboldt County. The first settlers were engaged in trade with the northern California miners and in the production of lumber. Early agricultural products included potatoes, wheat, and oats as well as butter and cheese. Although settlement by Americans began in the 1850s, there were only twelve Danes in the county in 1860.[45]

The first Dane, as well as probably the first white person, to enter Humboldt Bay after the Mexican War was Hans Henry Buhne, a seaman. His father had been a captain and shipowner, and the son followed the tradition and became a mate on a whaler. In 1847 the ship came to San Francisco for provisions and Buhne visited with his countryman Leidesdorff. The whaler lay in the Samoan Islands when word arrived of the gold discovery in California. Whaling was forgotten, and the ship headed for Chile, where it took on freight and passengers and arrived in San Francisco on June 1, 1849. Buhne experienced good fortune in the Auburn gold fields, but then suffered dropsy. Without a doctor and with no means of transportation, he lay in his tent helplessly awaiting death. One day a miner appeared with oxen and was told of the sick Dane who needed transportation to Sacramento. The driver happened to be not only a fellow Dane, but also from Buhne's hometown of Flensborg. Buhne was then removed to Sacramento and on to San Francisco by his countryman, and there he lived with two shipmates while he recuperated. Even though he was not fully recovered, he became second mate on the schooner *Laura Virginia* with the assignment to find a harbor close to the mines of Trinity County in northern California. There in 1850 Buhne crossed the bar in a small boat, sounded the bay, and brought the schooner in. Buhne later returned and kept a boardinghouse on Buhne's Point and also piloted vessels across the bar. His varied business ventures included a packet line to San Francisco.[46]

One portion of the Danes in Humboldt County followed the tradition of Buhne and made their living by shipping, fishing, or related maritime activities. One of the most famous men in the region was Hans D. Bendixen, who built 113 vessels of various sizes between 1868, when he arrived, and 1900, when he retired. He had learned the ship building trade at Aalborg and Copenhagen, and then spent five years in a San Francisco shipyard. His shipyard at Fairhaven covered fourteen acres and included a rooming house, a trading center, and a sawmill and employed 150 men. Even though his shipyard was twice damaged by flood and once destroyed by fire, he received $250,000 for it when his failing health forced him into retirement. He was buried at Thisted, the place of his birth, and he made the town a recipient of part of his estate.[47]

The Danes who settled in Humboldt County and were not engaged in maritime activity either operated shops and stores in the towns of Ferndale, Loleta, and Arcata or worked in agricultural occupations in the countryside. The first sizable migration of Danish farmers came in the period from 1873 to 1878. They originated from various localities in Denmark, but a large portion came from Slesvig. Most of these early settlers had lived previously at various places in California, especially at Petaluma, and in Marin County, The migration from Denmark continued into the twentieth century, although in diminished numbers, and in most instances the migrant traveled directly from Denmark to Humboldt County without stopping at other places. Obviously the later migrants knew of the area and possibly went to join relatives and friends already there.

Most of the agricultural practices had been established prior to the Danish migration, but the Danes helped in agricultural development. In 1875 two Danes bought some land covered with trees and scrub and, after they had cleared the land, sowed it with clover. The venture showed a profit and the prices of land, then potentially productive, increased in value.[48] The region was ideally suited for dairying because extremes in temperature were rare and the fog and moist sea air contributed to the growth of grass. So with good land management and the introduction of clover and alfalfa, dairying became profitable. Shipping butter was more economical than freighting cattle, hogs, and grain.[49]

Solvang is the newest and the most publicized of the Danish concentrations in California. The early settlers planned a ranching, dairying, and agricultural community, but the primary activity in contemporary times is tourism. Although initially the design of the buildings followed the California pattern, some later buildings such as Bethania church, dedicated in 1928, and those designed by Ferdinand Sorensen followed the Danish style. Major publicity came in 1947, when the *Saturday Evening Post* featured a report on the buildings and on an annual festival with Danish costumes, dancing, and performances called Danish Days. Blessed with a lovely climate, and nearness to Los Angeles, visitors came to Solvang in increasing numbers. The Danish residents recognized tourism's economic significance, so they expanded shops in the Danish style and constructed tourist facilities.[50]

The settlement began in 1911 when the Danish American Colony Corporation purchased a block of approximately 9,000 acres of land in the Santa Ynez Valley for the purpose of establishing a Danish community with a folk school. The initial organizers were the Rev. J. M. Gregersen, a proponent of the folk-school movement, the Rev. Benedict Nordentoft, and Peder P. Hornsyld, both former faculty members of Grand View College in Des Moines. Already in 1906 Nordentoft and Gregersen had gone to the West Coast to visit Danish communities and to examine the possibility of opening another folk school.[51]

Four years later, in the summer of 1910, Nordentoft and Gregersen called on Mads J. Freese, a Slesvig Dane, living in Salinas. Freese had not only maintained his Lutheran ties and helped to start a Danish congregation, but had also prospered in production of sugar cane and in real estate. He thought more men were needed to support a colonization project, so they established the Danish American Colony Company, with Lorentz Petersen of Arcata as the president and Freese in charge of land sales. They examined one potential site at Laytonville, midway between San Francisco and Humboldt County, but arable land was limited. Then, in July 1910, Freese spotted a notice in the Salinas newspaper for land forty miles north of Santa Barbara that was being offered for sale. The committee examined the land and found it suitable.[52]

The folk school, first called the Solvang Youth School and later Atterdag College in honor of a Danish king, was opened immediately in 1911 and initially shared the same building with Bethania Lutheran Church. In 1914 a separate three-story building for the school was constructed on a hill overlooking the town and opened its doors to Danish people from all over the United States until 1937, when it became the victim of declining enrollments and the depression.

By October 1912, 182 Danes, primarily friends of the developers, had migrated, and forty-one students were enrolled in the school. Land sales, however, were sluggish, so in September 1913 Pastor Gregersen left for Nebraska and Iowa to promote the sale of land. He was successful and the colony became stable. Of the inhabitants who settled in the early days or drifted in later, most had been born in Denmark but had lived in the United States for some time. The Solvang Danes did not originate from a single region in Denmark, but represented various sections.[53]

Because the farmers lived on their land and not in Solvang, the commercial sector of the town developed slowly. A barn and a hotel were built first in 1911, and in 1917 a dairy was established on the west end of town.[54] Solvang continued to be an ordinary agricultural town until the mid-1940s, when it became a tourist attraction. Today it is a town with a population of 2,500 and a tourist business attracting 2 million visitors each year.

On the Pacific coast, north of California, there are four significant Danish communities. Two are in the metropolitan settings of Portland, Oregon, and Tacoma-Seattle, Washington, while two are in the more rural settings of Junction City, Oregon, and Enumclaw, Washington.

Junction City was the settlement founded by the Grundtvigian A. C. Nielsen, who had lived at Clinton, Iowa, and had participated in the creation of the colonies of Tyler and Withee. A religious individual, he hoped to draw Danes together into communities large enough to support a church and pastor. At the same time, he worked as a real-estate agent and was well informed about orchards, dairies, and poultry. His long-range goal was to follow the Junction City settlement with others along the West Coast.[55]

Nielsen's colony at Junction City had been preceded two years earlier with a settlement begun by P. L. C. Hansen, a United Danish Lutheran pastor from Portland. In 1900 Hansen secured an option on 1,280 acres near Eugene and invited settlers from the Midwest to buy portions of the tract. The settlement was called Danebo and maintained its own congregation, Bethesda. Although Bethesda retained its Danish heritage, the congregation began using English in its worship in 1920. Danebo further lost its Danish identity when in the 1960s the city of Eugene expanded its boundaries and annexed the area.[56]

In 1902 Nielsen purchased a ranch east of Junction City and divided the 1,600 acres into tracts of ten to sixty acres. Although the land had been farmed extensively with crops such as wheat, the Danes were able to succeed through intensive and mixed farming practices. The climate also appealed to the Danes because it was moderate and much like that of Denmark. Nielsen advertised in both *Dannevirke* and *Den Danske Pioneer* and within months Danes were migrating west. A church was established that same year, but Nielsen's dream of a folk high school was never realized. Settlers came from both Denmark and Danish settlements in the United States, and in the 1920s several families left Askov, Minnesota, but the Oregon settlement remained small.

With the mixed farming procedure the Danes planted wheat for sale and restored the nitrogen through manuring the soil and planting legumes that also provided pasture for cattle. They also planted orchards that included apple and cherry trees. Although the Danes of Junction City also readily assimilated, they did so more slowly than the Danes at Danebo. Not until 1937 did the church introduce the English language, and their Danish identity is being maintained. In 1961 civic leaders introduced the annual Scandinavian Festival, and in several instances residents call attention to their Danish heritage through architectural designs of homes and business establishments.[57]

The other rural settlement at Enumclaw was not an organized colony, but had been started in the 1880s by Danes and Danish Americans looking for agricultural land. Information on Washington was distributed through the promotional activities of Henry Villard of the Northern Pacific Railroad. In the early 1880s he sent 126 agents to Europe, including Denmark, to encourage migration to the American West and also placed notices in the newspapers pointing out the advantages of settling along the route of his railroad.[58]

While some Danes obtained employment in lumbering, most took up small-scale farming. Many had holdings of five to ten acres on which they grew vegetables, berries, fruit trees, and hay, and also raised dairy cattle, pigs, and chickens. The Danish author Carl Hansen, a resident of Washington, confessed that the acreage was not as impressive as that of the prairie farmer, but the work was not as demanding.[59]

The urban Danes of Portland and Seattle are not as readily identifiable, but they settled in large enough numbers to enable them to establish churches, lodges, and retirement homes. As in San Francisco, the Danes held many different occupations, but they were especially prominent in construction, cartage, and furniture manufacture.[60]

The Danish population of the Pacific Northwest was not large, especially in comparison to that of the Swedes and Norwegians. In 1910, for example, Washington had 7,804 Danes and Oregon 3,215, while the combined Norwegian and Swedish population for the two states was six times larger.

# Part IV: *Danish American Innovations*

## CHAPTER 10

# *Danish American Institutions*

### I *The Danish Brotherhood in America*

THE Danish Brotherhood evolved from some Danish veterans groups and was shaped by the work of Mark Hansen. Hansen had fought in the war against the Germans in 1848 and had migrated to the United States in 1861. His first employment was freighting flour from Omaha to the Colorado gold fields in ox-drawn wagons, but a few months after his arrival, when the American Civil War began, he joined the Nebraska Cavalry. His military service ended when he contracted a fever in Louisiana and returned to Omaha to recover. Later, as more Danes settled in Omaha, he and other veterans of the European wars met to reminisce. The veterans not only relived the battles but also helped each other when one or another comrade needed aid. There were similar organizations in other Danish settlements called the Danish Brothers in Arms (*De Danske Vaabenbrødre*), and in 1881 Hansen tried to unify them into a single, cohesive society.[1]

Hansen was aided in the recruitment efforts by P. H. Johnsen, an agent for the railroad, who could use his pass to travel to Danish communities. But the organization was weak because of the emphasis on military rules for the meetings, and the military preoccupation discouraged the younger men from joining. The introduction of songs into the meetings helped a little, but within a year some members realized that a new name and new directions were necessary. At the 1882 convention in Omaha, where the delegates from the five lodges of Omaha, Neenah, Davenport, Racine, and Moline met, J. P. Paulsen of Davenport introduced the resolutions favoring change. The old supreme officers strenuously objected, and when they realized that the battle was lost, they, along with Hansen, grabbed the war chest and departed.[2]

The remaining members drafted a new constitution and bylaws and named the new organization the Danish Brotherhood. The constitution called for the unification of all Danes in the United States, not only the veterans, in order to perpetuate the memories of Denmark. But it also established a program of insurance for death, sickness, and disability that would be administered on the lodge level with assistance from the central organization if the burden on a specific lodge became too heavy. The delegates returned to their lodges and they approved the new direction. The Omaha lodge also approved and ordered the old treasurer to turn over the treasury of the Danish Brothers in Arms to the new organization.[3]

But Hansen carried the conflict to the pages of the *Pioneer*, a newspaper he had founded in 1872 to assist in forming the veterans' groups. Other opposition came from Lutheran pastors, especially F. L. Grundtvig, who objected to the office of chaplain, a position established in the veterans' organizations, which the Brotherhood had kept for public relations reasons. The church leaders also objected to the practice of conducting meetings in secret. But when the clergy began attacking the *Pioneer* as well, Hansen and the Brotherhood joined forces in facing a common enemy. Sophus Neble eventually became the owner and editor of the paper and Hansen turned to other businesses and his brickyard.[4]

The opposition of the church slowed the growth of the Brotherhood, but it could not stop it altogether. The expansion of the organization was directly related to immigration, and by 1889 there were thirty-four lodges, with 1,432 members. In 1902 the numbers increased to 145 lodges, with 8,347 members, and by 1907 the Brotherhood had grown to 255 lodges, with 17,173 members. The dramatic growth near the turn of the century was related to the goodwill developing in the Danish Church. The Brotherhood eliminated the office of the chaplain, and secrecy was dropped. At the Brotherhood convention in Des Moines in 1898 several teachers from Grand View College talked of harmony and invited the delegates to visit the school. Both organizations benefited from the new understanding.[5]

The changes made in the organization's rules also reflect the nature of the Danish community in America. In 1910, for example, members were admitted even though they could not speak Danish as long as they could understand it. In 1919 the constitution was amended so that lodges could permit discussions in English if the situation warranted it. By 1931 the language requirement was dropped and men were admitted if only one parent was of Danish descent. In 1935 the records of the society were kept in English rather than Danish. Finally, in 1939, men married to Danish women could become social members of the society.[6]

The Danish Brotherhood continues to function at the present time and maintains a membership of 11,000. For its members it provides life insurance, burial aid, help in sickness or old age, and aid to certain children's homes. It is also important as a sponsor of such functions as social gatherings, dramatic performances, dances, and picnics and makes available tapes for instruction in Danish and a kit on Danish folk-dancing. The Danish Sisterhood in America is largely an auxiliary and was formed in 1893.[7]

A smaller, though significant, society is Dania of California and Nevada. Organized in 1879 in Oakland for social reasons, Dania soon expanded throughout California. It also broadened its goals to help sick and unemployed Danes and to preserve Danish culture. Its peak membership year was 1930, when the society numbered 3,289. During its centennial year, 1979, Dania's membership stood at slightly more than 1,000, and although its membership is smaller, it continues its initial goals and also supports Aldersly, a home for the aged in San Rafael, California.[8]

## II *Danish Folk Schools*

One of the unique institutions that helps explain life in the Danish American community is the folk high school. There were numerous educational agencies, but only five schools were folk high schools in the Grundtvigian tradition. They were Elk Horn, Iowa (1878), Ashland, Michigan (1882), Nysted, Nebraska (1887), Danebod, Minnesota (1888), and Solvang, California (1911). The support for these schools came from Danes throughout the nation, but each community benefited from the school because it became the intellectual, social, and cultural center of the Danish settlement and the local people participated in the events.

The roots of the folk-school movement were in Denmark, and one of the factors which promoted the folk school was the rise of Danish nationalism. Danish power had been declining while that of the neighboring Germany was rising. An infusion of nationalism was necessary to prevent the disappearance of Denmark and to revive the spirit of the Danish people so they would make a stand. As a result the Danish heritage from the Viking days was examined and the people were taught to speak the Danish language with pride. It was not by accident that the first folk school was started at Rødding in Slesvig, where the Danish language was under pressure and where the German language was used in schools on every level of education, in churches, and in the courts.

Another root was the developing liberalism in all of Europe, including Denmark. Liberalism required a greater participation in government by the common people and that in turn required an educated and informed citizenry. Education on the elementary level was insufficient in most cases and education on the university level was limited to a few and, in addition, followed the traditional course of study rather than meeting the needs of society.[9] Into this context came the catalyst, N. F. S. Grundtvig, who advanced the idea of establishing schools for the common people with a course of study that stressed character development and not just the accumulation of information. More specifically the schools would aid the student to better understand Danish cultural heritage, clarify his view of human relationships, and deepen his understanding of spiritual reality.[10]

By 1862 there were fifteen folk schools in Denmark and a pattern of policy and procedure began to take shape. Most of the students were from a rural background and possessed a minimal amount of learning, derived mainly from the elementary schools. They generally were between the ages of eighteen and twenty-four and lived at the school for the term. The men attended the winter term and the girls the summer term, although eventually the schools became coeducational. The school was not geared to improve the economic condition of the student or to lead to a new occupation but to enrich the person intellectually and spiritually. Because of this orientation there were no entrance exams, no course exams or grades, and no diplomas.[11]

The school had residential accommodations, with students and teacher often living in the same building and eating meals together. The building was usually owned by the president, although on occasion in the United States the church or community owned the property. In Denmark the school received state support, but in America the economic needs were the concern of the president. Most schools were aided by an association of supporters called *Højskolesamfund.*

The subjects most commonly taught included history (Israel, ancient church, Danish, and American), mythology, mathematics, physics, geography, penmanship, grammar, Swedish gymnastics, literature (Danish and American), and folk-dancing. The courses varied from time to time and from school to school, depending on the interest and specialization of the teachers, and included on occasion marksmanship, care of domestic animals, and sewing. English was a necessity because the folk school attracted the recent immigrant who was interested in learning the American way in a secure setting.[12]

The method of teaching was primarily the lecture method, although there were some books. There was also a great deal of singing and group activities. The school at Nysted followed this schedule:

8:00 Breakfast, Devotion (short sermon, Scripture reading, Danish hymn)
9:00 Arithmetic and Language
11:00 President's Lecture
12:00 Lunch
1:00 American History, Gymnastics, Lecture (history or current events)
Evening Games, dances, songs, concerts, and plays.[13]

The opponents of the folk school basically argued from two different positions. One group, composed of the more religiously pious people and generally members of the Inner Mission, criticized the worldly aspects of the schools. They preferred to support schools that were Christian and taught Christianity. The folk schools included much material that preceded Christianity or material that was peripheral. The charge was accurate, although many would argue its validity. The folk school did not attempt to inculcate beliefs and convert students, but the teachers were Christian and the context of the school was also Christian.[14]

The other conflict was between the purists, who tried to preserve the school as it developed originally, and the practical-minded, who were willing to adjust to the American setting. Kristian Anker bought the Elk Horn school in 1890 and began to change the traditional pattern. He added such courses as business, teacher training for both the public and parochial schools, and a college-preparatory program. The purists insisted that they did not want academic institutions and that education of the spirit was the goal, and not the accumulation of knowledge. Other purists said that it was an accommodation to American life. The defenders of Anker's innovations said that the folk school must adjust to the surrounding conditions, and that even the original folk schools had practical courses. It was better to attend a Danish school and hear Danish than to go to a college where only English was spoken. Anker seemed to have the best of the argument, as his enrollment increased, and a critic, Carl Hansen of Danebod, complained that "the one that follows the folk school tradition with the goal of personal development must always man the pumps to keep from sinking."[15]

Mortensen estimated that approximately 10,000 to 12,000 students attended folk schools in America. Any appraisal of the schools' impact using numerical standards would find the movement unimportant. A. Th. Dorf, a folk-school leader, expressed this pessimism when he wrote, "The great majority of our people neither know nor care to know what the folk school is." Another Danish American, living at the turn of the century, believed the school would only work with an ideal instructor dealing with ideal pupils. "As might be expected," he stated, "this method is not conducive to any very intense intellectual activity."[16]

Judging from the devotion and loyalty of many people, however, there was a qualitative aspect that was important. Men kept trying to start schools, and even after failures they did not give up. Schools that were destroyed by fire were rebuilt. And the experience of the school remained with the ones who participated for the rest of their lives. Mortensen, who attended the school at Nysted and taught at Danebod, maintained that the leaders communicated and conveyed to the students "a world view which transcended humanism and touched deep sources of enlightenment and inspiration."[17]

The biggest problem was the competition with the American educational system and the American approach to education. Time spent in schools leading to a diploma often meant a better job or more money. The folk school was geared to developing the mind and spirit without financial rewards. Although some of the folk-school teachers were scholars and graduates of the University of Copenhagen, they generally did not cater to the desire of American students to accumulate academic credit.[18]

There were other reasons for the limited development of the folk-school system. The financial support was insufficient. Danes did not contribute in large amounts to any Danish educational programs or to their churches and charities. As a result too much of the burden was placed on the president of the school, who not only had to administer the institution and give lectures but was probably also the pastor of the local congregation. The scattered distribution of the Danish people and the poor transportation system further discouraged people from attending the schools away from home. Finally came the Americanization pressures and the decline of immigration, so that the enrollment was completely inadequate.[19] In spite of all hardships and exertions the folk-school movement was important to the Danish American people. It perpetuated the Danish heritage and language, but at the same time it served as an agency to lead the recent immigrants into the American way of life.

## III *The Danish American Press*

The Danish Americans, like other ethnic groups, purchased newspapers in their own language, but the support they gave was not impressive. There never was a daily Danish paper in America, and most of the fifty Danish weeklies lasted a few years and then stopped. Only a handful achieved any kind of stability and large circulation.[20]

*Den Danske Pioneer,* one of the two newspapers still being published, reached the largest circulation of any Danish American paper when in 1914 it had 39,913 subscribers.[21] Mark Hansen, a founder of the Danish Brotherhood, began the *Pioneer* in 1872. In the early days of the paper Hansen demonstrated some sympathy for the church, especially the folk high-school movement, but an unfortunate incident occurred when Pastor O. L. Kirkeberg, a Norwegian president of the Elk Horn folk school, named the school "Leif Erikson's Minde" in memory of an Icelander and not a Dane. Hansen insisted that a Danish name would be more appropriate. Another subject of controversy between Kirkeberg and Hansen was related to the mission of the church in the Omaha–Council Bluffs area. When Kirkeberg was in search of a base for a congregation there, he received considerable opposition from Danes affiliated with other denominations, from Socialists, and from Danes not interested in religion. Kirkeberg believed that Hansen should speak out against these groups, but that he lacked the courage to do so. Kirkeberg also charged that Hansen, who had come to America as a Mormon but had abandoned the group, was editing a paper "for Mormons, socialists, and atheists." Hansen responded that Kirkeberg and the ministers were trying to dominate the Danish community, and the feud between the *Pioneer* and the church was underway.[22]

The second person who worked with the *Pioneer* and who developed it into a leading paper was Sophus Neble. Neble came to the United States in 1883 to please his fiancée, who wanted him to become a farmer. After attempting farming in Wisconsin and realizing that he was not suited for that pursuit he traveled to Omaha to apply for a position on the *Pioneer* staff as typesetter, a trade he had learned in Denmark. He obtained the position and over the next few years assumed more and more responsibilities with the publication. Finally, in 1887, when Neble talked to Hansen about a reassignment of tasks, Hansen offered to sell the newspaper. Even though Neble lacked sufficient funds, the sale was completed.[23]

Neble, both as editor and then as owner, maintained Hansen's policy on church relations. He printed letters from correspondents or articles by his staff that ridiculed the pastors and attacked the institutional church as being corrupt and not responsive to the needs of the people. The *Pioneer* reported on lodge activities, dances, and other secular events, but it ignored church functions or the work of the church in charities and education. Eventually in the 1890s Neble's running battle with the church subsided, but not until the 1920s did the *Pioneer* give the church sympathetic coverage.[24]

Neble has been labeled a Socialist, but he identified himself in Danish political terms as a Radical Liberal and not a Social Democrat. His second wife was indeed the daughter of "Sorte" Hansen, a Danish American Socialist, but he never supported a Socialist for president. He was a Democrat and boosted William Jennings Bryan, the Nebraska Democrat. Both Neble and Hansen were dissatisfied with King Christian IX, and because of their attacks on him and the government the *Pioneer* was banned from Denmark from 1886 to 1898.[25] Many of the Danish migrants agreed with Neble's views on Danish politics and then accepted his position on the church, the Danish Brotherhood, and the Democratic party.[26]

Neble became a leader in the Danish American community, and in 1894 began a fund to help the Nebraska drought victims. In 1899 he collected more than $9,000 for needy workers' families during the labor strife and lockout in Denmark. In 1925 he received recognition for his leadership and was knighted by the Danish king. The honor pleased him, but he never wore the medal in the United States because he was an American citizen. He did wear it, however, on one occasion when he had an audience with the king. His actions showed his love for Denmark and the willingness to help the country, but he reminded all Danes that "America has given us the bread and freedom that our fatherland denied us."[27]

After Neble's death his wife continued to publish the newspaper, but in 1958 some Chicago investors bought the paper and brought it to Elmwood Park, a western suburb, where it is currently being published by Hjalmar Bertelsen. Its present circulation stands at approximately 3,500.

The other Danish newspaper being published today is *Bien* (The Bee), now a Los Angeles journal. *Bien* began in 1882 at San Francisco and reached its peak circulation of 5,000 in the 1940s. The editor whose name was associated with most of

*Bien*'s history, and who also wrote *Danske i California*, was Sophus Hartwick. To increase subscriptions, Hartwick went to the towns and farms of the West and encouraged the formation of Danish clubs and associations. At the same time he lined up correspondents from the local regions, reported the activities of the clubs in his paper, and sold subscriptions. His audience consisted primarily of West Coast Danes. The present circulation of *Bien* is approximately 3,500.[28]

A publisher whose paper no longer exists, but who became successful, was Christian Rasmussen. He began his newspaper in Chicago, but after a while moved his operation to Minneapolis, a city that had few Danes. Rasmussen was a Republican, a conservative, and a Grundtvigian, and his paper sold primarily in the rural Midwest. The *Ugebladet* (1881–1959) reached its peak circulation in 1914, with an impressive 22,500. He also published the two-volume *Danske i Amerika*, the first volume of which was written largely by P. S. Vig.[29]

The various church bodies also had their own newspapers, which in many instances did not limit themselves to religious matters. *Bikuben*, the Mormon paper, was published from 1876 to 1935. *Dannevirke*, the Grundtvigian paper, included information from Denmark, current events, and news from the Danish communities in addition to religious matters. Its peak circulation was 3,000.[30]

The foreign-language press, like the folk-school movement, played a dual role. On the one hand it maintained the language and knowledge of the homeland and promoted identification with the Danish community, but at the same time it educated the new immigrants on American history and geography and made them familiar with outstanding Americans. Most editors, such as Neble, encouraged Danes to remember Denmark but to become good citizens and to love America for providing a home.[31]

The circulation figures for the Danish American newspapers also reflect the dramatic change that took place in the Danish American community during the World War I period. In 1910 the circulation of the seven leading Danish papers was 72,000. This meant that one out of three first-generation Danes and one out of six of the first and second generations subscribed. In 1930 the circulation had dropped to 37,800. That meant one out of every five first-generation Danes subscribed, as well as one out of twelve for the first and second generation.[32] The implication was clear: the language was not being used and the papers intended to provide cohesiveness to the community were not being read.

CHAPTER 11

# *Danish American Socialism*

THE Socialist movement in Denmark, which took official form in 1871 with the establishment of the Social Democratic party, was interrelated with life and activity in America. One of the early promotors of migration to America, Mogens Abraham Sommer, joined the Socialist movement in its infancy in Denmark and helped organize some workers' rallies. Although he also loaned money to Louis Pio, one of the leaders, Sommer's personality and his continued association with religion led to his ouster from the party.[1]

Louis Pio, the most noted leader of the movement in the early days, was born of Danish parents, but his heritage included a French noble lineage. After he graduated from the University of Copenhagen with a degree in philosophy, he taught school for a time and also served in the army and in the postal service. Although he later claimed his conversion to socialism took place when, as a lad, he had seen a landlord beat a poor shoemaker because the man could not pay his rent, he more than likely became associated with socialism as the result of his experience in the Paris Commune in 1871. The first issue of *Socialistiske Blade* appeared in July 1871, anonymously, but within a month the justice minister identified Pio as the editor.[2]

Pio was present in Copenhagen in April 1872, when the bricklayers went on strike, so the Socialist leaders, Pio, Poul Geleff, and Harald Brix, called for an open-air meeting to support the strikers and the International. The police feared violence, and when the leaders refused to call off the rally, they were arrested and charged with crimes against public authority and order, crimes against religion, and violation of police regulation. Pio was sentenced to six years in prison, Geleff to five years, and Brix to four. After an appeal, a higher court reduced the terms to five years for Pio and three for the other two men.[3]

Prison conditions were harsh, and Pio's physical health suffered. The diet of smoked and salted horsemeat, bread, and thin beer was inadequate, and during his incarceration Pio developed ulcers and lost ten teeth. So debilitated did the three become that the government released them in 1875 before the sentences had been fully served, so as not to create martyrs. The one accomplishment for Pio during this time was his mastery of foreign languages. He was permitted to read in prison, and there he learned most of the eleven languages he knew.[4]

After regaining his strength, Pio resumed editing the Socialist newspaper. He was not satisfied, however, and yearned for a stronger voice in policy formation. He stressed political action and winning elections while the trade-union leaders preferred short-range goals that would improve wages and working conditions. Pio's discontent with the direction the party was taking coincided with financial problems with the newspaper and the growing fear that he might again be subjected to yet another prison term.[5] As a consequence Pio began to develop a plan to lead Danish workers to America. His motivation, however, was not the welfare of the workers but a program for bringing unity to the party and to end the mounting indebtedness.[6]

The scheme may have been original, or it may have been suggested by men like Sommer or by the writings of Rasmus Sorensen. Of particular interest to Pio was the state of Kansas, and in 1876, when Geleff was sent to the United States to search for vacant land, he was instructed especially to consider Kansas. One reason for choosing Kansas was that it was isolated, and like Utah for the Mormons, isolation was necessary for molding a Socialist community according to ideological blueprints. Another possibility was the salesmanship of the agent in Copenhagen representing the Kansas Pacific Railroad.[7] Geleff also visited other locations in America as well as the Danish community in Chicago, where he lectured to 300 listeners about communism and socialism.[8] Geleff returned to Denmark with a favorable report and Pio promoted the idea of a Socialist colony in Kansas.

Using his newspaper, Pio demanded that the government work against unemployment and provide 200,000 kroner for workers wishing to migrate to the United States.[9] Pio also published a pamphlet telling about Kansas, the railroads, and his hope for the colony. He reported that the colonists would leave in April, approximately three weeks after some trusted men had gone on ahead to select a site and purchase supplies. He also described the labor that would be necessary on arrival in Kansas, such as building log cabins, breaking the soil, planting maize, and digging a well, but he did not spell out the rules for the colony. All he promised was that the new association would be Socialist and that the goal was to help the poor improve their lot. The payment for the migrant was 400 kroner for a male and 230 for each female.[10]

Meanwhile Pio and Geleff negotiated with the police for a payment of money on the condition that the two would close the newspaper and migrate to America. The money came from several private firms and Pio was promised 20,000 kroner and Geleff 10,000 if they would leave by April 30, 1877. That schedule would coincide with Pio's plans, and they could gain some money for the Socialist venture or for the discharge of some debt payments. For some reason, however, either because of the pressure from the police or the impending financial collapse of Pio's newspaper, the departure date was advanced to March 23, 1877. Instead of notifying fellow Socialists, the two men left on separate ships for Scotland and then continued on to New York.[11] In New York they went to the designated people for their money, but Pio received only 10,000 kroner and Geleff a mere 1,500. Pio and Geleff quarreled about the division of the funds, so Geleff broke his association with Pio and settled instead in Chicago.

The premature and secret departure of the leaders came as a shock to the fellow Socialists in Denmark, and the Socialist cause was damaged for many years to come.[12] Geleff later expressed remorse over his actions, but Pio denied that he had betrayed socialism and instead insisted that it was an opportunity to test Socialist principles. Geleff quickly came out with a pamphlet telling his version of the affair including his complaints against Pio.[13]

Geleff took a position with *Heimdal*, the Danish newspaper that published his pamphlet, and later, in association with

Frederiksen, became a land agent in Colorado. He started Fowler, Colorado, in the 1890s, selling the land for $40 to $75 per acre. By 1910 the value of the land had increased to $150 per acre, but the Danish population remained limited to approximately thirty families. At one time in 1901 he owned a little store in Pueblo, and edited "The Colorado Investor." He also wrote humorous articles for the *Pioneer*, and it amazed some of the readers that he could have been the frightful revolutionist he was pictured to be. In 1920 the Social Democrats in Denmark paid for his passage back to Europe and there he died a tired and impoverished man.[14]

Pio, along with Augusta Jorgensen, whom he later married, and fifteen others left for their Kansas colony, near Hays, in May 1877. Included in the number was A. William "Sorte" Hansen, Pio's personal secretary, who had accompanied him from Denmark. Hansen agreed with Geleff that he had been cheated by Pio, but nevertheless Hansen went along to Kansas.[15]

In Kansas each person contributed to the purchase of land and equipment and worked with zeal to show the principles of socialism in operation. The men worked vigorously with the land by day, but then in the evening they argued constantly about the practical application of Socialist theory. The women were no better and quarreled about the distribution of tasks. After six weeks the land and equipment were sold and each person received $30. That part of Kansas was not the most conducive to successful agriculture and rain did not follow the plow west. However, discord more than environmental factors caused the collapse.[16]

The veterans of the Socialist colony scattered and eventually adjusted to the capitalist atmosphere. Hansen worked in a quarry and a farm near Grand Island, Nebraska, for a while and then joined his wife and daughter in Chicago, where he found employment as an agent for Frederiksen's bookstores in various Danish settlements. He gave it up because of the lack of books.[17] He had worked for Bing and Grøndahl in Denmark, so he then found employment in a Chicago porcelain factory, and frequently attended the gathering at the Round Table. He continued to participate in Socialist matters, even though he maintained that the Kansas failure showed the impracticality of socialism. On business trips to New York he visited a childhood friend and fellow Socialist, Fritz Schuman, but ideologically they had parted ways. Schuman had grown tired of waiting for reform through peaceful legislation and supported the anarchist solution, while Hansen held that violence and murder were more destructive of society than beneficial.[18]

Pio also found his way back to Chicago where he held several jobs in journalism while his wife gave music lessons. One of the first of his positions was with the Methodist publication *Den Kristelige Talsmand*, an appointment resulting from the kindness of an old family friend rather than religious conviction. Contrary to expectations, both Geleff and Pio were well received by the Chicago Danes. Those with Socialist sympathies had criticized the two men when word came to Chicago about their hurried departure from Denmark, but soon all was forgiven. Frederiksen, owner of *Heimdal*, gave Geleff a position and the columns of the paper were used to defend their action.[19] Even Consul Dreier and the "better" Danes received Pio and Geleff with friendship and sought their company. The only ones who showed some hostility were Martin and Henry Hertz, sons of the police commissioner of Copenhagen, who had been instrumental in convincing Pio and Geleff to leave. These two brothers had migrated to Chicago, where Martin operated a tobacconist's shop and Henry became a political leader in the Republican party. One evening Dreier had invited Geleff and Henry Hertz to a whist party, but when Hertz arrived at the consulate and learned that Geleff was expected, he expressed his regrets and left.[20] But even this coolness did not last long and soon Hertz, Pio, Geleff, and others all joined at the Round Table.

In 1879 some Socialists, including the Norwegian Markus Thrane, began *Den Nye Tid* and asked Pio to serve as editor. But he was no longer the agitator he had been, so after six months the directors fired him. His life in Chicago must have been frustrating. During his seventeen years in the city his occupations included that of professor, editor, translator, notary public, clerk of a customs house, county architect, and realtor, and he lived at least at eleven different addresses.[21]

Eventually Pio, like Geleff, entered the real-estate business. He secured a position from the Florida East Coast Railway Company and promoted a settlement called White City near Fort Pierce on the east coast of the state. The support for the project came from the wealthy industrialist Henry M. Flagler, and Pio hoped to attract Scandinavians to the community. Pio wrote a booklet which was distributed from the Florida booth he operated at the Columbian Exposition in Chicago in which he mentioned many places along the railroad line but called special attention to prosperous Danes already in the areas raising fruit trees and pineapples.[22] Although the project was not a success, Pio attracted several Danish Americans from Chicago, including one faithful veteran from the Kansas colony.[23]

Pio died in 1894 of typhus and his daughter had the ashes taken from Chicago for burial in Denmark. His wife continued to earn money to support herself and in 1897 was appointed Tenement Inspector by the mayor of Chicago. She retained her interest in socialism and continued to write and talk about the topic that had occupied her husband's career.[24]

While the names of Pio and Geleff are known in Denmark but not in the United States, the most famous Danish American Socialist was Laurence Gronlund. When Gronlund migrated to the United States in 1867 he continued on to Milwaukee, where he taught German and resumed his study of law. Two years later in 1869 he was admitted to the Chicago bar, but he evidently was not happy in the legal profession. He may well have turned to socialism after reading Pascal's *Pensées*, and in 1878 he gave up law and took up journalism and lecturing on political topics.[25]

Gronlund had some contact with the Danish community in Chicago, but there is no indication as to the specific year. Dreier gave him permission to sleep in the back part of the drug store in return for cleaning the shop and filling small prescriptions. After a short time it became evident that the two men could not work together and Gronlund left.[26] He moved to New York, and in 1883 was earning $10 a week and saving $3 to help publish his book *The Cooperative Commonwealth*, which appeared in 1884. The purpose of the book was to "persuade nonsocialist readers that the capitalist system must collapse and that a socialist order satisfying all social and humanitarian ideals should replace it."[27] Although Gronlund hoped for the revolution, he rejected the idea of class conflict, and later in his life he moved steadily away from Marxism yet remained a Socialist to the end. When Gronlund's book was discussed in Wilken's Cellar, Frederiksen thought it was rubbish, as bad as anything that had been written on national economics. Pio, mindful of Frederiksen's failures, did not think that Frederiksen's experiences made him a qualified judge.[28] Yet Gronlund's work was especially influential on Eugene Debs and Edward Bellamy, and their leadership and writing were important in the development of American socialism.[29]

Even though Pio and Geleff could not convince many Danish Socialists to migrate to Kansas, many came to the United States on their own and found employment in Chicago as laborers. The picture of the Danish Socialist community in Chicago is drawn best not by Pio, but by Christian Botker, editor of *Revyen*. Botker had worked on a provincial newspaper in Denmark, but following his migration in 1891 he found work at the terra-cotta factory at Perth Amboy. After a short stay he continued on to Chicago, and in 1892 he returned to journalism, until he began his own newspaper in 1895. It was an independent Socialist paper that did not have the endorsement of the Socialist Labor party. The party instead created *Arbejderen* as its official paper for the Danes and Norwegians in 1896. The editor, John Glambeck, called *Revyen* "reformist," which meant that Botker looked for social reform through existing political institutions.[30] But Glambeck could not capture the Socialist readership and three months after the newspaper began publication a split took place that further reduced the subscription lists, and the creditors claimed the paper.[31] Botker in turn kept his readership loyal with a lively paper that carried political news, local news, and a gossip column in addition to his Socialist material. Botker's style revealed itself in a report about a fire in Mrs. Jensen's boardinghouse which he summed up by saying that "everything was a complete loss and 200 bed bugs lost their lives."[32] His subscription list was generally between 2,000 and 3,000, but it increased to 5,000 during World War I.

The ideology of the Danish Socialists cannot be given in a single statement because like Socialists in other places there were differences of opinions and different spokesmen. The socialism most Chicago Danes supported and which Botker articulated was, as Glambeck said, reformist, and not revolutionary. The programs included municipal ownership of the streetcar system and electrical power plants, an eight-hour day, women's suffrage, free books for public schools, and guarantees of the right to strike and boycott. These and other goals were respectable and received the same support from the progressive wings of the Democratic and Republican parties.[33] The leadership came primarily from a few intellectuals and politicians whose hope was to improve the lot of the worker through social legislation and through strikes and boycotts. The aim of the Socialist party, Botker reported in 1912, was to secure for the workers the products of their labor and to get rid of the parasitic luxury class. "He who will not work, shall not eat."[34]

As a Socialist opinion-maker Botker also had enemies. He attacked Theodore Roosevelt just as Roosevelt attacked the Socialists, even though they both favored reform. He also opposed union leader Samuel Gompers, who dedicated his life to labor organizations, because of Gompers's faith in capitalism.[35] Nor did he spare the left wing of the Socialist groups. Daniel De Leon was censured for advocating radical methods and Botker objected to William Haywood's appointment to the Socialist Party Executive Committee because Haywood had anarchistic and syndicalistic tendencies.[36]

When World War I broke out in Europe, American Socialists were not united on policy, but Botker urged the Danes to be pacifists even though some in the Socialist party favored the Kaiser. Support for a German monarch was too much to ask from a Dane.[37] Then, when the United States did enter the war, he abandoned pacifism and urged the Danes to support the United States in the war against the Germans.[38] Botker gave up the paper in 1921 and with it his voice in the Socialist movement when he sold the paper to Frank Phillipsen. He accepted a position as an Inspector of United States Navigation at Chicago Municipal Pier.[39]

On the local level the Socialists accomplished little and weakened the movement by divisiveness. An indication that Danish Socialists were weak is suggested by their need to form a union with other Scandinavians. All of the socialist groups were open to all Scandinavians and only the Danish Socialist Society used the term Danish.[40] The various groups that formed and failed were such groups as the Scandinavian Socialist Society, organized in 1895; the Karl Marx Club, a discussion club; and *Friheden* (Liberty), a discussion club that split from the Karl Marx Club in 1909.[41]

The primary function of these groups was to promote candidates and win elections, but the Danish Socialist Society, for example, provided sick benefits. The Karl Marx Club provided an arena for clarification of ideology. It even developed a position statement for the Danish Socialists to refrain from Danish patriotic undertakings out of fear that such involvement would retard the development of class consciousness and the revolution. There may have been some lighter social moments among the members as well because the *Revyen* states that "the comrades parted about 3 o'clock in the morning."[42]

Numerically it is hard to establish the size of the Socialist movement among the Danes. While many joined the organizations, most Danes remained aloof and would only show support at election time. But even then there were few votes. The Danes had strong representation in Chicago's fourteenth, fifteenth, and thirty-fourth wards, but in 1900 each ward gave Debs only 500 to 600 votes. The Scandinavian Socialist Society had only 480 members in 1915 and one of its picnics attracted only 1,200 people in 1919.[43] During the 1920s Danish socialism declined even more and the Danes, if they participated in politics at all, did so under the banners of the two major parties.

CHAPTER 12

# *Denmark or America?*

## I *Rebild, Denmark, and the Aalborg Archives*

SHORTLY after the turn of the century a Racine journalist suggested that a society be created for the purpose of maintaining cultural ties between the United States and Denmark. The immediate concern was to provide an agency that would sponsor tours of Danish artists to Danish American communities. The proposal found a sympathetic audience and in 1906 the Danish American Society was formed, with Henry Hertz as president. Three years later, in 1909, the society enlarged its horizons and planned a project which called for a special Danish American Day at the Aarhus Exposition. Max Henius was assigned the task of convincing Americans visiting Denmark that summer to place Aarhus into their itinerary for the Fourth of July.[1] The idea was publicized among the Danish Americans, and Henius also addressed a large crowd at the annual Constitution Day picnic at Chicago's Riverview Park in support of the project.[2]

The event was a tremendous success and Henius, overjoyed, sent a cablegram from Denmark to Hertz with the information. Twelve hundred Danish Americans had registered and Henius and his friends planned to make it an annual event, although the location would not necessarily be at Aarhus.[3]

About the same time Henius and other Danish Americans decided to obtain some heath land that would be set aside for preservation. Much of the heath was being turned into productive farm land, and in other places the beech trees were growing over the heather. Even though heath land was not productive, many Danish immigrants had an emotional attachment to the heath. In November 1909, C. Bech, the father of the Danish consul in Chicago, spoke to a group at the Red Star Inn and reported that a tract of land had been selected. It was an area of 200 acres in the Rebild Hills south of Aalborg.[4]

The Danish Americans then set about collecting 140,000 kroner for the purchase of the land.[5] In 1911 the transaction was completed and in 1912 the land was turned over to Denmark as a national park, to be managed on the same principles as a national park in the United States. Although the presentation ceremony was planned for July 4, it was postponed until August 12 because of the death of the king. Since then, however, the celebrations have been held on American Independence Day and thousands of people have listened to Danish and American speakers. In 1927 a loudspeaker system was introduced so that visitors could scatter over the heath-covered hillsides to listen to the proceedings. Then in 1933 the Lincoln Log Cabin was erected to serve as a museum for artifacts and pictures contributed by Americans.[6]

An offshoot of the Rebild Hills project was the establishment of an archives of Danish American documents. The Danes in the United States had scattered and there remained some smoldering resentment from earlier controversies, so that it was almost impossible to identify a single location in America as a depository for Danish American material. Henius, in 1929, advanced the proposal of using Sohngaardsholm Manor House in Aalborg for the archives. The building had been constructed by his father, Isidore Henius, and the city of Aalborg had obtained possession of it. The Aalborg city leaders made it available for the archives and Henius hired Svend Waendelin of the University of Chicago as the librarian. Henius's own materials were deposited there, along with many other materials contributed by Danish Americans. The archives were opened in 1932 and were initially called the Dan-American Archives, although later the name was changed to Danes Worldwide Archives.[7]

During World War II the building was taken over for use by the Germans, so the materials were removed. When the Germans left, the costs of rehabilitating the old building and repairing the scars of military occupation were too great, and for years the materials were housed in five cramped rooms in an apartment complex. The collection, however, is being moved to new and larger quarters provided by the city of Aalborg.[8]

## II *Danish Assimilation and Persistence*

In spite of the rapid assimilation of the Danish immigrant group some cultural aspects remained even after the Danes became Americans, and some features have persisted to the present day. The question of assimilation, in contrast to cultural maintenance, is a matter of perspective. Should more emphasis be placed on the loss of ethnic attributes or on their retention? The issues are two sides of the same coin. Of importance here is not merely those traditions that were lost or retained but the functions the traditions performed.

Assimilation occurred faster in the cities than in rural areas, and Chicago was no exception. Already in 1883 Frederiksen published *Scandinavia*, a monthly journal that was issued in English. Possibly the Scandinavians had not learned sufficient English to make the enterprise profitable and it ceased publication after only three years. The pressure for assimilation was there, however, and the issue was discussed by P. Koch in one of the articles of the journal. He advised the Scandinavians to become Americans. "No half-way measure will do." "Become americanized [*sic*] as thoroughly and as rapidly as possible! Go among the Americans; settle among them; adopt their habits of living and thinking; above all, speak and write the English language exclusively."[9]

The assimilation of the Chicago Danes varied according to individuals, and many settled in the Danish neighborhoods while others scattered over Chicago and suburbs. There were also different generations of Danish immigrants. Those Danes who came in 1880 were different from the ones who came in 1910, and were already on the road to Americanization. The churches, clubs, bars, and neighborhoods all contributed to maintaining the Danish language, foods, and customs, but in employment and travel the setting was American.

The claim to the loyalty they felt to both Denmark and the United States can be substantiated by their response to an honor bestowed by the Danish king. From time to time the

Danish monarch recognized the work and contributions of some Danish Americans by honoring them with membership in the Order of the Knights of Dannebrog.

It was not only a reward for faithful service to the Danish American community but also a symbol of continued association with Denmark. Some opposition to this practice came from individuals who were hostile to the Danish monarchy for policies implemented during the period before constitutional reform. Other persons, such as the Chicago landscape architect Jens Jensen, were concerned over the possibility that a caste of knights could be established in America.[10] This rather unrealistic fear probably was more an expression of concern on the objector's part lest the acceptance of this honor be interpreted as lack of complete loyalty to the United States. Even though accepting this distinction from a foreign ruler indicated that loyalty to the United States was not without reservations, no one seriously believed that the recipients compromised their allegiance. When Henry Hertz and Max Henius were knighted, the editor of *Revyen* defended the act because he realized that it was in recognition of charitable work performed by the two men for Danish Americans. He also observed that the critics, if they were suddenly presented with the honor, would be more than willing to accept it.[11]

The greatest pressure for Americanization came during World War I. It was an organized, purposeful program that was directed against many ethnic groups, not just the Danes. Failure to cooperate could lead to denunciation. The Jacob A. Riis League, named after a Dane who Americanized rapidly, was formed to promote American patriotism among Danish Americans.[12] The president of the Chicago chapter of the league, Max Henius, favored assimilation and offered several suggestions for hastening the process. He praised the foreign-language press for always having contributed to Americanization, but he hoped for a greater emphasis in explaining American ideas and customs to the readers. He also suggested that all societies of foreign-born people keep the minutes in English, and that nationalistic and racial groups avoid becoming political blocs.[13]

But in spite of all the pressure, aspects of the Danish heritage remained. Noel Chrisman, in a study of the Danes of the San

Francisco Bay area, concluded that Danish ethnicity and identification continued to be expressed through voluntary organizations, newspapers, and certain types of business establishments. The voluntary organizations included the lodges, singing societies, and orchestras. The newspaper for the West Coast that dedicated itself to the publicizing of social group activity and today exists as the most visible Danish element in the Bay area is *Bien*. And finally there were businesses that catered to Danish customers, including travel agencies, restaurants, bakeries, taverns, delicatessens, and funeral homes. In the earlier part of the century the organizations and their activities were visible to the general public, while in more recent times information relative to the ethnic functions was generally limited to the members of the ethnic group.

Chrisman, therefore, sees the voluntary associations as unifiers of ethnic groups in an urban setting and considers the use of language, foods, and entertainment involved in the activity of the associations as the display of Danishness. The primary goal, nevertheless, is the maintenance of the organization, and those requirements that perpetuate certain Danish traits, such as Danish birth, are eliminated if the restrictions threaten the continued existence of the organization.[14]

The perpetuation of Danish culture during the first half of the century was more easily achieved in the rural areas than in the cities because the isolation prevented contact with conflicting cultures. The shops in the small towns were often Danish, the church which the rural people attended was Danish, and most of the neighbors were Danish. In the cities limited aspects of social life, such as societies and clubs, were associated with the Danes, but in the country much more of the daily life took place in a Danish context. While the clubs dominated city life, churches dominated rural life. But as the rural isolation broke down and the churches became American in order to survive, societies were formed in the rural districts to perpetuate some aspects of Danish life. Because societies have a greater chance of gaining members in a city than in sparsely populated rural areas Danish ways survive more frequently in urban settings.

An example of the development of interest in the Danish heritage is to be found in the Twin Cities of Minneapolis and

St. Paul. Only 2,600 Danes resided in the Twin Cities at the turn of the century, but, as urban America grew, more Danes and their descendants moved to Minneapolis and St. Paul. Danish churches and organizations were founded, but not until 1948 was the Danish American Fellowship organized to assist and coordinate the activities of the small Danish societies. Today the society sponsors an annual Danish Day celebration, gymnastics and dancing lessons, and charter flights to Denmark. The membership exceeds 1,000, and that includes Danish Americans who travel into the Twin Cities from Askov.[15]

At the same time Danes in rural concentrations have tried to capitalize on their Danish identity. Kimballton, Iowa, has displayed a copy of the "Little Mermaid," and the neighboring town of Elk Horn boasts a windmill imported from Denmark. Askov, Minnesota, stages an annual Rutabaga Festival at the end of August that highlights Danish dancing and *aebleskiver* (ball pancakes). The Danish Ladies Aid of the Askov church has published a book of favorite recipes—in English. And during the Bicentennial year, 1976, the streets and buildings were given Danish names.[16]

One of the measures of durability of Danish customs was the celebration of Danish festivals. Constitution Day (June 5) was celebrated by the Chicago community and many other places prior to World War II, but only on a small scale or with little regularity after that time.[17] In more recent times the event is celebrated at the various Danish old people's homes. Another June celebration, St. Hans Day (June 23), has not received as much attention as Constitution Day. In Denmark the bonfires were lit to frighten away the witches, while in the United States celebrations were on a smaller scale and the fire was used to heat wieners and bratwurst.[18]

The festival of Fastelavn or Shrovetide was highlighted with a contest called "*Slaa Katten af Tønden*" (Knock the Cat from the Barrel). A keg containing a cat was suspended by a rope a few feet in the air so that participants could take turns hitting the barrel with a club. The one who freed the terrified cat or knocked loose the last piece of wood, if no cat had been found, was declared the winner. The winner was crowned "King of the Cats" and his female companion, or the winner of the contest among the women, was titled "Queen of the Cats." In Nebraska the barrel was taken outside and suspended about ten feet in the air so that riders could gallop full tilt at it in their attempt to release the cat.[19] Fastelavn parties are still being held, and one of the activities involves the breaking of barrels filled with candy using a baseball bat as the club.[20]

Probably the festival with the greatest continuity is Christmas. At Christmas each family can celebrate the event within a small unit and not be dependent on large numbers of Danes. Each family can decide the extent to which Danish customs, such as dancing around the tree, will be used, and the kinds of foods that will be prepared in the traditional manner. There is also enough of a similarity to the non-Danish Christmas celebrations to encourage the observance of the event.[21]

Other examples of the Danish heritage that remained for a while in the rural setting were implements and articles of Danish make or inspiration. Several wooden windmills of the Dutch type were built by Danes and operated in Nebraska and North Dakota. They were soon replaced by other machines, but remained as tourist attractions. Other examples were spinning wheels, wool carders, carpenters' tools, wooden shoes, and feather beds.[22]

The last and possibly the most significant aspect of the Danish tradition is the language. Each family unit decided the extent of the language training its children should have. Conversation around the house was not sufficient, however, and some form of instruction was necessary. Few schools taught it, so the churches gave instruction because the knowledge of the language was necessary to appreciate a Danish church service. Many parishioners were less interested in Denmark or its language than were the pastors. The pastors tried to teach the songs, customs, and the language, but not many of the Danes took advantage of the opportunity.[23]

Although knowledge of Danish is not currently a prerequisite for participation in Danish events, many of the societies, such as the Danish American Fellowship of the Twin Cities and the Danish American Athletic Club of Chicago, provide classes in Danish.

Much of the recent interest in Danish America is scholarly

in nature or associated with academic institutions. In 1964, three years after the merger of the Danish Church with the Lutheran Church in America, some Danes hoped to retain some identity in the larger body and also keep up their old friendships. This led to the formation of the Danish Interest Conference and the publication of a semimonthly journal, *Kirke og Folk,* that treated both religious topics and matters of the Danish heritage.[24]

The Danish American Heritage Society (DAHS) was founded in 1977 and in July 1980 had a membership of 450. It also publishes a semiannual journal, the *Bridge*, which includes important contributions to the study of Danish American life. A project sponsored by the DAHS in cooperation with Grand View College, and headed by Thorvald Hansen of Grand View, is preparing a comprehensive list of Danish American historical materials in the United States, Canada, and Denmark libraries and depositories.[25]

During the Bicentennial year the Danish American Language Foundation was established for the specific purpose of ensuring the continued publication of the two Danish language newspapers, *Pioneer* and *Bien*. Dana College, of Blair, Nebraska, a four-year college of Danish heritage, carries on the tradition and sponsors "Sights and Sounds of Christmas" and the Danish Folk Dancers, and prides itself in the Lauritz Melchior Memorial Room and a collection of Bing and Grøndahl plates.[26]

The retention of Danish customs and traditions by the Danes in America was largely a social-psychological decision for both the first generation of immigrants and their descendants. Each person responded in his own way, but Erling Duus captured a familiar theme. In describing his grandparents Duus said, "Of course, they learned to speak good English and they lived in an American world that they became somewhat at home in, but the spiritual center of their lives was Danish America." Duus then went on to report that the grandparents on one occasion traced their steps back to Denmark for a visit, and suddenly on their return to America realized that they had become Americans.[27]

# *Notes and References*

## *Introduction*

1. Enok Mortensen, "Looking Back and Looking Forward," *Bridge: Journal of the Danish American Heritage Society,* May 1978, pp. 5–11. Earlier attempts at establishing a historical society were made in 1905, 1927, and 1932.

2. Milton M. Gordon, "Assimilation in America: Theory and Reality," *Daedalus,* Spring 1961, pp. 263–85.

3. United States Immigration Commission, *Immigration in Industries* 23 (Washington, D.C., 1911), p. 192. *United States Census of Population, 1930* (Washington, D.C., 1930).

4. *United States Census of Population, 1930.*

5. Membership of the two synods was 47,000 and the number of Danish Americans plus the Americans with at least one Danish parent was 509,564. See page 88.

6. David Bunce, "A Profile of an Ethnic Community: Scandinavians in Chicago, 1880–1900" (thesis, The Flinders University of South Australia, 1976), p. 26.

7. John H. Bille, "A History of the Danes in America," *Transactions of the Wisconsin Academy of Sciences, Arts, and Letters,* March 1896, pp. 7, 36.

8. Kristian Hvidt, *Flight to America: The Social Background of 300,000 Danish Emigrants* (New York, 1975), pp. 170, 171.

9. A. William Hoglund, *Finnish Immigrants in America, 1880–1920* (Madison, Wisconsin: University of Wisconsin Press, 1960), pp. 121–23.

10. F. M. Paulsen, "Danish-American Folk Traditions: A Study in Fading Survivals" (Ph.D. dissertation, Indiana University, 1967) p. 23. The buttermakers are also widely traveled Danes.

11. *Skandinaven,* September 4, 1889.

12. O. N. Nelson, *History of the Scandinavians and Successful Scandinavians in the United States* (Minneapolis, 1893), p. 66. Peter Riismøller, *Rebild: The Fourth of July Celebrations in Denmark* (Copenhagen, 1952), pp. 92, 93, 103. Philip S. Friedman, "The Danish Com-

munity of Chicago, 1860–1920" (master's thesis, Northwestern University, 1976), pp. 32, 34; Bille, p. 8.

13. Theodore C. Blegen, *Norwegian Migration to America: An American Transition* (Northfield, Minnesota: The Norwegian-American Historical Association, 1940), pp. 172, 173.

14. *Danish Times*, February 20, 1931.

15. Max Henius, ed., *Den danskfødte Amerikaner* (Chicago, 1912), pp. 170, 171.

*Chapter One*

1. Jørgen Bukdahl et al., *Scandinavia Past and Present through Revolutions to Liberty* (Copenhagen: Edvard Henriksen, 1959), 1:463.
2. W. Glyn Jones, *Denmark* (London: Ernest Benn, 1970), p 32.
3. Bukdahl, 1:464; Jones, p. 32.
4. Bukdahl, p. 466.
5. Jones, p. 35.
6. Bukdahl, 1:506, 508, 510.
7. Waldemar Westergaard, *The Danish West Indies under Company Rule* (New York: Macmillan Co., 1917), p. 37; Jones, p. 243.
8. Jones, pp. 243–44.
9. Ibid., pp. 244–45.
10. Ibid., p. 245.
11. Bukdahl, 1:546.
12. Ibid., 1:548; John Danstrup, *A History of Denmark* (Copenhagen: Wivel, 1949), p. 75.
13. Bukdahl, 2:645, 646; Jones, p. 39.
14. P. G. Lindhardt, *Grundtvig: An Introduction* (London: S.P.C.K., 1951), p. 5.
15. Palle Lauring, *A History of the Kingdom of Denmark* (Copenhagen: Høst & Son, 1960), 260; Jones, p. 57.
16. Lauring, pp. 204, 211.
17. Bukdahl, 2:722, 723, 726; Lauring, p. 212.
18. J. P. T. Bury, ed., *The Zenith of European Power, 1830–1870*, Vol. 10 of *The New Cambridge Modern History* (Cambridge: Cambridge University Press, 1960), p. 219.
19. Lauring, p. 213. Waldemar Westergaard, *Denmark and Slesvig (1848–1864), with a Collection of Illustrative Letters by Daniel Bruhn, Including His Letters from California and Nevada (1864–1872)* (Copenhagen: Nyt Nordisk, 1946), pp. 23–25.
20. Bukdahl, 2:729.
21. Ibid., pp. 729, 760.

22. Lauring, pp. 222, 230; Bukdahl, 2:760. Nebraska Danes named their dogs "Bismarck" especially when the dog was vicious. A. W. Christensen, *A Story of the Danish Settlement in Dannevirke* ([n. p.], 1961), p. 58.
23. Peter Riismøller, *Rebild: The Fourth of July Celebrations in Denmark* (Copenhagen, 1952), p. 52; Kristian Hvidt, *Danes Go West: A Book about the Emigration to America* (Copenhagen, 1976), p. 158.
24. Hvidt, *Flight to America*, p. 141.
25. Bukdahl, 2:760–62.
26. Ibid., p. 1004.
27. Lauring, pp. 232, 233.
28. Henning Ravnholt, *The Danish Co-operative Movement* (Copenhagen: Det Danske Selskab, 1947), pp. 18, 19, 33, 34.
29. Ibid., pp. 32, 34.
30. Ibid., pp. 48, 49.
31. Jones, p. 72.
32. Bukdahl, 2:831.
33. Ibid., pp. 832, 833.
34. Ibid., p. 832.
35. Jones, p. 84.
36. Bukdahl, 2:832.
37. Jones, pp. 76, 77; Hvidt, *Flight to America*, p. 145.

## *Chapter Two*

1. *Statistical Abstract of the United States, 1943–1971.*
2. Kristian Hvidt, *Flight to America: The Social Background of 300,000 Danish Emigrants* (New York, 1975).
3. Ibid., pp. 39–41, 45, 50, 60.
4. Ibid., pp. 73, 74.
5. Ibid., p. 74. Even though much of the study on the age of the migrants offered a static picture of the period, Hvidt did observe some trends. In the 1860s and 1870s the average age of the migrants was higher than the average from 1885 to 1890. Hvidt interpreted the first period as one reflecting an escape from poverty while the second was more a quest for adventure. Kristian Hvidt, *Danes Go West* (Copenhagen, 1976), p. 138.
6. Kristian Hvidt, "America Fever Strikes Denmark," *Danish Journal*, Special issue (1976), p. 26.
7. Hvidt, *Flight to America*, pp. 84, 86, 93, 101.
8. Peter Riismøller, *Rebild: The Fourth of July Celebrations in Denmark* (Copenhagen, 1952), p. 40.
9. Hvidt, *Flight to America*, pp. 118, 124, 128, 132.

10. Ibid., p. 118.
11. Riismøller, p. 44.
12. Erling Duus, *Danish-American Journey* (Franklin, Mass., 1971), p. 18; Boy Jessen, *Living Under Three Flags* (New York: Vantage Press, 1959), pp. 141, 143.
13. Hvidt, *Flight to America*, p. 139.
14. Hvidt, *Danes Go West*, p. 172.
15. Cora E. Fagre, comp., *The Lars Strandskov Family* (Boulder, Colorado: Estey Printing Co., [n.d.]).
16. Edward Young, *Labor in Europe and America* (Philadelphia: S. A. George & Co., 1875), pp. 704, 745–47.
17. Ibid., pp. 704, 739–44.
18. Ibid., pp. 704–705, 805. Other items were included in the report but were excluded from this study for the sake of reducing the length of the list and because comparison was made impossible through the utilization of different units of measure.
19. Ibid., pp. 707, 708.
20. Ibid., p. 702.
21. Ibid., p. 816.
22. Louis Pio, "A Consular Report on the Situation of the Workingman in Denmark," *Scandinavia*, January 1886.
23. Hvidt, *Flight to America*, pp. 113, 114.
24. Soren J. M. P. Fogdall, *Danish-American Diplomacy 1776–1920* (University of Iowa Studies in the Social Sciences, Vol. 8, no. 2; Iowa City, [1922]), pp. 110, 111.
25. *Staten Nebraska i de Forenede Stater, Nordamerika dens Hjaelpekilder og Fordele* (Copenhagen: Carl Lund, 1871). Another example is Sophus Listoe, *Om Udvandringen til Amerika: Staten Wisconsin som et Hjem for den Skandinaviske Invandrer* (Copenhagen: A. Fribergs, 1870).
26. Philip Taylor, *The Distant Magnet: European Emigration to the USA* (New York: Harper & Row, 1971), pp. 74, 75.
27. *Vejviser til Union Pacific Jerbanens Land* (Copenhagen: E. Ferslev, 1870). *Frit Land in Nord Dakota* ([n.p.], [*Soo Line*] 1901).
28. Arne Hall Jensen, *Den dansk-amerikanske Historie* (Copenhagen: Arthur Jensens Forlag, 1937), p. 94.
29. Taylor, p. 116.
30. Hvidt, *Danes Go West*, pp. 180–82; Jensen, p. 94.
31. Hvidt, *Danes Go West*, pp. 200, 202.
32. Ibid., p. 210.
33. Ibid., pp. 212, 213.
34. Ibid., pp. 177, 216, 218.
35. Taylor, pp. 126, 127.

36. "Til de danske Emigranter." Pamphlet in Archives, Lutheran School of Theology at Chicago.

37. *United States Census of Population.*

38. Ibid.

*Chapter Three*

1. *Danske i Amerika* (Minneapolis, 1907), 1:16–21. Awnsham Churchill and John Churchill, *A Collection of Voyages and Travels* (London: Awnsham and John Churchill, 1704), p. 562. Enok Mortensen, *The Danish Lutheran Church in America: The History and Heritage of the American Evangelical Lutheran Church* (Philadelphia, 1967), pp. 19–21. A beautifully written account is Thorkild Hansen, *The Way to Hudson Bay: The Life and Times of Jens Munk* (New York: Harcourt Brace & World, 1965).

2. *Danske*, 1:40.

3. Carlo Christensen, *De forste danske i New York* (Copenhagen, 1953), pp. 20–28.

4. Knud Fabricius, L. L. Hammerich, and Vilh Lorenzen, eds., *Holland Danmark Forbindelserne Mellem de To Lande Gennem Tiderne* (Copenhagen: Jespersen og Pios Forlag, 1945), pp. 150, 159, 161, 182.

5. Christensen, p. 68.

6. Ibid., pp. 83, 91, 92, 101.

7. Ibid., p. 118; J. H. Innes, *New Amsterdam and Its People* (New York: Charles Scribner's Sons, 1902), pp. 108, 111.

8. Christensen, pp. 148–52.

9. Thomas P. Christensen, *A History of the Danes in Iowa* (Solvang, California, 1952), p. 21. George T. Flom, "The Danish Contingent in the Population of Early Iowa," *Iowa Journal of History and Politics* 4 (1906): 222, 223.

10. O. N. Nelson, *History of the Scandinavians and Successful Scandinavians in the United States* (Minneapolis, 1893), p. 58. J. Taylor Hamilton and Kenneth G. Hamilton, *History of the Moravian Church: The Renewed Unitas Fratum 1722–1957* (Bethlehem, Pennsylvania: Moravian Church in America, 1967), pp. 45–48.

11. Flom, p. 224.

12. Hamilton, p. 191.

13. *Danske*, 1:47, 65.

14. Ibid., 1:48. P. S. Vig, "Otto Krogstrups Selvbiografi samt Beretning og om hans Virksomhed og Død i Amerika," *Kirkehistoriske Samlinger* (1903–1905), V Raekke, 2:198.

15. *Danske*, 1:45.

16. Henry P. Johnston, "Christian Febiger: Colonel of the Virginia Line of the Continental Army," *Magazine of American History*, March 1881, pp. 188–203.

17. *Danske*, 1:150, 151.

18. Ibid., p. 96.

19. Flom, pp. 229, 230.

*Chapter Four*

1. William Mulder, *Homeward to Zion: The Mormon Migration from Scandinavia* (Minneapolis, 1957), p. 104.

2. Ibid., pp. 9, 34. Jørgen W. Schmidt, *Oh Du Zion i Vest: Den Danske Mormon Emigration 1850–1900* (Copenhagen: Rosenkilde og Bagger, 1965), p. 21.

3. Andrew Jenson, *History of the Scandinavian Mission* (Salt Lake City: Deseret News Press, 1927), pp. 3, 7; Kenneth O. Bjork, *West of the Great Divide: Norwegian Migration to the Pacific Coast, 1847–1893* (Northfield, Minnesota: Norwegian-American Historical Association, 1958), pp. 76, 77; Mulder, p. 38.

4. Mulder, pp. 36, 39.

5. Jenson, p. 9; Mulder, p. 41.

6. Mulder, pp. 42, 46, 47; Jenson, pp. 19, 21, 28.

7. Peter O. Hansen, the translator of the *Book of Mormon*, married a Danish girl shortly after his arrival in Denmark, and when she had given birth to a child, Hansen sent mother and child to Utah. Later he wrote to Heber C. Kimball, leader in the church, for permission to marry a Norwegian girl, but evidently the reply was negative. Helge Seljaas, "Polygamy among the Norwegian Mormons," *Norwegian-American Studies* (Northfield, Minnesota: Norwegian-American Historical Association, 1977), p. 155; Mulder, pp. 91, 109, 240.

8. Mulder, p. 48.

9. Ibid., pp. 104, 107, 108, 110.

10. Ibid., p. 61.

11. Ibid., pp. 79, 80; Jenson, p. 87.

12. Mulder, pp. 104, 137; Bjork, pp. 106, 107; Jenson, p. 48. The numbers exclude children under eight years of age.

13. Alfred Christiansen, "Scandinavians and the New Zion in the West," *American Scandinavian Review*, Autumn 1972, p. 269; Jenson, p. 88.

14. Bjork, p. 112.

15. Jenson, p. 87.

16. Flom, p. 239; Bjork, pp. 112, 117; Mulder, pp. 142, 147, 168, 337.
17. Mulder, pp. 192, 194, 210, 222.
18. Ibid., pp. 223, 240.
19. Ibid., pp. 62, 63, 248, 250, 346; Helen Z. Papanikolas, *The People of Utah* (Salt Lake City: Utah State Historical Society, 1976), p. 178.
20. Mulder, pp. 258, 260–63.
21. Ibid., pp. 286, 287.
22. William Mulder, "Mormons from Scandinavia, 1850–1900. A Shepherded Migration," *Pacific Historical Review*, August 1954, p. 246.
23. The Navajo called him "Kagoochee" or "Crooked Feet." Albert R. Lyman, "Bishop Jens Nielson History and Genealogy," Historical Department of the Church of Jesus Christ of Latter-Day Saints.

*Chapter Five*

1. John M. Jensen, *The United Evangelical Lutheran Church* (Minneapolis, 1964), pp. 5, 6; P. S. Vig, "The United Danish Evangelical Lutheran Church in America," typed, box 7, Vig Papers, Nebraska State Historical Association; Hal Koch, *Grundtvig* (Yellow Springs, Ohio: The Antioch Press, 1952), p. 61.
2. Jens Christian Kjaer, *History of the Church of Denmark* (Blair: Lutheran Publishing House, 1945), p. 76; Poul Hartling, ed., *The Danish Church* ([n.p.]: Det Danske Selskab, [n.d.]), pp. 58–59.
3. Johannes Knudsen, *Danish Rebel* (Philadelphia: Muhlenberg Press, 1955), pp. 44, 176.
4. Hartling, pp. 63, 64.
5. Knudsen, pp. 98, 185.
6. Jensen, p. 8.
7. Enok Mortensen, *The Danish Lutheran Church in America: The History and Heritage of the American Evangelical Lutheran Church* (Philadelphia, 1967), p. 15.
8. Knudsen, pp. 4, 115.
9. Ibid., pp. 5, 37, 102, 115, 147.
10. Kjaer, p. 85; Hartling, p. 72. In 1868 the government permitted groups of twenty families or more to set up free churches.
11. James J. Raun, "Danish Lutherans in America, to 1900" (unpublished Ph.D. dissertation, University of Chicago, 1930), pp. 22–25. Vilhelm Beck, *Memoirs*, ed. P. C. Nyholm (Philadelphia, 1965), pp. 5, 15. John Jensen, a leading historian of the United Evangelical

Lutheran Church, prefers to keep the Danish word *Indre* in connection with Mission instead of Inner.

12. Raun, pp. 27–29; Jensen, pp. 10–11.
13. Raun, p. 62; Jensen, p. 26.
14. Thomas P. Christensen, "Danish Settlement in Wisconsin," *Wisconsin Magazine of History*, September 1928, p. 35.
15. Raun, p. 77; Jensen, p. 62.
16. Jensen, pp. 56, 57.
17. Ibid., p. 62.
18. Raun, p. 77. Enok Mortensen, "Our Father's Church We Build," typed, Lutheran School of Theology at Chicago, Record Group 4, Box 14. Jensen, p. 48. Paul C. Nyholm, *The Americanization of the Danish Lutheran Churches in America* (Minneapolis, 1963), p. 91.
19. Jensen, pp. 51, 62. Clausen ordained Nielsen at St. Ansgar, Iowa, in 1871 and Nielsen ordained Rasmus Andersen in 1872. H. Fred Swansen, *The Founder of St. Ansgar: The Life Story of Claus Laurits Clausen* (Blair, Nebraska, 1949), p. 178. Examples of Danish-Norwegian disagreements are given in Nyholm, p. 90.
20. Mortensen, pp. 44–45; Jensen, p. 49; Nyholm, p. 92.
21. Mortensen, p. 49.
22. Christensen, p. 36.
23. Jensen, p. 63. In 1874 the faculty of Concordia Seminary, St. Louis, after examining the matter at the request of a Racine congregation, found Adam Dan a heretic and Grundtvigianism heresy. *Evangelisk Luthersk Kirketidende,* July 1874, pp. 477–82; August 1874, pp. 494–99.
24. Mortensen, p. 53; Jensen, p. 64.
25. Jensen, pp. 67, 68.
26. Ibid., pp. 74, 75. William E. Christensen in *Saga of the Tower: A History of Dana College and Trinity Seminary* (Blair, Nebraska, 1959), p. 37, maintains that the Blair synod was basically Inner Mission, but because of Beck's advice to join the strongly Grundtvigian Danish Church, the Blair synod was neutral and that the Danish Church took the offensive against the Inner Mission.
27. Jensen, pp. 76, 81; Raun, pp. 83, 84. Mortensen considers this incident to be the real schism in Danish Lutheranism, p. 119.
28. Thomas P. Christensen, *A History of the Danes in Iowa* (Solvang, California, 1952), p. 102; Jensen, pp. 82–84.
29. Jensen, pp. 82–84; Christensen, *Saga*, p. 11.
30. Jensen, pp. 85–87.
31. Ibid., pp. 88–92.
32. Ibid., pp. 217, 218, 221.
33. Mortensen, p. 49.

34. Ibid., p. 94; Theo. P. Beck, *The Professor P. S. Vig* (Blair, Nebraska, 1946), p. 47; Jensen, pp. 106–108. Vig later wrote: "He [Helveg] was a minister's son from Denmark, a graduate of the university; I was a farmer's son who had merely sniffed at the phial of learning in the authorized pharmacy. He was a Grundtvigian; I half Indre Mission. He was a Danish Dane; I a Danish American" (Beck, p. 47). The history of the seminary and the controversy is told in Thorvald Hansen's *School in the Woods: The Story of an Immigrant Seminary* (Askov, Minnesota, 1977).
35. Raun, p. 160.
36. Christensen, "Wisconsin," p. 31.
37. L. Henningsen, *Dansk Folkesamfund i Amerika, 1887–1912*, (Aarhus: S. Jensen Sort, 1914), pp. 4, 5.
38. Mortensen, pp. 90, 91; Jensen, p. 108; Raun, p. 163. Helveg was president of the Luck chapter of the society and Vig opposed the group (Hansen, p. 89).
39. Dannevirke was the earthen defense wall built by the Danish Queen Thyra in the tenth century (Jensen, pp. 109–14, 117); John H. Bille, "A History of the Danes in America," *Transactions of the Wisconsin Academy of Sciences, Arts, and Letters*, March 1896, p. 15; Beck, *Vig*, pp. 61–63; Hansen, pp. 87, 88.
40. Jensen, pp. 120–22.
41. Raun, p. 90.
42. Jensen, pp. 127, 128.
43. P. C. Jensen, *A History of the Iowa District of the United Evangelical Lutheran Church, 1897–1957* (Blair, Nebraska: Lutheran Publishing House, [1957]).
44. Beck, *Vig*, p. 73.
45. J. M. Jensen, pp. 143–47.
46. Thorvald Hansen, *We Laid Foundation Here . . . The Early History of Grand View College* (Des Moines, 1974), pp. 25, 30, 38, 39.
47. Mortensen, pp. 134–36.
48. Christensen, *Iowa*, p. 163; Hansen, p. 111.
49. Christensen, *Iowa*, pp. 64–66; Hansen, pp. 45, 122.
50. Cora E. Fagre, comp., *The Lars Strandskov Family* (Boulder, Colorado: Estey Printing Co., [n.d.]); Nyholm, p. 80.
51. J. M. Jensen, pp. 195–99; Nyholm, pp. 419–28; Mortensen, p. 249.
52. Nyholm argued that the Americanization of the United Church had been achieved by 1960 so that union with the Danish Church, and therefore association with the Danish heritage, was not meaningful (pp. 407, 408).
53. Nyholm, pp. 246, 253.

54. Ibid., p. 119.
55. Ibid., p. 174.
56. Christensen, *Iowa*, p. 121.
57. Nyholm, pp. 171–72; Mortensen, p. 207.
58. J. M. Jensen, p. 179.
59. Mortensen, pp. 177–78; Peter L. Petersen, "Language and Loyalty: Governor Harding and Iowa's Danish-Americans During World War I," *Annals of Iowa*, Fall 1974, p. 409.
60. Christensen, *Iowa*, p. 124.
61. Nyholm, p. 176; Mortensen, p. 175.
62. J. M. Jensen, p. 140.
63. Ibid., pp. 164, 168, 170.
64. Nyholm, pp. 134, 139, 178; J. M. Jensen, p. 181; Mortensen, p. 241.
65. Christensen, *Iowa*, p. 50.
66. Ibid.; O. M. Norlie, *History of the Norwegian People in America* (Minneapolis: Augsburg Publishing House, 1925), p. 268.
67. O. N. Nelson, *History of the Scandinavian and Successful Scandinavians in the United States* (Minneapolis, 1893), 2:49. Enok Mortensen, "The Value of Our Heritage," *Lutheran Tidings*, July 1962, p. 5.
68. Raun, pp. 58, 62; Mortensen, *Danish Lutheran Church*, p. 28.
69. J. M. Jensen, pp. 133, 135, 219, 223.
70. Christensen, *Iowa*, p. 108.
71. Sorenus J. M. P. Fogdall, "The Dano-Norwegian Baptists in America" (master's thesis, University of Chicago, 1915), pp. 6–9.
72. Mortensen, *Danish Lutheran Church*, p. 26. M. C. Carstensen, "The First Fifty Years," *Seventy-Five Years of Danish Baptist Missionary Work in America* (Philadelphia, 1931), p. 5.
73. Norlie, p. 182; Nels S. Lawdahl, *De Danske Baptisters Historie i Amerika* (Morgan Park, Illinois, 1909), p. 17. Lawdahl's book is largely a collection of congregational histories.
74. Carstensen, p. 5.
75. Ibid., pp. 6–9, 13.
76. Lawdahl, pp. 19–22.
77. Peter Riismøller, *Rebild: The Fourth of July Celebrations in Denmark* (Copenhagen, 1952), p. 90; Fogdall, p. 67.
78. P. Stiansen, *History of the Norwegian Baptists in America* (Wheaton, Illinois: The Norwegian Baptist Conference of America, 1939), pp. 89, 92, 93. Hauge reported that the Danes usually joined the church as individuals but the Norwegians came in groups (Stiansen, p. 36). The reason for the division of the conference in 1910 was largely nationalistic, based on the belief that mission work would be

more effective if directed to the nationalities separately (Fogdall, p. 99). When Hauge concluded that the Sabbath should be observed on Saturday instead of Sunday, his parishioners accused him of heresy and he spent much of his later life as missionary to the Sioux. See T. P. Christensen, "Danish Settlement in Minnesota," *Minnesota History: A Quarterly Magazine*, December 1927, p. 367.

79. Stiansen, pp. 99, 103, 105, 107.
80. Ibid., pp. 286, 301.
81. Christensen, "Minnesota," pp. 369–71.
82. Fogdall, pp. 90, 99; Lawdahl, p. 533.
83. Arlow W. Andersen, *The Salt of the Earth: A History of Norwegian-Danish Methodism in America* (Nashville, 1962), p. 18; S. N. Gaarde, *Methodistkirken i Danmark, 1858–1908* (Esbjerg: Kristelig Bogforenings Forlag, 1908), p. 1.
84. Andersen, pp. 12–17.
85. Ibid., pp. 42, 44, 62.
86. "Historical Section: History of Norwegian-Danish Methodism," *Journal and Yearbook with Historical Section of the Sixty-fourth Annual Session: Norwegian-Danish Conference of the Methodist Church* (1943), p. 58; Andersen, p. 35.
87. Andersen, pp. 8, 114, 120.
88. Evelyn Geneva Anderson, "History of the Norwegian-Danish Conference of the Methodist Episcopal Church in the United States" (master's thesis, University of Colorado, 1940), p. 77.
89. Andersen, pp. 163, 281.
90. Ibid., pp. 6, 327.
91. Don F. Neufeld, ed., *Seventh-Day Adventist Encyclopedia* (Washington, D.C.: Review & Herald Publishing Association, 1966), pp. 338, 760.
92. Ibid., pp. 550–51.
93. Ibid., pp. 801, 1222.
94. *Danske i Amerika* (Minneapolis, 1907), 1:258, 259.

## *Chapter Six*

1. Thomas P. Christensen, "Danish Settlement in Wisconsin," *Wisconsin Magazine of History*, September 1928, p. 19; *Danske i Amerika* (Minneapolis, 1916), 2:119, 145.
2. H. Fred Swansen, *The Founder of St. Ansgar: The Life Story of Claus Laurits Clausen* (Blair, Nebraska, 1949), p. 169. Clausen edited *Emigranten*, a newspaper for Norwegians and Danes, but gave up the venture after only seven months.
3. Christensen, pp. 20, 21; George T. Flom, "The Danish Con-

tingent in the Population of Early Iowa," *Iowa Journal of History and Politics* 4 (1906): 231. The publication date for the *Haandbog* was 1847.

4. Enok Mortensen, *The Danish Lutheran Church in America: The History and Heritage of the American Evangelical Lutheran Church* (Philadelphia, 1967), p. 23; Peter Riismøller, *Rebild: The Fourth of July Celebrations in Denmark* (Copenhagen, 1952), p. 38.

5. Christensen, p. 21; *Danske*, 1:337–49.

6. Soren J. M. P. Fogdall, *Danish-American Diplomacy 1776–1920* (University of Iowa Studies in the Social Sciences, Vol. 8, no. 2; Iowa City, [1922]), p. 101.

7. Christensen, pp. 22, 23; *Danske*, 1:189.

8. Christensen, p. 24; Riismøller, p. 89; Mortensen, p. 24.

9. Flom, p. 232; Albert O. Barton, "The Scandinavian Element in Wisconsin," *Wisconsin: Its History and Its People, 1643–1924*, ed. Milo M. Quaife (Chicago: The S. J. Clarke Publishing Co., 1924), 121. *Danske*, 1:253, 254.

10. *Danske*, 1:254, 259, 260; anon., *Commemorative Biographical Record of the Counties of Brown, Kewaunee, and Door, Wisconsin* (Chicago: J. H. Beers & Co., 1895), p. 261.

11. Anton Jarstad, "The Melting Pot in Northeastern Wisconsin," *Wisconsin Magazine of History*, June 1943, p. 428.

12. Christensen, pp. 25, 26.

13. Kristian Hvidt, *Danes Go West* (Copenhagen, 1976), p. 74.

14. Jarstad, p. 428.

15. Nicholas C. Burckel, ed., *Racine: Growth and Change in a Wisconsin County* (Racine: Racine County Board of Supervisors, 1977), pp. 80, 88, 104, 105. *Racine Sunday Bulletin*, October 28, 1956.

16. Anon., *The History of Racine and Kenosha Counties, Wisconsin* (Chicago: Western Historical Co., 1879), pp. 397, 398. *Emmaus Lutheran Church, Racine, Wisconsin, 1851–1976.* [By the congregation.]

17. Burckel, pp. 101, 528.

18. *Danske*, 2:176; Christensen, pp. 24, 25, 28. *Seventy-fifth Anniversary, 1873–1948: Danish Lutheran Church of West Denmark.* [By the congregation.]

19. *Danske*, 2:174, 175; Christensen, pp. 29, 30.

20. *Danske*, 2:194–96; Enok Mortensen, *Schools for Life: A Danish-American Experiment in Adult Education* (Askov, Minnesota, 1977), pp. 119, 120.

21. Christensen, pp. 31, 32; Thomas P. Christensen, *A History of the Danes in Iowa* (Solvang, California, 1952), p. 35. *Nazareth Danish*

*Evangelical Church, Withee, Wisconsin, 1893–1943.* [By the congregation.] *Den Danske Koloni ved Withee, Wisconsin* ([n.p.]: Den Dansk Koloniforening, 1908). See also Harald A. Pedersen, "Acculturation among Danish and Polish Ethnic Groups in Wisconsin" (Ph.D. dissertation, University of Wisconsin, 1949).

22. American Lutheran Church Archives, Dubuque, Iowa, Miscellaneous Danish Churches.

23. John W. Dasef, *History of Montcalm County, Michigan* (Indianapolis, Indiana: B. F. Bowen & Co., 1916), p. 350; Mortensen, *Danish Lutheran Church*, pp. 68, 69; Flom, p. 232; August Rasmussen, *Pioneer Life in the Big Dane Settlement: Montcalm County, Michigan, North America, 1856–1902* (n.p., n.d.), pp. 1–25. Many of the early settlers originated from Holbaek and Hallebyøre, Zealand.

24. Dasef, pp. 351, 355, 356. American Lutheran Church Archives.

25. *Michigan History Magazine*, Autumn 1940, p. 441.

26. E. M. Favrholdt, *Labour in the Vineyard: Fifty-five Years History of the Danish Lutheran Church in Manistee, Michigan, 1868–1923.* [By the congregation.]

27. *Danske*, 2:210.

28. Mortensen, *Schools*, pp. 36–46.

## *Chapter Seven*

1. Kristian Hvidt, *Flight to America: The Social Background of 300,000 Danish Emigrants* (New York, 1975), p. 171.

2. Other cities in 1900 with sizable Danish populations were New York, 5,621; Omaha–Council Bluffs, 3,539; San Francisco, 2,171; Racine, 2,815; and the Twin Cities, 2,679.

3. *Danske i Amerika* (Minneapolis, 1916), 1:239; *Skandinaven*, February 2, 1892; *Scandia*, December 27, 1913. Christian Nielsen, "Halfems Aar i Chicagos Danske Koloni 1837–1927" (typescript at Northwestern University).

4. *Scandia*, August 11, 1900.

5. Paul F. Cressy, "Population Succession in Chicago," *American Journal of Sociology* 44 (1938–1939): 59–69.

6. Philip S. Friedman, "The Danish Community of Chicago, 1860–1920" (master's thesis, Northwestern University, 1976), pp. 41, 49.

7. Morris Salmonsen, *Brogede Minder: Fra Fyrretyve Aars Ophold i Chicago* (Copenhagen, 1913), p. 25; Friedman, pp. 38, 39.

8. *Skandinaven*, February 2, 1892; Friedman, pp. 43, 48; *Proceedings of the Board of Education of the City of Chicago: July 13, 1890 to June 28, 1899* (Chicago: Board of Education, 1899), p. 254.

9. Swansen, p. 198; Salmonsen, p. 32.

10. *Album of Genealogy and Biography 1899*, Chicago Foreign Language Project; Nielsen, p. 16.

11. *Revyen*, October 24, 1903; November 21, 1903.

12. *Dansk Tidende*, October 9, 1925; Friedman, p. 50.

13. *Revyen*, December 16, 1899.

14. Ibid., January 3, 1903.

15. *Dansk Tidende*, August 1, 1924. Statistics for remigration were not collected until 1908. From that date until 1914 the average return rate was between 8 percent and 9 percent of the annual migration.

16. H. Einar Mose, *The Dania Society of Chicago* (Chicago, 1962), p. 11.

17. *Revyen*, March 14, 1896; October 3, 1896. *Skandinaven*, September 27, 1896. The committee included Adam Dan, Henry Hertz, and M. Salmonsen. *Skandinaven*, September 27, 1896. There was also an argument as to whether the statue should be in a standing or sitting position.

18. *Revyen*, September 3, 1898; February 11, 1899.

19. Ibid., February 6, 1909.

20. Ibid., May 30, 1906; February 6, 1909. Noel J. Chrisman, in "Ethnic Influence on Urban Groups: The Danish-Americans" (Ph.D. dissertation, University of California, Berkeley, 1966), points out that visible expression of ethnicity is difficult without ethnic associations. For more information on the Chicago orphanage see Enok Mortensen, *The Danish Lutheran Church in America: The History and Heritage of the American Evangelical Lutheran Church* (Philadelphia, 1967), p. 76.

21. *Revyen*, June 11, 1910; *Skandinaven*, June 8, 1920; *Dansk Tidende*, June 12, 1925.

22. *Dansk Tidende*, July 9, 1926.

23. Mose, pp. 8, 9, 20; *Scandia*, August 18, 1900; September 1, 1900.

24. The table top was approximately four feet in diameter and constructed of wood that has been described in different sources as oak or mahogany. After the passage of Prohibition in the United States it was sent to Denmark, where it was placed in Wivel's Café near Tivoli Gardens. *Danish Times*, May 27, 1927. At the present time it is located in the Danes Worldwide Archives at Aalborg, although the table top there is made of walnut and attached to an ornamental base.

25. Marion Tuttle Marzolf, "The Danish-Language Press in America" (Ph.D. dissertation, University of Michigan, 1972), p. 40.

26. Mary Kay Norseng, "Clemens Petersen in America," *Scandinavian Studies*, Autumn 1976, pp. 348–403; *Dansk Biografisk Leksikon*

(Copenhagen: J. H. Schultz, 1935); *Lakeside Directory of Chicago 1878–1879* (Chicago: Reuben Donnelly, 1879).

27. Salmonsen, pp. 68, 69; Mose, p. 26.

28. *Aalborg Stiftstidende*, October 12, 1934.

29. A. T. Andreas, *History of Chicago* (Chicago: A. T. Andreas, 1886), 3:455.

30. Mose, p. 26; Kristian Hvidt, *Danes Go West* (Copenhagen, 1976), p. 279. Frederiksen published an English paper, *Scandinavia*, from 1883 to 1886, but it was not successful.

31. Henry Hertz to Martin Hertz, March 1, 1872; August 19, 1872. Personal file, Archives, Aalborg.

32. *Revyen*, March 30, 1901.

33. Ibid., November 24, 1917. Henry Hertz, personal file, Archives, Aalborg.

34. Anon., *Max Henius* (Chicago: Max Henius Memorial Committee, 1937), pp. 22, 31, 33, 41.

35. *Max Henius*, pp. 60, 201.

36. *Revyen*, May 26, 1900; August 25, 1900; Mose, p. 11; Aase Bak, "Dansk-Amerikanske Kunstnere, 1850–1914" (thesis, Aarhus University, 1979), pp. 50, 73; *New York Times*, December 10, 1922; *New York Evening Journal*, August 24, 1923. Gelert's studio was located in back of Dreier's pharmacy.

37. *Revyen*, February 28, 1914.

38. *75th Anniversary: The Danish Evangelical Lutheran Trinity Church, 1872–1947*. [By the congregation.]

39. Nyholm, p. 167.

40. *The Illinois District of the United Evangelical Lutheran Church Celebrates Its Golden Jubilee, 1897–1947* (Blair, Nebraska: Lutheran Publishing House, 1947).

41. *Salomons Almanak: De Forenede Staters danske almanak, haand- og aarborg* (Seattle: Danish Publishing House of the Pacific Coast, 1916).

42. Marzolf, p. 35.

43. Friedman, p. 59.

44. David Bunce, "A Profile of an Ethnic Community: Scandinavians in Chicago, 1880–1900" (thesis, The Flinders University of South Australia, 1976), pp. 41, 54, 55, 60.

45. Mose, pp. 2, 6, 9, 17, 21.

46. *Revyen*, July 24, 1892.

47. Salmonsen, p. 34.

48. *Scandia*, August 18, 1900; September 1, 1900.

49. Friedman, p. 78. Having sold its property in the Humboldt Park area, Dania, in 1980, meets at different sites while it and other

Scandinavian societies search for a building suitable for joint ownership. Dania's membership stands at 135.

50. *Revyen*, February 27, 1909; March 3, 1909; *Skandinaven*, January 19, 1892.

51. *Revyen*, December 9, 1905.

52. *St. Peter's Evangelical Lutheran Church, Dwight, Illinois 1876–1941.* [By the congregation.] *Danske i Amerika* (Minneapolis, 1907–1916), 2:61, 62.

53. Thomas P. Christensen, "Danish Settlements in Minnesota," *Minnesota History: A Quarterly Magazine*, December 1927, p. 367.

54. Floyd Sorensen, "The Development of a Cooperative Community: Clarks Grove, 1863–1912" (typed manuscript, Minnesota Historical Society, 1934). Franklyn Curtiss-Wedge, comp., *History of Freeborn County, Minnesota* (Chicago: H. C. Cooper, Jr. & Co., 1911), p. 443.

55. Sorensen, pp. 6, 7; Curtiss-Wedge, p. 454.

56. Sorensen, pp. 8–17; Curtiss-Wedge, p. 455. The first cream separator in the United States was imported by Jeppe Slifsgaard of Fredsville, Iowa.

57. Cora E. Fagre, comp., *The Lars Strandskov Family* (Boulder, Colorado: Estey Printing Co., [n.d.]).

58. Thomas P. Christensen, *A History of the Danes in Iowa* (Solvang, California, 1952), p. 34.

59. Enok Mortensen, *Seventy-five Years at Danebod* (Tyler, Minnesota, 1961), pp. 7, 8.

60. Christensen, *Iowa*, pp. 133–34.

61. Mortensen, *Seventy-five*, p. 7.

62. Ibid., pp. 75, 77.

63. A. E. Tasker, *Early History of Lincoln County* (Lake Benton, Minnesota: The Lake Benton News Print, 1936), p. 41.

64. Enok Mortensen, *Schools for Life: The Grundtvigian Folk Schools in America* (Askov, Minnesota, 1977), pp. 86–87, 91–93.

65. Mortensen, *Seventy-five*, p. 39. Kristian Østergaard, "The Danish Settlement at Tyler, Minnesota," *Scandinavia*, April 1924, p. 23.

66. Anker M. Simonsen, *Builders with a Purpose* (Askov, 1963), pp. 9, 51. Edmund DeS. Brunner, *Immigrant Farmers and Their Children* (Garden City, New York: Doubleday, Doran & Co., 1929), p. 162.

67. Christensen, "Minnesota," p. 382; Simonsen, pp. 47, 49.

68. Brunner, p. 161.

69. Paul C. Nyholm, *The Americanization of the Danish Lutheran Churches in America* (Minneapolis, 1963), p. 123.

70. Ibid.; Simonsen, pp. 23, 28, 45.

71. Christensen, "Minnesota," p. 383; Brunner, pp. 175, 176.

72. P. C. Jensen, *A History of the Iowa District of the United Evangelical Lutheran Church 1897–1957* (Blair, Nebraska: Lutheran Publishing House, [1957]), pp. 4, 5; *Pressing On . . .: 1871–1971, Nazareth Lutheran Church* [Cedar Falls]. [By the congregation]. The first Dane in Iowa was Niels Christian Boye who in 1837 settled in Muscatine County and in 1842 took his merchandising business to Iowa City. See George T. Flom, "The Danish Contingent in the Population of Early Iowa," *Iowa Journal of History and Politics*, April, 1906, p. 233.

73. *Danske i Amerika* (Minneapolis, 1907), 1:270–71; Christensen, *Iowa*, pp. 89, 90.

74. Edward S. White, *Past and Present of Shelby County, Iowa* (Indianapolis: B. F. Bowen & Company, 1915), p. 127.

75. Enok Mortensen, *The Danish Lutheran Church in America: The History and Heritage of the American Evangelical Lutheran Church* (Philadelphia, 1967), p. 69; Mortensen, *Schools*, p. 22; Christensen, *Iowa*, p. 78.

76. Christensen, *Iowa*, p. 85; Mortensen, *Schools*, pp. 26, 30.

77. Christensen, *Iowa*, p. 87; *Des Moines Register*, March 6, 1966.

78. Christensen, *Iowa*, p. 87; H. F. Andrews, ed., *History of Audubon County, Iowa* (Indianapolis: B. F. Bowen & Company, 1915), p. 294.

79. *Den Danske Pioneer*, September 7, 1916.

80. Velinda Rovn Nielsen, comp., *Ringsted, Iowa, 1899–1974: History of Our Heritage* (Ringsted, Iowa, n.p., n.d.), p. 6; Christensen, *Iowa*, p. 93.

81. Nielsen, *Ringsted*, pp. 8, 9.

82. Christensen, *Iowa*, pp. 94–95; Axel H. Andersen, ed., *Andersen's Yearbook, 1919* (Omaha: Axel H. Andersen, 1919). Another Danish community in Iowa, but one that did not fit the patterns was a settlement of religious dissenters in Story and Hamilton counties. See Thomas P. Christensen, "Little Copenhagen" (typed manuscript, State Historical Society of Iowa, Iowa City, Iowa).

83. Andrews, p. 293.

84. Nielsen, *Ringsted*, p. 100.

85. Ibid., pp. 100–104; Andrews, p. 293.

## *Chapter Eight*

1. *Danske i Amerika* (Minneapolis, 1907), 2:316, 317.

2. G. B. Christiansen, *Recollections of Our Church Work* (Blair, 1930), p. 99. *75th Anniversary 1874–1949: Our Savior's Danish Evan-*

*gelical Lutheran Church, Omaha, Nebraska.* [By the congregation.] Arthur C. Wakeley, *Omaha: The Gate City and Douglas County, Nebraska* (Chicago: S. J. Clarke Publishing Co., 1917), 1:398.

3. Howard P. Chudacoff, *Mobile Americans: Residential and Social Mobility in Omaha 1880–1920* (New York: Oxford University Press, 1972), p. 65.

4. Letter from N. O. Berthelsen, Omaha, to author, September 18, 1979.

5. Ellen Kiechel Partsch, *Howard County, The First 100 Years* ([n.p., n.d.]), p. 2. Hannibal had settled at Mouse Lake, Wisconsin, in 1856 but instead of becoming a farmer, he worked as a colonization agent in the United States and Denmark. He used *Fremad* to publicize the Nebraska settlement. Albert O. Barton, "The Scandinavian Element in Wisconsin," *Wisconsin: Its History and Its People 1634–1924*, ed. Milo M. Quaife (Chicago: The S. J. Clarke Publishing Co., 1924), p. 121.

6. Inventory of the County Archives of Nebraska, No. 47, Howard County (St. Paul), WPA. December 1941, Lincoln.

7. *Danske*, 2:81.

8. A. W. Christensen, *A Story of the Danish Settlement in Dannevirke* ([n.p.], 1961), pp. 5, 7, 9.

9. Enok Mortensen, *Schools for Life: The Grundtvigian Folk Schools in America* (Askov, Minnesota, 1977), pp. 57–60.

10. Ibid., pp. 64, 73.

11. Partsch, p. 15.

12. Alfred C. Nielsen, *Life in an American Denmark* (Des Moines, 1962), p. 62.

13. Roy C. Bang, *Heroes Without Medals* (Minden, Nebraska: Warp Publishing Co., 1952), pp. 44, 261, 264.

14. Ibid., pp. 44, 213.

15. Partsch, p. 5; A. W. Christensen, pp. 6, 7.

16. Nielsen, p. 16.

17. Partsch, p. 15.

18. Nielsen, pp. 20, 22.

19. A. W. Christensen, p. 35; Partsch, p. 15.

20. Boy Jessen, *Living Under Three Flags* (New York: Vantage Press, 1959), p. 156; A. W. Christensen, pp. 17, 37.

21. G. B. Christiansen, pp. 194, 214; A. W. Christensen, pp. 14, 36.

22. Thomas P. Christensen, "The Danish Settlements in Kansas," *Collections of the Kansas State Historical Society, 1926–1928*, 17: 300–302; John H. Bille, "A History of the Danes in America," *Transactions of the Wisconsin Academy of Sciences, Arts, and Letters*, March 1896, p. 27.

23. G. B. Christiansen, p. 250.
24. Sister Anna Poulsen, *Eben-Ezer: The History of 70 Years of Christian Mercy Work in Colorado* (Brush, Colorado: Eben-Ezer Lutheran Care Center, Corp., 1978).
25. Olga S. Olsen, "An Historical Study of the Danish Immigrants in South Dakota" (master's thesis, University of South Dakota, 1940), pp. 4–7. "South Dakota Danes," typed manuscript, Vig Papers, Nebraska State Historical Society, Lincoln.
26. Olsen, pp. 7, 8; *Dannevirke*, July 16, 1886; September 13, 1893; September 18, 1887; "South Dakota Danes," Vig Papers.
27. "South Dakota Danes," Vig Papers.
28. Olsen, pp. 13–15. "South Dakota Danes," Vig Papers.
29. "South Dakota Danes," Vig Papers; Olsen, p. 15; Thomas P. Christensen, "The Danes in South Dakota," *South Dakota Historical Collection* 14 (1928):540. Other Danish communities in the general area were at Lodi, Irene, and Beresford.
30. *Danske*, 2:439.
31. Olsen, pp. 18, 20; "South Dakota Danes," Vig Papers.
32. "South Dakota Danes," Vig Papers; Olsen, pp. 36, 37; Thomas P. Christensen, *A History of the Danes in Iowa* (Solvang, California, 1952), p. 30.
33. Waldemar C. Westergaard, "History of the Danish Settlement in Hill Township, Cass County," *Collections of the State Historical Society of North Dakota* 1 (1906), pp. 153, 155. *Rural Cass County: The Land and People* ([n.p.], Cass County Historical Society, 1976), p. 434.
34. Westergaard, p. 157.
35. Ibid., pp. 163, 164.
36. Ibid., p. 165.
37. P. C. Jensen, "History of the North Dakota District of the United Danish Evangelical Lutheran Church in America: A Brief Account of the First 30 Years (Danish Period)," p. 5, located in Wartburg Theological Seminary, Dubuque, Iowa.
38. Ibid., pp. 5, 6; Paul C. Nyholm, *The Americanization of the Danish Lutheran Churches in America* (Minneapolis, 1963), p. 122.
39. John M. Jensen, *The United Evangelical Lutheran Church* (Minneapolis, 1964), pp. 138, 139.
40. P. C. Jensen, p. 8. Mortensen says that the school stressed the afterlife while a Grundtvigian folk school dealt with the temporal life. See *Schools*, p. 121. Anon., *Seventy-five Years of Kenmare and the Gooseneck Area* ([n.p.], [1972]).
41. Anon., *Pioneers and Progress* (Bismarck, Burke County and White Earth Valley Historical Society, 1972), p. 796.

42. *Seventy-five Years of Kenmare and the Gooseneck Area.*

43. Cora E. Fagre, comp., *The Lars Strandskov Family* (Boulder, Colorado: Estey Printing Co., [n.d.]).

44. P. C. Jensen, pp. 12, 13; Christensen, *Iowa*, p. 37; *History of the Nathanael and Volmer Lutheran Churches of Dagmar, Montana 1907–1975.* [By the congregation].

45. Fagre, *The Lars Strandskov Family.*

46. John L. Davis, "Danes Came to Central Wharton County in 1894 Bringing Church, Language, Culture," *People* 6 (January-February, 1976):6.

47. Thomas P. Christensen, "Danevang, Texas," Southwestern Historical Quarterly 32 (1928–1929): 67.

48. Grace C. Grantham, "The Danes in Wharton County" (master's thesis, Texas College of Arts and Industries, 1947), p. 18.

49. Christensen, p. 69. "Danevang," Pamphlet in Archives, Lutheran School of Theology at Chicago.

50. Christensen, "Danevang," p. 70.

51. Susan Lucas and Sara Clark, "Community Celebration in Danevang," in Francis E. Abernethy, ed., *The Folklore of Texas Cultures* (Austin: The Encino Press, 1974), p. 192; Grantham, p. 34.

52. Lucas, p. 192; *Danevang Community Anniversary, Danevang, Texas, 1894–1944* ([n.p.], [n.d.]), pp. 63–65, 68; *Houston Chronicle Magazine*, December 14, 1947.

## *Chapter Nine*

1. Max Henius, ed., *Den danskfødte Amerikaner* (Chicago, 1912), pp. 12–14, 189, 194; *Our Saviour's Danish Evangelical Lutheran Church, Bridgeport, Connecticut, 1894–1944.* [By the congregation].

2. H. Hansen, *Perth Amboy* (Kolding: Konrad Jørgensens Bogtrykkeri, 1920), pp. 34, 35; William C. McGinnis, *History of Perth Amboy, New Jersey, 1851–1962* (Perth Amboy: American Publishing Co., [n.d.]), 4:13.

3. Hansen, p. 39.

4. Walter Green, *The Story of Terra Cotta* (New York: Tobias A. Wright, 1920), p. 134; McGinnis, p. 13; *Perth Amboy Evening News*, May 5, 1939.

5. Marion Tuttle Marzolf, "The Danish-Language Press in America" (Ph.D. dissertation, University of Michigan, 1972), p. 95.

6. Peter Riismøller, *Rebild: The Fourth of July Celebrations in Denmark* (Copenhagen, 1952), pp. 85, 87; Kristian Hvidt, *Danes Go West: A Book about the Emigration to America* (Copenhagen, 1976), p. 281.

7. Enok Mortensen, "Looking Back and Looking Forward," *Bridge: Journal of the Danish American Heritage Society*, May 1978, p. 8; Archives of Baron Joost Dahlerup, Letters No. 1577, 1578. New-York Historical Society, New York, N.Y., May 25, 1933, May 27, 1933.

8. Sophus Hartwick, *Danske i California og California historie: beretninger om de danskes liv og virke fra de tidligste pioner dage* (San Francisco, 1939, 1:41–43; J. M. Guinn, *History of the State of California and Biographical Record of Coast Counties, California* (Chicago: The Chapman Publishing Co., 1903), p. 584.

9. Hartwick, 1:51–54.

10. Ibid., pp. 57–60.

11. John A. Hawgood, ed., *First and Last Consul: Thomas Oliver Larkin and the Americanization of California* (Palo Alto: Pacific Books, 1970), p. 95.

12. Ibid., pp. 92, 96. The heirs sold the property for $90,000 and the purchaser later sold it for fifteen times as much.

13. David Lavender, *Westward Vision, The Story of the Oregon Trail* (New York: McGraw-Hill, 1963), pp. 332–36.

14. Thomas R. Cox, *Mills and Markets: A History of the Pacific Coast Lumber Industry to 1900* (Seattle: University of Washington Press, 1974), p. 22; Ruby J. Swartzlow, *Lassen: His Life and Legacy* (Mineral, California: Loomis Museum Association, 1964), pp. 11, 12, 21.

15. Hartwick, 1:72, 109–14.

16. Allan Nevins, *Fremont: Pathmarker of the West* (New York: D. Appleton-Century, 1939), pp. 217–22.

17. Ibid., p. 234.

18. George P. Hammond, ed., *The Larkin Papers* (Berkeley: University of California Press, 1951), 4:302, 348.

19. Ibid., 4:393.

20. Swartzlow, p. 23; Nevins, p. 250.

21. Hartwick, 1:126.

22. Ibid., pp. 219–23. Funck, a sailor and ship carpenter, had left his ship in 1847 and helped construct the water wheel at Sutter's mill. Paul E. Vandor, *History of Fresno County, California with Biographical Sketches . . .* (Los Angeles: Historic Record Co., 1919), 2: 1674. Peter Riismøller, *Rebild: The Fourth of July Celebrations in Denmark* (Copenhagen, 1952), p. 56.

23. Hartwick, 2:519; Jack McNairn and Jerry Mullen, *Ships of the Redwood Coast* (Stanford: Stanford University Press, 1945), p. 90.

24. Cox, pp. 23, 124, 125; Hartwick, 1:180.

25. Hartwick, 2:5, 19.

26. Ibid., 2:520. Edward M. Stensrud, *The Lutheran Church and*

*California* (San Francisco [n.p.], 1916), p. 33. Stensrud's book was a promotion for "Scandinavian-American Colonies of California," five miles north of Marysville, Yuba County.

27. Hartwick, 2:858–60.

28. Ibid., 1:246–55.

29. Danes who arrived in California in the 1850s and who preferred agriculture to urban occupations settled in Alameda County east of the Bay. This never became a Danish center, however, and many Danes later migrated to Watsonville and Salinas near Monterey Bay, where Danish communities, churches, and lodges were to flourish. The first Danes in Salinas came in 1867 and more arrived in the next decade. By 1880 the settlement was large enough to support a Lutheran congregation (Hartwick, 1:521, 673, 674).

30. Page Smith and Charles Daniel, *The Chicken Book* (Boston: Little Brown & Co., 1975), pp. 233–35; *Petaluma Argus-Courier, Centennial Edition 1855–1955*, August 18, 1955. The Danes who migrated to Sonoma County and Petaluma in the early days came primarily from South Jutland or from those parts of Denmark occupied by the Germans. The migration to Petaluma was not a wave, but a continuous flow that lasted into the twentieth century. Although some settlers came directly from Denmark, most had lived in various places in California. In the 1930 census there were 629 Danes listed for Sonoma County who were native Danes and 836 persons born of Danish parents. Thomas J. Gregory, *History of Sonoma County, California . . . with Biographical Sketches* (Los Angeles: Historic Records Co., 1911), pp. 497, 485, 577. Honoria Tuomey, *History of Sonoma County, California* (Chicago: The S. J. Clarke Publishing Co., 1926), 1:9, 17, 142, 412.

31. Vandor, 1:62.

32. Hartwick, 1:224–25.

33. Vandor, 1:252.

34. G. O'Hara Taaffe, *California som det er* (Copenhagen: Th. Michaelsen & Tillge, 1869); Hartwick, 1:226, 227.

35. Vandor, 1:252; Lilbourne Alsip Winchell, *History of Fresno County and the San Joaquin Valley* (Fresno: A. H. Cawston, 1933), pp. 110, 113, 120; Virginia E. Thickens, "Pioneer Agricultural Colonies of Fresno County," *California Historical Society Quarterly*, March 1947, p. 19.

36. Winchell, pp. 87, 122.

37. Ibid., p. 139.

38. Thickens, p. 32.

39. Vandor, 1:262–63.

40. Hartwick, 1:261; Kenneth O. Bjork, *West of the Great Divide:*

*Norwegian Migration to the Pacific Coast, 1847–1893* (Northfield, Minnesota: Norwegian-American Historical Association, 1958), p. 220.

41. Bjork, p. 220; Hartwick, 1:590.
42. Vandor, 1:263.
43. Hartwick, 2:593.
44. Personal information about the Danes of Fresno can be obtained from the biographical sketches from Vandor's *History of Fresno County* and Hartwick's *Danske i California.* Drawing generalizations from books such as this should be done cautiously; one must remember that sampling methods were not used. The sketches in Vandor were paid for by each person described and Hartwick selected prominent Danes, so the tendency in both books was to include the more successful members of the community. Also, because of the time of publication, those were selected who had reached maturity at that time. Bearing these limitations in mind, the two books do nevertheless contribute to a larger and more intimate picture of the Danish community in Fresno. The total number of Danes whose biographical sketches were included was 145, but not in every instance was the type of information category the same or was it completely provided.

Of the 145 people, 128 listed their place of origin. Fifty-seven percent were from Jutland and 42 percent were from the islands, including Copenhagen. The Jutland population, therefore, was higher in Fresno than one would expect from the Hvidt sources, which indicated that 40 percent migrated from places in Jutland. The two books also listed those Danes who migrated from Slesvig, but who are not included in Hvidt's figures because Slesvig was part of Germany. If those individuals are added and 16 percent of the Danes in Fresno were from that province, the number of Danes from Jutland would be raised to 65 percent of the Fresno community.

The average age at the time of migration was twenty-three; and 83 percent of them migrated when they were between fifteen and twenty-nine. Hvidt's statistics show that 55 percent were in that bracket. Ninety percent were single at the time of migration, but 91 percent of the Fresno Danes, including those who migrated with wives, married Danes or Danish American girls. Five percent married Americans and 3 percent married Scandinavians.

The Lutherans predominated, and among those who listed religious affiliation 90 percent were Lutheran. No religious information, however, was given for 47 percent. Only 20 percent listed a political party, and of those who did, 69 percent were Republican.

45. Owen C. Coy, *The Humboldt Bay Region 1850–1875* (Los Angeles: California Historical Association, 1929), pp. 61, 109, 111, 114.
46. John Carr, *Pioneer Days in California* (Eureka, California:

Times Publishing Co., 1891), p. 420; Hartwick, 2:610; Coy, p. 268.

47. McNairn, p. 80; Hartwick, 2:617.

48. Leigh H. Irvine, *History of Humboldt County with Biographical Sketches . . .* (Los Angeles: Historic Record Co., 1915), pp. 394, 500, 522; Hartwick, 2:624.

49. *75th Anniversary, 1899–1974: Our Savior's Lutheran Church, Ferndale, California.* [By the congregation].

50. Enok Mortensen, *Schools for Life: The Grundtvigian Folk Schools in America* (Askov, Minnesota, 1977), p. 112.

51. Gloria Houston, "The Origins, Development, and Significance of Atterdag College: A Danish Folk High School in America" (Ph.D. dissertation, University of California at Los Angeles, 1971), pp. 69, 70, 72.

52. Hartwick, 2:510–11.

53. Houston, pp. 105, 107–108; Owen H. O'Neill, *History of Santa Barbara County* (Santa Barbara, California: Harold McLean Meier, 1939), p. 387. Church Records, Bethania Lutheran Church, Solvang, California. Marcus Christian Nielsen from Mors illustrates how widely some Solvang residents had traveled. He had migrated to Michigan in 1883 when he was twenty-one, and found employment as a woodchopper. He continued on to Minnesota in 1891 and helped found the Danish settlement in Tyler. Four years later he went to Danevang, Texas, where he owned a cotton gin and blacksmith shop. In 1911 he left for Solvang, where he became a partner with Sophus Olsen in a grocery store (O'Neill, p. 72).

54. Hartwick, 2:515.

55. John Alden Olson, *The Danish Settlement of Junction City, Oregon* (San Francisco: R and E Research Associates, 1975), p. 4; *Through Five Decades: The History of the Lutheran Church, Junction City, Oregon, 1902–1952.* [By the congregation].

56. *Diamond Jubilee 1900–1975: Bethesda Lutheran Church, Eugene, Oregon, 97402.* [By the congregation].

57. Olson, pp. 27, 28, 48–57; *Through Five Decades.*

58. Jorgen Dahlie, "A Social History of Scandinavian Immigration: Washington State 1895–1910" (Ph.D. dissertation, Washington State University, Pullman, 1967), p. 15.

59. Henius, pp. 164, 165.

60. Clarence B. Bagley, *History of King County, Washington* (Chicago: The S. J. Clarke Publishing Co., 1929), 1:816, 824.

### *Chapter Ten*

1. *Danish Brotherhood in America: Eighteenth National Conven-*

*tion 1931, Detroit* [By the DBIA]; *Danske i Amerika* (Minneapolis, 1907), 1:214.

2. *Danish Brotherhood . . . Detroit. Danske i Amerika* 1:214–15.
3. *Danish Brotherhood . . . Detroit. Danske i Amerika* 1:215.
4. *Danske i Amerika* 1:215, 216.
5. Ibid., 1:219. *Danish Brotherhood . . . Detroit.*
6. Typed copy of "DBIA Conventions: Landmark Decisions." Danish Brotherhood in America, Omaha, Nebraska.
7. Interview with Diana Doyle, Omaha, Nebraska. *Danish Brotherhood in America: 24th National Convention, Racine, Wisconsin, September 19–24, 1955.* [By the DBIA]. John P. Johansen, *Immigrant Settlements and Social Organizations in South Dakota* (Brookings: South Dakota Experiment Station, [1937]), p. 22.
8. Sophus Hartwick, *Danske i California og California historie . . .* (San Francisco, 1939), 1:337; Noel J. Chrisman, "Ethnic Influence on Urban Groups: The Danish-Americans" (Ph.D. dissertation, University of California, Berkeley, 1966), pp. 65–68; Howard R. J. Petersen, Omaha, Nebraska, to author, January 17, 1980.
9. Thorvald Hansen, *We Laid Foundation Here: The Early History of Grand View College* (Des Moines, 1974), pp. 15, 16. Enok Mortensen, *Schools for Life: The Grundtvigian Folk Schools in America* (Askov, Minnesota, 1977), pp. 10–12.
10. Hansen, p. 16.
11. Mortensen, p. 14; Hansen, p. 16.
12. Jean B. Kern, "A Folk School in Iowa" (typed manuscript in Iowa Historical Society, Iowa City); Alfred C. Nielsen, *Life in an American Denmark* (Des Moines, 1962), pp. 26, 117.
13. F. M. Paulsen, "Danish-American Folk Traditions: A Study in Fading Survivals" (Ph.D. dissertation, Indiana University, 1967), p. 267.
14. Mortensen, p. 20.
15. Ibid., pp. 31, 32, 81; Kern, "A Folk School in Iowa."
16. Mortensen, pp. 63, 125; John H. Bille, "A History of the Danes in America," *Transactions of the Wisconsin Academy of Sciences, Arts, and Letters*, March 1896, p. 5.
17. Mortensen, p. 6. A student of Danish folklore considers the folk schools a clearing house for Molbo tales—nitwit stories based on the residents of Mols—and pastor stories that on occasion were not particularly uplifting, but still a part of Danish life (Paulsen, p. 184).
18. Hansen, p. 18; P. H. Holm-Jensen, *The People's College* (Blair: Danish Lutheran Publishing House, 1939), p. 129.
19. Holm-Jensen, p. 129.
20. Paulsen, p. 19.

21. Marion Tuttle Marzolf, "The Danish-Language Press in America" (Ph.D. dissertation, University of Michigan, 1972), p. 118.
22. Thomas P. Christensen, *A History of the Danes in Iowa* (Solvang, California, 1952), pp. 106, 107; Mortensen, p. 26.
23. *Danish Brotherhood . . . Detroit*; Marzolf, p. 57.
24. John M. Jensen, *The United Evangelical Lutheran Church* (Minneapolis, 1964), pp. 156–59; Marzolf, p. 75.
25. Marzolf, pp. 61, 68.
26. Jensen, p. 159.
27. Marzolf, pp. 77, 81, 158.
28. Marzolf, pp. 91–93; Chrisman, pp. 43–57.
29. Marzolf, pp. 83, 118.
30. Ibid., pp. 109, 118.
31. Ibid., p. 3.
32. Ibid., p. 167.

*Chapter Eleven*

1. Kristian Hvidt, *Danes Go West: A Book about the Emigration to America* (Copenhagen, 1976), pp. 160–61; *Revyen*, March 2, 1901.
2. *Dansk Biografisk Leksikon* (Copenhagen: J. H. Schultz, 1935); John Danstrup and Hal Koch, *Danmarks Historie: De nye Klasser, 1870–1913* (Copenhagen: Politikens Forlag, 1965), 12:64.
3. Danstrup, pp. 69, 70; Kenneth E. Miller, "Danish Socialism and the Kansas Prairie," *Kansas Historical Quarterly*, Summer 1972, p. 157.
4. Miller, p. 158.
5. Ibid.
6. Hvidt, p. 162.
7. Miller, pp. 160, 164.
8. *Heimdal*, August 11, 1876.
9. Miller, p. 159; Hvidt, p. 162.
10. Louis Pio, *Kansas Efter forskellige Rejseberetninger* (Copenhagen: S. Larsen, 1877), p. 33.
11. *Den Danske Pioneer*, August 12, 1909; Thomas Thomsen, "De Danske Skillingsvisers Syn Paa Amerika og Paa Udvandringen Dertil 1830–1914" (typed manuscript, Udvandrerarkivet, Aalborg). Thomsen also lists some of the migrants accompanying Pio.
12. Hvidt, pp. 162, 163.
13. Miller, p. 162; *Den rene, skaere sandhed om Louis Pio og mig selv* (Chicago: Heimdal, 1877).
14. *Revyen*, January 5, 1901; September 24, 1910; clipping, Biographical Section, Udvandrerarkivet, Aalborg. Geleff wrote *Haandbøg for Udvandrere til Amerika* in 1883 under the name of Harald

Brede, probably because of restrictions placed on his writings in Denmark.

15. *Revyen*, August 16, 1909. Hansen was called "Sorte" or "Black" because his hair and complexion were dark and he looked more like a Spaniard than a Dane (*Chicago Posten*, June 30, 1910).

16. Miller, pp. 165–67.

17. H. Einar Mose, *The Dania Society of Chicago* (Chicago, 1962), p. 28.

18. *Revyen*, February 17, 1906; *Den Danske Pioneer*, August 12, 1909; *Chicago Posten*, June 30, 1910.

19. *Lakeside Directory of Chicago, 1878–1879*. Marion Tuttle Marzolf, "The Danish-Language Press in America" (Ph.D. dissertation, University of Michigan, 1972), p. 41.

20. Letter from Martin Hertz to parents, June 13, 1877; personal file, Udvandrerarkivet, Aalborg; Hvidt, p. 164.

21. *Scandinavien*, March 15, 1884; *Lakeside Directory of Chicago*; Marzolf, p. 42. His occupation as professor indicated that he had no other occupation to list because he did not teach. He did write several items, including a Danish cookbook, a Scandinavian-English dictionary, and "The Sioux War in 1862" for the April 1884 issue of *Scandinavia*, in which the Scandinavians were champions of civilization and the Indians were barbarians.

22. *Østkysten af Florida* ([n.p.], 1893).

23. Miller, p. 168.

24. *Revyen*, June 30, 1917.

25. Stow Persons, ed., *The Cooperative Commonwealth by Laurence Gronlund* (Cambridge, Massachusetts: Harvard University Press, 1965), p. x; *Dictionary of American Biography*.

26. *Chicago Posten*, June 23, 1910.

27. Persons, p. xii.

28. *Chicago Posten*, June 30, 1910.

29. Persons, pp. xii, xvii, xxv; Howard H. Quint, *The Forging of American Socialism* (Indianapolis: The Bobbs-Merrill Co., 1952), pp. 28, 30.

30. Marzolf, pp. 101, 102.

31. *Revyen*, May 5, 1900.

32. Marzolf, pp. 101, 102.

33. *Revyen*, November 21, 1903; January 11, 1913.

34. Ibid., September 21, 1912.

35. Ibid., January 11, 1909.

36. Ibid., June 22, 1912; January 4, 1913.

37. Ibid., January 28, 1922.

38. Marzolf, p. 140.

39. *Danish Times*, July 22, 1922.
40. *Revyen*, February 6, 1909.
41. Ibid., October 16, 1909.
42. Ibid., May 27, 1911.
43. Ibid., November 10, 1900; July 3, 1919.

*Chapter Twelve*

1. *Max Henius* (Chicago, 1937), pp. 64, 67.
2. *Revyen*, July 10, 1909.
3. Ibid., July 10, 1909; *Henius*, p. 67.
4. *Revyen*, November 13, 1909.
5. Ibid., February 12, 1910.
6. Kristian Hvidt, *Danes Go West* (Copenhagen, 1976), p. 288; *Henius*, p. 201.
7. *Henius*, p. 142.
8. Interview with Mrs. Inger Bladt, Aalborg, June 8, 1979.
9. *Scandinavia*, June 1884.
10. *Danish Times*, July 17, 1925.
11. *Revyen*, August 10, 1907.
12. *Skandinaven*, May 14, 1918.
13. *Americanization Bulletin*, December 1, 1918. Department of Interior, Bureau of Education.
14. "Ethnic Influence on Urban Groups: The Danish-Americans" (Ph.D. dissertation, University of California, Berkeley, 1966), pp. 24, 41, 61, 148.
15. Danish American Heritage Society, "Newsletter No. 4, April 1979"; letter from Mrs. Medora Petersen, Askov, Minnesota, January 7, 1980.
16. Letter from Enok Mortensen, Solvang, California, November 27, 1979; letter from Mrs. Medora Petersen, Askov, Minnesota, January 7, 1980.
17. F. M. Paulsen, "Danish-American Folk Traditions: A Study in Fading Survivals" (Ph.D. dissertation, University of Indiana, 1967), p. 56.
18. Ibid., p. 58. Danish American Athletic Club, Chicago.
19. Interview with Arnold N. Bodtker, July 27, 1980; Ellen Kiechel Partsch, *Howard County, The First 100 Years* ([n.p.], [n.d.]), p. 46.
20. Susan Lucas and Sara Clark, "Community Celebrations in Danevang," in Francis E. Abernethy, ed., *The Folklore of Texas Cultures* (Austin: The Encino Press, 1974), p. 195; letter to Membership, Danish American Athletic Club, February 4, 1980.

21. For a description of a Danish Christmas dinner see Paulsen, pp. 60, 61.

22. Waldemar C. Westergaard, "History of the Danish Settlement in Hill Township, Cass County," *Collections of the State Historical Society of North Dakota* 1 (1906), p. 159; Partsch, p. 6.

23. A. W. Christensen, *A Story of the Danish Settlement in Dannevirke* ([n.p.], 1961), p. 26. Cora E. Fagre, comp., *The Lars Strandskov Family* (Boulder, Colorado: Estey Printing Co., [n.d.]).

24. Danish American Heritage Society, "Newsletter No. 3, September 1978."

25. Ibid., "Newsletter No. 4, April 1979"; "Newsletter No. 5, November 1979."

26. Ole Kjaer Madsen and Niels-Peter Albertsen, eds., *'You'll Never Regret the Voyage': US '76 Danish Participation* (Copenhagen: Danish Bicentennial Committee, [1976]). Dana College, "Dana Campus Guide."

27. Erling Duus, *Danish-American Journey* (Franklin, Massachusetts, 1971), p. 72.

# *Selected Bibliography*

For additional references to books and articles see notes section.

ANDERSEN, ARLOW W. *The Salt of the Earth; a History of Norwegian-Danish Methodism in America.* Nashville: Parthenon Press, 1962.

BABCOCK, KENDRIC. *The Scandinavian Element in the United States.* 1914. University of Illinois Studies in the Social Sciences, 12:7.

BECK, THEO. P. *The Professor P. S. Vig.* Blair, Nebraska: Danish Lutheran Publishing House, 1946.

BILLE, JOHN H. "A History of the Danes in America." *Transactions of the Wisconsin Academy of Sciences, Arts, and Letters* 11 (March 1896): pp. 1–48.

CHRISMAN, NOEL J. *Ethnic Influence on Urban Groups: The Danish-Americans.* Ph.D. dissertation, University of California, Berkeley, 1966.

CHRISTENSEN, A. W. *A Story of the Danish Settlement in Dannevirke.* [N.p.] [By the author], 1961.

CHRISTENSEN, CARLO. *De første danske i New York.* Copenhagen: Nyt nordisk forlag, 1953.

CHRISTENSEN, THOMAS P. "Danevang, Texas." *Southwestern Historical Quarterly* 32 (1928–1929): 67–73.

———. "The Danish Settlements in Kansas." *Kansas Historical Collections, 1926–1928,* 17, 300–305.

———. "Danish Settlements in Minnesota." *Minnesota History* 8 (December 1927): 363–85.

———. "Danish Settlements in Wisconsin." *Wisconsin Magazine of History* 12 (1928): 19–40.

———. *A History of the Danes in Iowa.* Solvang, California: Dansk folkesamfund, 1952.

CHRISTENSEN, WILLIAM E. *Saga of the Tower: A History of Dana College and Trinity Seminary.* Blair, Nebraska: Danish Lutheran Publishing House, 1959.

CHRISTIANSEN, G. B. *Recollections of Our Church Work.* Blair, Nebraska: Lutheran Publishing House, 1930.

DANISH BAPTIST GENERAL CONFERENCE OF AMERICA. *Seventy-five Years of Danish Baptist Missionary Work in America.* Philadelphia: American Baptist Publication Society, 1931.

*Danske i Amerika*, 2 vols. Minneapolis: C. Rasmussen Co., 1907–1916.

DUUS, ERLING. *Danish-American Journey*. Franklin, Massachusetts: Gauntlet Books, 1971.

HANSEN, THORVALD. *School in the Woods: The Story of an Immigrant Seminary*. Askov, Minnesota: American Publishing Co., 1977.

———. *We Laid Foundation Here . . . The Early History of Grand View College*. Des Moines: Grand View College, 1974.

HARTWICK, SOPHUS. *Danske i California og California Historie*. 2 vols. San Francisco: [n.p.], 1939.

HENIUS, MAX. *Den danskfødte Amerikaner*. Chicago: Gyldendalske Boghandels Forlag, 1912.

HVIDT, KRISTIAN. *Danes Go West*. Copenhagen: Rebild National Park Society, 1976.

———. *Flight to America: The Social Background of 300,000 Danish Emigrants*. New York: Academic Press, 1975.

JENSEN, JOHN M. *The United Evangelical Lutheran Church*. Minneapolis: Augsburg Publishing House, 1964.

LAWDAHL, N. S. *De danske Baptisters historie i Amerika*. Morgan Park, Illinois: Forfatterens forlag, 1909.

MARZOLF, MARION. *The Danish-Language Press in America*. Ph.D. dissertation, University of Michigan, 1972.

MILLER, KENNETH E. "Danish Socialism and the Kansas Prairie." *Kansas Historical Quarterly* 38:2 (1972): 156–68.

MORTENSEN, ENOK. *The Danish Lutheran Church in America. The History and Heritage of the American Evangelical Lutheran Church*. Philadelphia: Board of Publications, Lutheran Church of America, 1967.

———. *Seventy-five Years at Danebod*. Tyler, Minnesota: Danebod Lutheran Church, 1961.

———. *Schools for Life: A Danish-American Experiment in Adult Education*. Askov, Minnesota: Danish-American Heritage Society, 1977.

MOSE, H. EINAR. *The Dania Society of Chicago*. Chicago: Dania Society, 1962.

MULDER, WILLIAM. *Homeward to Zion: The Mormon Migration from Scandinavia*. Minneapolis: University of Minnesota Press, 1957.

NELSON, O. N. *History of Scandinavians and Successful Scandinavians in the U. S.*, 2 vols. Minneapolis: Nelson and Co., 1893–1897.

NIELSEN, ALFRED C. *Life in an American Denmark*. Des Moines: Grand View College, 1962.

NYHOLM, PAUL. *The Americanization of the Danish Lutheran Churches in America*. Minneapolis: Augsburg Publishing House, 1963.

Paulsen, Frank M. *Danish-American Folk Traditions: A Study in Fading Survivals*. Ph.D. dissertation, Indiana University, 1967.

Raun, James J. *Danish Lutherans in America to 1900*. Ph.D. dissertation, University of Chicago, 1930.

Riismøller, Peter. *Rebild*. Copenhagen: Hassings Forlag, 1952.

Salmonsen, Morris. *Brogede minder*. Copenhagen: Gyldendalske, Boghandel, 1913.

Simonsen, Anker. *Builders with a Purpose*. Askov, Minnesota: American Publishing Co., 1963.

Swansen, Hans F. *The Founder of St. Ansgar*. Blair, Nebraska: Lutheran Publishing House, 1949.

Westergaard, Waldemar C. "History of the Danish Settlement in Hill Township, Cass County, North Dakota." *Collections of the State Historical Society of North Dakota* 1 (1906): 153–80.

# Index